COURT SATIRES
OF THE
RESTORATION

John Harold
Wilson

OHIO STATE UNIVERSITY PRESS

COLUMBUS

The illustrations appearing on pages i, ii, v, ix, 1, and 2 are enlarged extracts from *Carriere at Nancy*, by Jacques Callot, and are used by permission of the National Gallery of Art in Washington, D.C., Rudolf L. Baumfeld Collection. The illustration appearing on the front and back endsheets, an enlarged extract from *Combat at the Barrier*, by Jacques Callot, is used by permission of the Metropolitan Museum of Art, New York City, Gift of Edwin de T. Bechtel, 1957, and has been reproduced from *Eyes on the World*, by Esther Averill, published by Funk and Wagnalls Publishing Company, Inc. (1969).

Library of Congress Cataloging in Publication Data

Wilson, John Harold, 1900–
    Court satires of the Restoration.

    Bibliography, p.
    Includes index.
    1. Satire, English. 2. English poetry—Early modern, 1500–1700. I. Title.
    PR1195.S3W55   821'.07   75-28021
    ISBN 0-8142-0249-7

TO EDWIN W. ROBBINS

CONTENTS

CONTENTS

ACKNOWLEDGMENTS

I am indebted to the officers of the Ohio State University who, by several periods of assigned research duty, made it possible for me to work in some of the world's great libraries: Harvard, Yale, Princeton, Columbia, the New York Public and the Folger Shakespeare in this country, and the British Museum, the Public Record Office, the Victoria and Albert, Cambridge University, and Oxford's Bodleian in England. To the long-suffering librarians and curators of those institutions I offer my thanks for their help and my apologies for the strains I imposed upon their patience. Finally I am grateful to the Editorial Board and the staff of the Ohio State University Press.

J. H. W.

INTRODUCTION

The purpose of this volume is to present a selection of typical Restoration Court satires—personal satires—from 1663 through 1690. The political satires of the period have been well represented by such modern collections as *The Roxburghe Ballads* and *The Bagford Ballads* and by the recent publication of the Yale *Poems on Affairs of State*. Court satires have been only incidentally represented in these collections; yet in some ways they are more interesting and useful than the political poems because they tell us a great deal about the lives and manners of Restoration high society. Partisan political satire is ephemeral; personal satire is more likely to be universal.

Written for the coterie of fashionable folk who frequented the Court, strolled in the galleries of Whitehall and in St. James's Park, drove in Hyde Park, gambled at the Groom Porter's lodgings, and thronged the playhouses, Court satires deal with Court personalities, literary and theatrical figures, and the intrigues and scandals which were the talk of the town. The Court poets seem to have been remarkably well informed, and usually, to judge by contemporary gossip as recorded in private letters, newsletters, diaries, and memoirs, their victims deserved the punishment of publicity.

Ideally, satire might be described as the product of indignation recollected in tranquillity. In literature satire is definable as a device for achieving rejection or repudiation by means of ridicule, which may vary in quality from good-natured raillery to mordant scorn. Its purpose is to render a person (or a group), an institution, an idea, or a practice ludicrous or contemptible. Its common devices are burlesque, parody, irony, exaggeration (or understatement), and invective.

A satirist may be moved by ethical, moral, or social indignation, by personal animus, or by downright malice. His point of view may be ideal, societal, or personal. Usually the best satire is written from an ideal point of view by a satirist inspired by ethical indignation. Laughter is never more than incidental to satire, and some satires approach tragedy in tone. Satire can be embodied in any artistic form.

In Restoration England personal libels and lampoons—or poems on private affairs—were relatively new. Reaching back to classical writers, the Court poets preferred the whips of Juvenal to the gentle scoldings of Horace. Except for fugitive, usually anonymous, political ballads, they had few recent models. In effect the Court satirists, asserting that they were moved by moral indignation, adapted the forms and methods of political satire to their own purposes, attacking their victims more for vice and folly than for political heresy. The result was social satire, as timely—and usually as vicious—as the prose of gossip columnists in modern periodicals.

Thousands of Court libels and lampoons must have been written in the years 1660 through 1700; hundreds have survived. Harleian MS. 7319 in the British Museum, "A Collection of Choice Poems," contains 755 satires, of which some 680 are personal libels. The fashion seems to have grown slowly; there are comparatively few Court satires to be found from the date of King Charles II's restoration (May 19, 1660) to about 1679. After that they multiplied fantastically during the last years of the reign and fell off during the brief reign of James II, perhaps because, with the breaking up of the Restoration coterie, the poets were losing both subject matter and audience. In the dour and proper reign of William and Mary, many of the Court libelers turned to political satire.

Most of the satires in the following collection appear in two or more manuscript collections, and some were printed singly or in various editions of the *Poems on Affairs of State* (1689–1716). Customarily Court satires were first passed around in manuscript and copied by gentlemen (or their secretaries) for their own collections, or copied by such scribes as "Captain" Robert Julian, styled "Secretary to the Muses," for the country trade. The manuscript collections in such major libraries as the British Museum, the Victoria and Albert Museum, the Bodleian, the Huntington, the Folger, Harvard, and Yale, are usually of two kinds: anthologies of satires, chronologically arranged and copied by professional writers into blank-leaved folios or quartos; and aggregations of satires in a variety of hands, often copies sent by the post to correspondents in the country, and later loosely bundled or bound together in a volume. Frequently in aggregations one comes across sheets still showing the creases resulting from folding the paper down to letter size. Of course there is no way of knowing whether such satires are the originals or early copies, but it is reasonable to suppose that they are closer to the originals than versions copied by later scribes into blank books, or printed in late seventeenth-century miscellanies.

Most of the Court satires were circulated without an author's name. There were sound reasons for satirists to remain anonymous. A poet was subject to suits for libel, for *scandalum magnatum*, or for violating the Licensing Act of 1662, which was stretched to include the circulation of manuscript political satires. (The Act expired in May, 1679, but it was replaced by royal proclamations and renewed from 1685 to 1695.) Moreover, courtiers were quick to defend their "honor," either with their own swords or with the clubs of hired bravos. Thus it was generally believed at the time that John Dryden was beaten in Rose Street on the night of December 18, 1679, at the instigation of someone libeled in an anonymous "Essay upon Satire," written by John, Earl of Mulgrave, but mistakenly attributed to his protegée, Dryden.[1]

Attribution in manuscript or print must always be suspect. Even the inclusion of a satire in the posthumous "Works" of a contemporary poet is no guarantee that he wrote it. Unscrupulous printers were always ready to pad out a thin sheaf of verses with any unattributed songs, lampoons, or libels at hand, and some of them were not above cannibalizing lesser poets to fill out the scrawny flesh of a volume. For example, after his careful examination of the 61 poems in Rochester's *Poems on Several Occasions* (1680), David M. Vieth concluded that 15 were certainly and 19 probably by Rochester; 2 and perhaps 1 more by Sir George Etherege; 3 by Aphra Behn; 3 by John Oldham; 2 and perhaps 1 more by Sir Carr Scroope; 3 and perhaps 2 more by Lord Dorset; 2 by Alexander Radcliffe; 1 by Thomas D'Urfey; 1 by Edmund Ashton; probably 1 by Sir Charles Sedley; probably 1 by Lady Rochester; and 4 of uncertain authorship. All were attributed to Rochester by the volume's original printer.[2]

If we cannot attribute specific satires to their authors, we know at least who some of the satirists were. Hardened sinners themselves, they were an envious, self-conscious lot, who rarely praised and often sneered at their rivals. Sometimes they wrote little critical essays in verse, praising their friends and attacking their poetical enemies. Thus in "Advice to Apollo," 1677, the poet asks the god of poesy to pardon the satiric muses of Charles Sackvile (Buckhurst), Earl of Dorset, and John Wilmot, Earl of Rochester, and to "strike" such upstarts as Sir Carr Scroope, John Dryden, Fleetwood Shepherd, and John Sheffield, Earl of Mulgrave,

> with th'affected train
> Who satire write, yet scarce can spell their name.[3]

Similarly, the author of "A Ballad [1682]" (verses quoted are in this collection unless footnoted) attacks as mere scribblers of satire John Baber; John ("Jack") Howe; Anthony Carey, Viscount Falkland; Fleetwood Shepherd; Henry Heveningham; Charles, Viscount Mordaunt; Dr. Charles Frazier; and William Fanshaw. In "To Julian" [1684], another poet ridicules the satiric squibs of Henry, Lord Eland; John, Earl of Mulgrave; Jack Howe, and John Cutts. The author of "Julian's Farewell to the Muses," 1685, complains about "Howe's envenomed pen," the "sharp, mercurial wit" of George Etherege, the empty thoughts of Lord Eland, and the "censorious wit" of Charles, Earl of Dorset. This running *poetomachia* seems to have been motivated more by malice than by critical judgment.

Rarely a daring poet admitted his authorship, usually in the last line of his satire. Thus "Advice, or a Heroic Epistle to Mr. Fr. Villiers" [1683], ends with

> Now to conclude at parting,
> All I have writ is certain,
> And so I end,
> Your faithful friend
> And servant, Roger Martin.

"A Letter to Julian in Prison," 1685, concludes

> So rest I till you hear from me again,
> Your real friend and servant,
>   Henry Maine.[4]

Similarly, "Satyr 1692/93" concludes

> This stingless satire's author, if you'd know,
> The dial speaks not, but it points
>   Jack Howe.[5]

Most of the poets were attached to the Court in some capacity or other and could pick up the gossip of the day in the Stone Gallery, the Privy Chambers, the Groom Porter's lodgings, or in nearby coffee houses and taverns. Some went to greater lengths. According to Bishop Burnet, Lord Rochester dressed a footman as a guardsman sentinel "and kept him all the winter long every night at the doors of such ladies as he believed might be in intrigues."[6] We are told by their rivals that Hugh, Lord Cholmondeley, used his footmen as spies to follow suspected sinners about town, and that Jack Howe sent forth his sisters to watch the actions of their friends and acquaintances. The author of "A Satyr" [1680], accused Ned Russell, third son of William, Earl of Bedford, of spying on the town.

> . . . Like a cur who's taught to fetch he goes
> From place to place to bring back what he knows;
> Tells who's i'th' Park, what coaches turned about,
> Who were the sparks, and whom they followed out.

Eight years later Sir George Etherege commented that Ned had spent most of his life jolting about the streets in a hackney coach "to find out the harmless lusts of the Town."[7] Finally, Captain Robert Julian, a busy purveyor of satires, trotted from coffee houses to bawdy houses with his pockets full of verses for sale, picked up the latest scandal, and passed it on to the stable of poets who supplied him with libels.

Lacking information, the Court poets boldly copied from each other or followed the general principle, "Give a bitch a bad name and you might as well hang her." Thus the widowed Frances, Duchess of Richmond, once reputed mistress to King Charles, endured the attacks of malicious libelers for the rest of her blameless life, becoming, in effect, a mythical harlot. Similarly the poets often magnified the affairs of known sinners into monstrosities of lechery; they were always ready to embroider fact with fiction. Lord Rochester defended "the lies in his libels" by saying that they "came often in as ornaments that could not be spared without spoiling the beauty of the poem."[8] A naive anonymous poet put the matter more simply in "Scandal Satyrd" [1682],

> Poets may add, but not base lies invent;
> Reforming, not defaming, is their talent.

Each fault I find, in downright truth I'll show it,
For I mean well, but am a scurvy poet;
But 'tis some merit to be dull and know it.[9]

"Satire," "lampoon" (once a drinking song), and "libel" (originally an attack on a single victim) were interchangeable terms in Restoration England. The favorite devices of the satiric poets were scurrilous invective, obvious irony, and occasionally burlesque—all written in the coarsest possible terms. The simplest form of satire was a ballad or a set of verses in iambic couplets, often (to judge by the title) designed to be sung to a popular broadside tune. Most of the satires were "shotguns," loaded with obscene epithets and scandalous charges against those whom the poet happened to dislike or envy, or about whom there was a deal of gossip at the moment. Letters of so-called advice to "Julian, Secretary to the Muses," or some other distributor of scandal, were numerous. More pretentious were imitations of the form, but not the tone, of Horatian satires, and "session" satires (imitating Suckling's "A Session of the Poets"), in which poets appeared before Apollo, lovers before Venus or Cupid, or suitors for a place at Court before King Charles II. The verses are often rough and the rhymes discordant. No matter; the poets aimed for liveliness, ribaldry, and vigor. As Addison wrote of a later generation of satirists, "Scurrility passes for wit, and he who can call names in the greatest variety of phrases is looked upon to have the shrewdest pen."[10]

Court satires were rarely printed, and manuscript copies were not easily obtained. On January 26, 1674, for example, Walter Overbury wrote to Sir Joseph Williamson at Cologne, "Sir Nic[holas Armourer] sent your excellency a song of a certain signior that came in with the Duchess of Modena ["Signior Dildo"], which if it is miscarried I must take care to write it anew, though it reaches and touches most of the ladies from Westminster to Wapping."[11] In 1682 Lady Campden wrote to Lady Rutland, "There are sad lampoons made of all the [Court] ladies, but I cannot get a copy of them."[12] Even when copies of such "sad lampoons" were available, some ladies were reluctant to handle them without tongs. Thus Lady Frances Brudenell wrote to Lady Hatton in 1680, "The lampoons that are made of most of the Town ladies are so nasty that no woman will read them, or I would have got them for you."[13]

Fortunate indeed was the gentlewoman who could say with Wycherley's Alithea in *The Country Wife*, "Why, pray, who boasts of any intrigue with me? What lampoon has made my name notorious?" Women were easy game for the Court satirists; they could not defend their honor with sword and dagger. Moreover, according to contemporary law and the still viable medieval myth, they were vulnerable; as women they were considered inferior beings, by nature given to frivolity, inconstancy, lechery, and adultery.

In 1685 Robert Wolseley described the ladies' plight. "Women's reputations . . . have been reckoned as lawful game as watchmen's heads, and 'tis thought as glorious a piece of gallantry by some of our modern sparks to libel a woman of honor as to kill a constable who is doing his duty. . . . How infamous, insipid, or ignorant soever the authors themselves are, their satires want not sting; for upon no better evidence than those poetical fables and palpable forgeries, the poor ladies, whose little plots they pretend to discover, are either made prisoners in their own houses or banished into the country during life; though so ill-colored generally is the spite and so utterly devoid of all common probability are the brutal censures that stuff up their licentious lampoons that 'tis not easy to determine which of the two deserve most to be laughed at, the fantastical foplings that write 'em or the cautious coxcombs that believe 'em."[14]

Mr. Wolseley overstated his case. No doubt some ladies suffered for an innocent flirtation magnified by a satirist into adultery, but certainly underlying most of the "poetical fables" is a great deal of prosaic, biographical fact. Sin flourished at the Restoration Court; many a gay blade boasted openly of his conquests, and many a titled trollop flaunted her wickedness brazenly, to the disgust of the respectable, the envious, and the unsuccessful. The "fantastical foplings" simply substituted "women" for "men" in Dryden's dictum that " 'Tis an action of virtue to make examples of vicious men."[15] The poets belabored vicious men, too, but they honestly believed that women were naturally sinful and more to blame than the men they tempted. In "Woman's Wisdom. 1683", an anonymous fopling wrote,

> Nature does strangely female gifts dispense,
> Lavish in lust and niggardly in sense.
> Those who have reason, women still detest,
> But court to their embrace a driv'ling beast.[16]

xvii

The misogynous author of "A Satire on the Court Ladies," 1680, picturing the typical wife as always lustful, concluded,

> While next her lust, the chiefest joy she takes
> Is slyly to deride the fool she makes.
> Nor will she to one lover be confined,
> But is as surely false as she is kind.
> Husband and lovers all she makes her prey,
> And for her ends by turns will all betray.

Significantly a gentleman could sue his adulterous wife in the spiritual courts for a divorce *a mensa et thoro* (a legal separation), or before the House of Lords for a divorce *a vinculo*. But in the spiritual courts a wife could rarely win unless she could prove her husband guilty of extreme cruelty, and until the nineteenth century no wife could sue her errant husband for a divorce *a vinculo*.[17] In Restoration England male promiscuity was not even a venial sin. Smugly secure in their masculine ethos, then, Court satirists felt justified in firing their blunderbusses at Court bawds, harlots, and adulteresses, occasionally hitting an innocent woman. They fired at men too—fops, fools, rakes, and rascals—and rarely hit an innocent man.

In effect, Restoration Court satires constitute a body of subliterature, interesting in itself, and often useful to the biographer and the social historian. From this well-fertilized soil came some masterpieces, for instance, the personal satires of Rochester, Dorset, Dryden, Swift, and Pope.

Because Court satires were written for and about the members of a close-knit coterie, who would immediately identify the *personae* of a satire even under nicknames, modern editorial identification is difficult. Peers changed their titles from time to time—when a son inherited his father's title, or a baron was promoted to viscount or earl. Wives of peers had an inconvenient habit of dying in childbed; many a peer had two or more wives in the course of his lifetime, each referred to only by his title. Lesser courtiers—Ladies of the Bedchamber, Maids of Honor, Gentlemen and Grooms of the Bedchamber, minor members of the royal household, and officers of the Guards—shifted their employments, changed their names by marriage or promotion, or resigned, perhaps to be replaced by a kinsman with the same surname.

The Court poets rarely used both given names and surnames. Unfortunately in their casts of characters there are often two or more people with the same surname; there were many Gerards and dozens of Villierses. Frequently, too, the poets called their victims by such nicknames as "King John," "Grandio," "wry-mouthed Tyzard," "Goliath," "Perkin," "Old Maggot," "the Lily Lass," and "Princely Nan," or they used only a given name with an epithet: "whistling John" (Berkeley), "villain Frank" (Villiers), "bold Frank" (Newport), "beardless Phil" (Kirke), "scabby Ned" (Villiers), or "well-bred Mall" (Howard). Often the context of a passage or the repeated use of an epithet helps to identify a character. Thus "Grandio" and "King John" are clearly cant names for John Sheffield, Earl of Mulgrave, who earned the titles by his arrogance and by his ill-advised addresses to Princess Anne. Occasionally a marginal gloss identifies the *personae* of a satire, but such glosses must be used with caution; often they are only the guesses of later transcribers.

Even more difficult is the identification of scandalous liaisons and episodes. Topical references are often so brief or cryptic as to defy explanation. Fortunately the period abounds in personal letters, diaries, and memoirs supplying items which, put together like the pieces of a jig-saw puzzle, serve to illuminate many references. Occasionally the literary detective must frankly admit that he cannot identify or explain a reference.

Most of the satires in this collection are drawn from the Harleian and Additional Manuscripts in the British Museum. Some are from collections in the Bodleian Library, Oxford University, notably MS. Don b. 8, Douce MS. 357, MS. Eng. Poet. d. 152, MS. Firth c. 15, and MS. Rawl. Poet. 81, 159, and 173. A very useful collection is Dyce MS. 43 in the Victoria and Albert Museum. Some satires are drawn from Harvard MSS. 633 and 636 F, from Folger MS. m. b. 12, and from the Ohio State Wentworth MS, "A Choyce Collection."[18]

From the many satires available I have chosen to reproduce those which seemed to me most interesting and most representative of their kind and date. I have modernized punctuation and spelling, and I have included in the notes only substantial textual variants. All dates are Old Style, but I have given them as if the year began on January 1 instead of on March 25 (e.g., January 1, 1682, not January 1,

1681/2). Dates in brackets after the titles of satires are conjectural. To reduce repetition, I have added in an appendix brief biographies of persons frequently mentioned.

J. H. W.

1. See C. E. Ward, *The Life of John Dryden*, 1961, pp. 143–44.

2. David M. Vieth, *Attribution in Restoration Poetry*, 1963, pp. 365–477.

3. *Poems on Affairs of State*, Yale, 1963, I, 392.

4. Victoria and Albert Dyce MS., II, 637.

5. MS. Holkham (Earls of Leicester), p. 129.

6. Gilbert Burnet, *History of His Own Time*, 1823, I, 486.

7. Additional MS. 34, 362, p. 132; *Letters of Sir George Etherege*, ed. Frederick Bracher, 1974, p. 185.

8. Gilbert Burnet, *Some Passages of the Life and Death of . . . John, Earl of Rochester*, 1680, p. 26.

9. Harleian MS. 6913, p. 209.

10. *The Spectator*, no. 451, August 7, 1712.

11. *Letters to Sir Joseph Williamson*, 1874, II, 132.

12. *Rutland MS*, II, 69.

13. Joan Wake, *The Brudenells of Deene*, 1953, p. 184.

14. Preface To Rochester's alteration of *Valentinian*, 1685.

15. *Of Dramatic Poesy*, ed. George Watson, 1962, II, 126.

16. Rawlinson MS. Poet. 159, f. 79.

17. See Frederick Clifford, *A History of Private Bill Legislation*, 2 vols., 1885.

18. For an excellent bibliographical analysis of these and other MSS, see W. J. Cameron, "A Late Seventeenth-Century Scriptorium," *Renaissance and Modern Studies*, VI, 1963, 24–52.

REFERENCES CITED BY SHORT TITLES

Boswell, Eleanor, *The Restoration Court Stage*, 1932.

Brown, Tom, *Amusements Serious and Comical*, ed. A. L. Hayward, 1927.

Browning, Andrew, *Memoirs of Sir John Reresby*, 1936.

———. *Thomas Osborne, Earl of Danby and Duke of Leeds*, 3 vols. 1944–51.

The Bulstrode Papers . . . Newsletters Written to Sir Richard Bulstrode, 1673–1675, 1896.

Burnet, Gilbert, *History of His Own Time*, 6 vols., 1825.

Calendar of Orrery Papers, ed. E. MacLysacht, 1941.

Calendars of State Papers, Domestic Series.

Calendars of Treasury Books.

Carte, Thomas, *The Life of James, Duke of Ormonde*, 6 vols., 1851.

Cartwright, Julia, *Sacharissa*, 1901.

Clarendon State Papers, 2 vols., 1763.

Cockayne, G. E., *Complete Baronetage*, 5 vols., 1900–1909.

———. *Complete Peerage*, ed. Vicary Gibbs, 13 vols., 1910–59.

Collins, Arthur, *The Peerage of England*, 8 vols., 1779.

Dalton, Charles, *English Army Lists*, 6 vols., rpt., 1960.

D'Aulnoy, Marie Catherine, *Memoirs of the Court of England in 1675*, ed. G. D. Gilbert, 1913.

Delpech, Jenine, *The Life and Times of the Duchess of Portsmouth*, 1953.

The Letters of John Dryden, ed. C. E. Ward, 1942.

The Ellis Correspondence, ed. Agar Ellis, 2 vols., 1829.

Letters of Sir George Etherege, ed. Frederick Bracher, 1974.

The Diary of John Evelyn, ed. E. S. De Beer, 6 vols., 1955.

Fea, Allan, *Some Beauties of the Seventeenth Century*, 1907.

The Gyldenstolpe Manuscript Miscellany, ed. Bror Danielson and David M. Veith, 1967.

Hamilton, Anthony, *Memoirs of Count Grammont*, ed. Gordon Goodwin, 2 vols., 1903.

Harris, Brice, *Charles Sackville, Sixth Earl of Dorset*, 1940.

Correspondence of the Family of Hatton . . . 1601–1704, ed. E. M. Thompson, 2 vols., 1878.

Hearne, Thomas, *Remarks and Collections*, 11 vols., 1885–1921.

Herbert Correspondence, ed. W. J. Smith, 1963.

Historical Manuscripts Commission Reports:

Fifth Report	*Finch MS*
Sixth Report	*Hastings MS*
Seventh Report	*Hodgkin MS*
Tenth Report	*House of Lords MS*
Bath MS	*Kenyon MS*
Beaufort MS	*Le Fleming MS*
Buccleuch MS	*Ormonde MS*
Denbigh MS	*Portland MS*
Downshire MS	*Rutland MS*
Egmont MS	*Stuart Papers*

Jusserand J. J., *A French Ambassador at the Court of Charles the Second*, 1892.

The Diary of Dr. Edward Lake, ed. G. P. Elliott, 1846.

The Lexington Papers, ed. H. Sutton-Manners, 1851.

London County Council, *Survey of London*.

London Marriage Licenses, 1521–1869, ed. Joseph Foster, 1887.

Luttrell, Narcissus, *A Brief Relation of State Affairs*, 6 vols., 1857.

Macaulay, Thomas, *The History of England*, 10 vols., 1849.

Macky, John, *Memoirs of the Secret Services of John Macky, Esq.*, 1733.

Middlesex County Records, Vol. IV, 1892.

Newsletters Addressed to Sir Richard Newdigate, The Folger Shakespear Library, Washington, D.C.

The Diary of Samuel Pepys, ed. H. B. Wheatley, 10 vols., 1893–99.

Poems on Affairs of State, editions of 1689, 1703, 1705, 1716.

Poems on Affairs of State, 1660–1714, Yale, 6 vols., 1963–71.
Vol. I, ed. George deF. Lord; Vol. II, ed. Elias F. Mengel; Vol. III, ed. Howard H. Schless; Vol. IV, ed. Galbraith M. Crump; Vol. V, ed. W. J. Cameron; Vol. VI, ed. Frank H. Ellis.

The Portledge Papers, 1687–1697, ed. R. J. Kerr and I. C. Duncan, 1928.

Price, Cecil, *Cold Caleb*, 1956.

Public Record Office, Lord Chamberlain and State Papers.

Complete Poems of John Wilmot, Earl of Rochester, ed. David M. Veith, 1968.

The Rochester-Savile Letters, 1671–1680, ed. J. H. Wilson, 1941.

Letters of Rachel, Lady Russell, 1854.

The Savile Correspondence, ed. W. D. Cooper, 1858.

Diary and Correspondence of Henry Sidney, ed. R. W. Blencoe, 1843.

Simpson, Claude M., *The British Broadside Ballad and its Music*, 1966.

A Complete Collection of State Trials, ed. T. J. Howell, 1812.

Memoirs of the Verney Family During the Seventeenth Century, ed. F. P. Verney and M. M. Verney, 2 vols., 1907.

Vernon, James, *Letters Illustrative of the Reign of William III*, 3 vols., 1841.

Westminister Abbey Registers, ed. J. L. Chester, 1876.

Letters Addressed from London to Sir Joseph Williamson, ed. W. D. Christie, 2 vols., 1874.

Wilson, J. H., *The Court Wits of the Restoration*, 1948.

———. *Nell Gwyn, Royal Mistress*, 1952.

———. *All the King's Ladies*, 1958.

Wood, Anthony, *The Life and Times of Anthony Wood*, ed. Andrew Clark, 5 vols., 1891–1900.

———. *Athenae Oxonienses*, ed. Philip Bliss, 4 vols, 1813.

———. *Fasti Oxonienses*, ed. Philip Bliss, 2 vols, 1815.

[ON THE LADIES OF THE COURT]

[*1663*]

The title of this early example of a shotgun satire is enclosed in brackets as conjectural; the original is without title or date. Probably it was written before September 16, 1663, when Lady Brudenell's husband Robert inherited as second Earl of Cardigan, and she became Lady Cardigan (line 30).

On September 30, 1660, James, Duke of York (the King's younger brother) secretly married Anne Hyde, daughter of Edward, Earl of Clarendon and Lord Chancellor. On May 21, 1662, King Charles II married Catherine of Braganza. Both the Queen and the Duchess had to have large entourages of servants: Ladies of the Bedchamber, Maids of Honor, Ladies of the Privy Chamber, and dressers. Most of the ladies libeled in this satire had some kind of post at Court, where, according to the cynics, virtue was a worthless commodity. Pepys reported (February 21, 1665) that "my Lady Castlemaine will in merriment say that her daughter (not above a year old or two) will be the first mayde in the Court that will be married."

The copy text is Bodleian MS. Don. b. 8, p. 179 ("Sir W. Haward's Collection").

Cary's face is not the best,
But she as useful as the rest,
Though not so much alluring;
She's near as good as Madam Wood
For pimping and procuring.   5

Strangely pleasant were their chats,
When Mayne and Steward played at flats,
Their marriage night so taught them;
Till Charles came there
And with his ware   10
Taught how their fathers got them.

3

Wells' broken vessels leak,
Though fools their freedom have to speak,
They take no honor from them;
Whilst thou art there   *15*
They are sure to bear
All that is laid upon them.

Warmestry's brows are black as coal,
Which makes me love her from my soul;
But, I fear, she's faulty.   *20*
For all her pride,
Her cony's wide;
She needs not be so haughty.

Boynton, Price and all the rest,
Take heed of leap-frog, though in jest,   *25*
Obey your reverend Mother,
Who warns you all
To none to fall
But Caesar and his brother.

Brudenell long was innocent,   *30*
But for the time she has misspent
She'll make amends hereafter.
Who can do more
Than play the whore
And pimp too for her daughter?   *35*

Shrewsbury hath sounding fits,
You'd think she'd almost lose her wits,
She lies so on the ground, sir;
But Jermyn's tarse
Will claw her arse   *40*
And make her soon rebound, sir.

Killigrew is whore enough,
And though her cunt be not so rough,

4

She makes it up in motion.
'Twill be good rent 45
When all is spent
And prove her better portion.

Shirley thinks she has got renown,
'Cause to the offers of the crown
She gave such bold denial. 50
'Tis clear as the sun
'Twas Carlisle's gun
That made her so disloyal.

Middleton, since thou dost swive
Thou art the simplest wench alive 55
To give such friends denial.
For Castlemaine
Shows thee the gain
To command the pintle royal.

Savile's eyes are full of fire, 60
Which makes appear her heart's desire,
But she's a close contriver;
For all agree
That Bates is he
That doth in private swive her. 65

Wetnall will not take a touch,
But yet, to show her lust as much,
She hath boys to grope her;
For now and anon
'Tis Hamilton, 70
But constantly Will Roper.

Hamilton's a crafty wench,
Who by speaking so good French
Hath overcome her knight, sir.
She doth but stay 75

Her marriage day,
And then she will be right, sir.

Scroope, they say, hath no good breath,
But yet she's well enough beneath,
And hath a good figary;   *80*
Or with such ease
She could not please
The King's great secretary.

Waldgrave now is out of date,
For all her servants now of late   *85*
Have found her breath so stinking!
She mourns her luck,
For they'll not fuck
Unless they have been drinking.

Leveston is yet but small,   *90*
But she's the fairest of them all,
And hath as many graces.
For she can kill
Whenso e'er she will,
Such charming in her face is.   *95*

Byron fain would conquer still,
But now she only hath the will;
Her killing power is over;
And yet 'tis plain
She hurt Dick Lane,   *100*
But he's like to recover.

---

1. *Cary*. Simona Cary, daughter of Sir Ferdinand Cary, was one of Queen Catherine's original Maids of Honor. In 1670 the King gaver her £2,000 bounty, presumably toward her marriage (*CTB*, 1670, p. 660). Since the poet charged her only with "pimping and procuring," an easy indictment, the chances are that she was reasonably virtuous.

4. *Wood.* Mary, Lady Wood, formerly Mary Gardiner, one of Queen Henrietta Maria's Maids of Honor, married in November, 1651, Sir Henry Wood in Paris. After the Restoration, Sir Henry became Clerk of the Board of the Green Cloth, and his wife became one of Queen Catherine's dressers. After Lady Wood died of smallpox in 1665, Pepys remarked (March 17, 1665) that she was "a good-natured woman and a good wife, but for all that it was ever believed she was as others were." Lady Wood's daughter, Mary, married Charles Fitzroy, Duke of Southampton, in 1671, and died November 15, 1680, aged seventeen.

7. *Mayne.* Barbara (Villiers) Palmer, Countess of Castlemaine, Lady of the Queen's Bedchamber, and the King's chief mistress; see Appendix, Cleveland. *Steward.* Frances Teresa Stuart, one of the Queen's Maids of Honor; see Appendix, Richmond. *at flats.* Lesbian practices. See "The Ladies' Complaint to Venus," c. 1691 (Lansdowne MS. 852, f.43) in which Venus scolds the ladies,

> you are to blame
> And have got a new game
> Called flats, with a swinging clitoris.

8. *marriage night.* According to gullible Mr. Pepys (February 8, 1663), Lady Castlemaine and Mrs. Stuart went through a mock wedding ceremony one night, "but in the close, it is said that Lady Castlemaine, who was the bridegroom, rose, and the King came and took her place with pretty Mrs. Stuart. This is said to be very true."

12. *Wells.* Winifred Wells, youngest daughter of Gilbert Wells of Twyford, Hants., was one of the Queen's original Maids of Honor, and one of the King's many mistresses. It was said that she had dropped a child during a Court ball, perhaps on December 31, 1662 (Pepys, February 8, 1663). On February 20, 1665, a gossip reported that the King had given her "£1,500 or £2,000" (*Sixth Report*, p. 337B). On September 7, 1672, the King gave her £2,150 (*CSPD*, 1672, p. 627), probably as a marriage portion. On July 14, 1673, she owned her marriage to Thomas Windham, one of the King's equerries, and the Queen appointed her as a dresser (*Williamson*, I, 104). She remained in the Queen's service until 1692.

18. *Warmestry.* Ellene or Hellene Warmestry was one of the Queen's Maids of Honor. She figures in Hamilton's *Memoirs of Count Grammont* (I, 105, 135; II, 29), "Miss Warmestre was brown; she had no shape at all, and still less air; but she had a very lively complexion, very sparkling eyes, [and] tempting looks." Although unmarried, she was "very quietly brought to bed in the midst of the Court." The father of her by-blow may have been William, Lord Taafe. Eventually she married John Machen, of Hills, Sussex.

22. *cony.* Vagina.

24. *Boynton.* Katherine, daughter of Colonel Matthew Boynton of Barniston, Yorks., was one of the Queen's Maids of Honor. In May or June, 1669, she married Colonel Richard ("Lying Dick") Talbot, a Gentleman of the Bedchamber to the Duke of York. Katherine died in 1678. *Price.* Henrietta Maria, daughter of Sir Robert Price, The Priory, Brecon., was also one of the Queen's Maids of Honor. On December 4, 1673, she married Alexander Stanhope of the Inner Temple, a widower and younger son of Sir John Stanhope of Elvaston, Derby. The King gave her a warrant for a dowry of £2,500. She died in October, 1674, and three years later Stanhope claimed the dowry, which was still unpaid (*Westminster Abbey Registers*; *CTB*, 1676–79, p. 582).

7

26. *reverend mother*. Bridget, wife of Sir William Sanderson (1586?–1676) was "Mother of the Maids of Honor" to the Queen until she died, January 17, 1682, aged eighty-nine.

30. *Brudenell*. Lady Anne, fourth daughter of Thomas Savage, Earl Rivers, was the second wife of Robert Brudenell (1607–1703), who inherited as second Earl of Cardigan on September 16, 1663. Lady Brudenell seems to have been respectable enough, but as the mother of the beautiful but indiscreet Anna-Maria, Countess of Shrewsbury, she was damned by association.

36. *Shrewsbury*. Anna-Maria (Brudenell), second wife of Francis Talbot (1623–68), eleventh Earl of Shrewsbury. See Appendix, Shrewsbury.

39. *Jermyn*. Henry Jermyn (1636–1708), Master of the Horse to the Duke of York and a handsome little man with a large head, was an irresistable lover. On August 17, 1662, Jermyn fought an impromptu duel with Captain Thomas Howard, his rival for Lady Shrewsbury's favors. Jermyn's second, Giles Rawlins, was killed, and Jermyn was seriously wounded (Pepys, August 19, 1662). *tarse*. Penis.

42. *Killigrew*. Probably Elizabeth, daughter of Sir William Killigrew, Vice-Chamberlain to the Queen. At this time Elizabeth was one of the Queen's dressers and unmarried; hence the emphasis on her "portion." She married Sir Francis Clinton (1635–93), son of the fifth Earl of Lincoln and a Gentleman of the Privy Chamber. Lady Clinton was buried in Westminster Abbey on December 11, 1677.

48. *Shirley*. Dame Anne Shirley, widow of Sir Thomas Shirley, an obscure lady, seems to have lived at the King's expense (see *CSPD*, 1665–66, p. 424). On December 22, 1663, the King gave her £50 as "royal bounty" (*CTB*, 1660–67, p. 565).

52. *Carlisle*. Charles Howard (c.1629–85), son of Sir William Howard of Naworth, Cumb., was created on April 30, 1661, Earl of Carlisle. In 1663 he was ambassador to Russia. According to Burnet (*Own Time*, II, 265), Carlisle "had been in great favor with Cromwell . . . and had then run into a high profession of religion, to the pitch of praying and preaching at their meetings. But after the Restoration he shook that off and run into a course of vice."

54. *Middleton*. The beautiful and notorious Jane Middleton, a famous beauty; see Appendix, Middleton.

57. *Castlemaine*. Barbara (Villiers) Palmer, Countess of Castlemaine, the King's chief mistress; see Appendix, Cleveland. *pintle*. penis.

60. *Savile*. Probably Lady Frances Savile, daughter of Thomas, Earl of Sussex. In June, 1668, she married Francis, Lord Brudenell, son of Robert, second Earl of Cardigan. In "Scandal Satired" [1682], Harleian MS. 6913, p. 209, she is described

> As grinning Brudenell, nown mother's brat,
> Famed for sly lust and pert provoking chat.

Lady Frances died June 6, 1695; her husband in 1698.

64. *Bates*. Possibly Charles Bates, a very minor courtier. He was the second husband of Anne, widow (1657) of Edward, Lord Clinton.

66. *Wetnall*. Elizabeth, daughter of Sir Henry Bedingfield of Oxborough, Norfolk, and wife of Thomas Wetenhall of East Peckham, Kent, was a flirt, but would not satisfy her lover, Hamilton (see *Grammont*, II, 95, 216).

68. *grope*. Touch, feel amorously.

70. *Hamilton*. Captain George Hamilton, younger brother of Anthony, author of *The Memoirs of Count Grammont*. George was an officer in the Horse Guards

at this time. After 1667 he took service in the French army, was created a count, and died at the Battle of Saverne in June, 1676. He married Frances Jennings, Maid of Honor to the Duchess of York.

72. *Hamilton.* Elizabeth (1641–1708), oldest daughter of Sir George Hamilton, married "her knight," Philiberte, Comte de Grammont, in December, 1663, and went to France with him November 3, 1664.

77. *right.* A cant term for sexually available.

78. *Scroope.* Lady Mary Scroope, a famous wit, was daughter of Sir Robert Carr of Sleaford, Lincs., widow of Sir Adrian Scroope, mother of the minor poet, Sir Carr Scroope, and one of the Queen's dressers. In 1663 she was mistress of Henry Bennet, Earl of Arlington, "The King's great secretary" of state (Jusserand, *A French Ambassador*, p. 151). Later she was the mistress of Henry Savile, Envoy to France (Cartwright, *Sacharissa*, p. 234). Lady Scroope died in 1685.

80. *figary.* Probably *figuerie*, a fig garden; obscene.

84. *Waldgrave.* Probably one of the daughters of Sir Henry Waldgrave, Bart., of Stoninghall, Norfolk. By two successive wives, Sir Henry had eleven sons and eleven daughters!

85. *servants.* Lovers.

90. *Leveston.* According to Lord Cornbury (*Beaufort MS*, pp. 52-53), this was Lady Elizabeth Livingston, daughter of James, Earl of Newburgh. Still very young, she was a "maid" of the Privy Chamber to the Queen.

96. *Byron.* Eleanor, daughter of Robert Needham, Viscount Kilmurry, was the second wife of John Byron, first Lord Byron, who died in 1652. Lady Byron had been one of the King's mistresses during the period of royal exile. According to John Evelyn, she had been the King's "seventeenth whore abroad" (Pepys, April 26, 1666). Lady Byron died on January 26, 1664.

100. *Dick Lane.* Richard Lane was a Groom of the Bedchamber to the King. The poet implies that Lady Byron "hurt" him by giving him venereal disease.

A BALLAD

[*1667*]

King Charles II had barely entered into his inheritance when a host of broken cavaliers who had lost everything but their lives in the civil wars descended upon Whitehall with petitions for the repayment of loans, for the return of sequestered estates, or for places in the government. In the new King's circumstances, he could do little or nothing to satisfy their demands. The embittered cavaliers referred to the Act of Indemnity and Oblivion (August 29, 1660) as an act of indemnity for the King's enemies and of oblivion for his friends.

No doubt the disgruntled cavalier who wrote "A Ballad" had been defeated in his own expectations and chose to lay the blame on a Court ruled by pimps, drabs, and cheats. He is unfair to Clarendon, an honest old man whose only fault was that he had passed his prime and was too rigid to cope with the new Restoration society.

The copy text is Add. MS. 34, 362, f. 18v. For an identical version see Bodleian MS. Don b. 8, p. 184. The satire is undated, but it must have been written before Clarendon was removed from office, August 30, 1667.

> Good people, draw near
> If a ballad you'd hear,
>   It will teach you the new way of thriving.
> Ne'er trouble your heads
> With your books or your beads;   5
>   The world's ruled by cheating and swiving.
>
> Ne'er prattle nor prate
> Of the miscarriages of state,
>   It will not avail you a button.
> He that sticks to the church   10
> Shall be left in the lurch,
>   With never a tatter to put on.

10

Old fatguts himself,
With his tripes and his pelf,
   With a purse as full as his paunch is,   *15*
Will confess that his Nanny
Fopdoodled her Jemmy,
   And his kingdom is come to the haunches.

Our Arlington Harry,
The prime Secretary,   *20*
   Was first of the smock a secretis;
Being esquire of the frock
And true to the smock,
   Now admitted to manage the state is.

And Dapper his clerk,   *25*
Being true to the mark,
   Was at once both his scribe and his setter;
But Joseph, we hear,
Would fain be a peer;
   Lord and lackey begin with a letter.   *30*

The controller Clifford
Was forced to stand stiff for't,
   To make his way to the table;
He had a friend at a shift
To give him a lift;   *35*
   Tom fool may thank G. for his bauble.

'Tis well for the Babs
That the pimps and the drabs
Are now in the way of promotion;
Else Villiers and May   *40*
Had been out of play,
   But Denham went off with a potion.

Next comes Castlemaine,
That prerogative quean;

If I had such a bitch I would spay her.   *45*
She swives like a stoat,
Goes to't leg and foot,
Level coil with a prince and a player.

6. *swiving.* Copulating. From AS *swifan*, to shake or move quickly.

10. *the church.* The Anglican, or Established Church.

13. *old fatguts.* Edward Hyde (1607–74), first Earl of Clarendon, a corpulent man, was Lord Chancellor from 1660 to 1667. He was accused of enriching himself at the expense of the state. He was removed from office on August 30, 1667, and impeached by the House of Commons in October. He fled abroad on November 29, 1667.

17. *fopdoodled.* Cheated, deceived. The poet accuses Anne Hyde (1637–71), daughter of Clarendon, of tricking James ("Jemmy"), Duke of York, into marrying her on September 3, 1660, seven weeks before her first child by the Duke was born. Since King Charles still lacked legitimate offspring, Anne's children were in the line of succession to the throne.

18. *haunches.* I.e., James, who should have married a princess, has debased his royal blood merely for the satisfaction of his loins.

19. *Arlington Harry.* Henry Bennet (1618–85) became Keeper of the King's Privy Purse (and ex officio pimp to the King) after the Restoration. He became First Secretary of State in October, 1662, and was created Baron Arlington in 1665 and Earl of Arlington in 1672. According to Thomas Carte (*Ormonde*, II, 147), Arlington "was a *fourbe* in his politics, loose in his principles, and thought to be a secret convert to the Roman Catholic religion." In 1674 he became Lord Chamberlain of the Household.

21. *the smock.* A chemise or loose undergarment of linen worn by women. *secretis.* The poet may have had in mind the Latin *secretus*: secret or private.

25. *Dapper.* Joseph Williamson (1633–1703) was at this time Keeper of the State Paper Office and Under-Secretary of State. A pliant and genial courtier, he was knighted on January 24, 1672, and succeeded Arlington as Secretary of State, 1674–79.

27. *Setter.* Pimp.

31. *Clifford.* Sir Thomas Clifford (1630–73), a fiery Roman Catholic, was appointed Comptroller of the Household on November 28, 1666. Thereafter he was successively a Commissioner of the Treasury (1667) and Lord High Treasurer (1672) until the Test Act forced him out of office.

36. *Tom fool.* Clifford. "G" has eluded me. Guineas? It was generally believed that Clifford owed his "bauble," the white wand of office borne by officers of the Royal Household, to his friend and patron, Henry Bennett, Lord Arlington.

37. *Babs.* Probably one was Dame Barbara Villiers, grandmother of Barbara, Lady Castlemaine, the King's reigning mistress. Dame Barbara (who died in 1672) had a house in King Street, a part of Whitehall just beyond the Privy Garden. The poet suggests that she procured for her granddaughter, Barbara. The other Bab was Baptist May (c. 1627–93), Keeper of the Privy Purse after Arlington, and his successor as pimp in ordinary.

42. *Denham.* Margaret (Brooke), wife of the eccentric poet Sir John Denham, was one of the Duke of York's mistresses. She died January 6, 1667, supposedly poisoned in a cup of chocolate by the Duchess of York's sister-in-law, Henrietta Hyde, later Countess of Rochester.

43. *Castlemaine.* Barbara, Countess of Castlemaine, the King's chief mistress; see Appendix, Cleveland. *quean.* Whore.

46. *stoat.* Ermine, reputedly lubricious.

48. *level coil.* On even terms. *a player.* According to the gossips, handsome Charles Hart, leading man of the King's Company of players, was one of Lady Castlemaine's numerous lovers (Pepys, April 7, 1668).

SIGNIOR DILDO

([*December*] *1673*)

Anne, Duchess of York died on March 31, 1671. On November 21, 1673, the Duke's second bride, Marie Beatrice d'Este, Princess of Modena, arrived in England with her mother, the Duchess Regent of Modena, and an entourage of Italian priests, ladies, and gentlemen. The new Duchess's arrival was the occasion for "Signior Dildo." On January 26, 1674, Walter Overbury wrote to Sir Joseph Williamson at Cologne, "Sir Nic[holas Armourer] sent your excellency a song of a certain senior that came in with the Dutchesse of Modena . . . it reaches and touches most of the ladys from Westminster to Wapping" (*Williamson Letters*, II, 132).

The artificial priapus, here aggrandized as "Signior Dildo," was not a novelty in England, but after the appearance of this popular ballad, it was often referred to only as the "signior." For example, in the epilogue to *The Mistaken Husband*, September, 1675, an actress says,

> To act with raw boys is loving without men.
> What will not poor forsaken women try?
> When man's not near, the Signior must supply.

Again, in "The Ladies' Complaint to Venus" [1691] (Lansdowne MS. 852, f.43) Venus complains,

> I am told with a vast long signior
> Some matrons do ease
> Their lust and do please,
> Though they have not been lain with these ten years.

"Signior Dildo" was first printed in *Poems on Affairs of State*, 1703. Attributing it to Rochester, David M. Vieth included the satire in his *The Complete Poems of John Wilmot, Earl of Rochester* (Yale, 1968). The ballad acquired many additional stanzas by later hands;

14

see "Additions to Signior Dildo," Bodleian MS. Don. b. 8., pp. 480–82.

Here the copy text is Harleian MS. 7319, p. 5, dated 1673. The satire is dated 1673 or 1674 in MS. Firth C. 15, p. 3; Harleian MS. 7317, p. 124; MS. Don. b. 8, p. 477; Dyce MS. 43, I, 119; and "A Choyce Collection," p. 10.

You ladies all of merry England
Who have been to kiss the Duchess's hand,
Pray, did you lately observe in the show
A noble Italian called Signior Dildo?

The Signior was one of her Highness's train   5
And helped to conduct her over the main,
But now she cries out, "To the Duke I will go;
I have no more need for Signior Dildo."

At the sign of the Cross in St. James's Street,
When next you go thither to make yourselves sweet   10
By buying of powder, gloves, essence or so,
You may chance get a sight of Signior Dildo.

You'll take him at first for no person of note,
Because he appears in a plain leather coat,
But when you his virtuous abilities know,   15
You'll fall down and worship Signior Dildo.

My Lady Southeske, Heaven prosper her for't,
First clothed him in satin, then sent him to Court.
But his head in the circle he scarcely durst show,
So modest a youth was Signior Dildo.   20

The good Lady Suffolk, thinking no harm,
Had got this poor stranger hid under her arm;

15

Lady Betty by chance came the secret to know,
And from her own mother stole Signior Dildo.

The Countess of Falmouth, of whom people tell   *25*
Her footmen wear shirts of a guinea an ell,
Might save the expense if she did but know
How lusty a swinger is Signior Dildo.

By the help of this gallant, the Countess of Rafe
Against the fierce Harry's preserved herself safe;   *30*
She stifled him almost beneath her pillow,
So closely she embraced Signior Dildo.

That pattern of virtue, her Grace of Cleveland,
Has swallowed more pricks than the nation has land;
But by rubbing and scrubbing so large it does grow   *35*
It is fit for just nothing but Signior Dildo.

Our dainty fine duchesses have got a trick
To dote on a fool for the sake of his prick;
The fops were undone did their graces but know
The discretion and vigor of Signior Dildo.   *40*

The Duchess of Modena, though she looks high,
With such a gallant is contented to lie,
And for fear the English her secrets should know,
For a gentleman usher took Signior Dildo.

The countess o'th' Cockpit (who knows not her name?   *45*
She's famous in story for a killing dame),
When all her old lovers forsake her, I trow,
She'll then be contented with Signior Dildo.

Red Howard, Red Sheldon, and Temple so tall
Complain of his absence so long from Whitehall.   *50*
Signior Bernard has promised a journey to go
And bring back his countryman, Signior Dildo.

16

Doll Howard no longer with his Highness must range,
And therefore is proffered this civil exchange:
Her teeth being rotten, she smells best below,   *55*
And needs must be fitted for Signior Dildo.

St. Albans with wrinkles and smiles in his face,
Whose kindness to strangers becomes his high place,
In his coach and six horses is gone to Bergo
To take the fresh air with Signior Dildo.   *60*

Were this Signior but known to the citizen fops,
He'd keep their fine wives from the foremen of shops;
But the rascals deserve their horns should still grow
For burning the Pope and his nephew Dildo.

Tom Killigrew's wife, North Holland's fine flower,   *65*
At the sight of this Signior did fart and belch sour,
And then her Dutch breeding farther to show,
Says, "Welcome to England, Mynheer Van Dildo."

He civilly came to the Cockpit one night
And proffered his service to fair Madam Knight.   *70*
Quoth she, "I intrigue with Captain Cazzo.
Your nose in mine arse, good Signior Dildo."

This Signior is sound, safe, ready, and dumb
As ever was candle, carrot, or thumb;
Then away with these nasty devices and show   *75*
How you rate the just merits of Signior Dildo.

Count Cazzo, who carries his nose very high,
In passion he swore his rival should die,
Then shut up himself to let the world know
Flesh and blood could not bear it from Signior Dildo.   *80*

A rabble of pricks, who were welcome before,
Now finding the porter denied 'em the door,

Mischievously waited his coming below,
And inhumanly fell upon Signior Dildo.

Nigh wearied out, the poor stranger did fly,   *85*
And along the Pall Mall they followed full cry.
The women, concerned, from every window,
Cried, "Oh, for Heaven's sake, save Signior Dildo!"

The good Lady Sands burst into laughter
To see how the ballocks came wobbling after,   *90*
And had not their weight retarded the foe,
Indeed't had gone hard with Signior Dildo.

17. *Southeske*. Anne (Hamilton), wife of Robert Carnegie, third Earl of Southeske, was successively mistress to Philip, Earl of Chesterfield, and to James, Duke of York. For her relations with York, see *Grammont*, I, 166–70.

21. *Lady Suffolk*. Barbara (1622–81), a daughter of Sir Edward Villiers and second wife of James Howard, third Earl of Suffolk, was Groom of the Stole to Queen Catherine.

23. *Lady Betty*. Lady Elizabeth Howard was the second daughter of Lord and Lady Suffolk. Against her parents' wishes she married Thomas Felton, a Groom of the Bedchamber, in July, 1675. For her character, see below "Ballad on Betty Felton."

25. *Falmouth*. Mary (Bagot), once Maid of Honor to the Queen, was the widow of Charles Berkeley, Earl of Falmouth, slain in a sea battle with the Dutch, June 3, 1665. Lady Falmouth had a very bad reputation, but in 1674 she married Charles, Lord Buckhurst (later Earl of Dorset). She died in September, 1679.

28. *swinger*. A very powerful person.

29. *Rafe*. Elizabeth (1647–90), widow of Josceline Percy, eleventh Earl of Northumberland (died May, 1670), married on August 24, 1673, Ralph ("Rafe") Montague.

30. *Harry's*. Perhaps "Harry's" *membrum virile*. Vieth suggests that the allusion may be to Rochester's friend, Harry Savile. At a house party at Althrop in September, 1671, Savile stole to Lady Northumberland's bedside in the dead of night and wakened her with his passionate declaration. Terrified, she rang her bell and Savile fled. See "Questions and Answers from Garroway's Coffee-House" (*POAS*, 1716, III, 67),

    Q. How came Montague to gain the widow from Savile?
    A. The one was witty in going to bed; the other wiser in cutting the bell-rope.

33. *Cleveland*. Barbara (Villiers), now Duchess of Cleveland; see Appendix.

34. *land*. Variant: "than the ocean has sand," Dyce MS. 43, I, 120.

37. *duchesses*. Probably the poet had in mind three Court ladies: the Duchess of Cleveland; Louise Keroualle, now Duchess of Portsmouth, who had displaced Cleveland as chief royal mistress; and Frances, widowed Duchess of Richmond.

41. *Modena*. Laura d'Este, Duchess of Modena, who had accompanied her daughter to England, left for Italy early in January, 1674.

45. *Cockpit*. "The countess" was probably Anna Maria, widow of Francis Talbot, Earl of Shrewsbury (see Appendix). She was indeed a "killing" dame in the sense that at least three men—Giles Rawlins, William Jenkins, and her husband—had died in quarrels about her. When the Duke of Albemarle died, January 3, 1670, Anna-Maria's lover, George, Duke of Buckingham, with whom she had been living openly for two years, moved into Albemarle's apartments in the Cockpit, an appendage to Whitehall Palace.

49. *Red Howard*. Anne (c. 1656–1703), younger daughter of William Howard, fourth son of Thomas, Earl of Berkshire. Anne became a Maid of Honor to the Queen in November, 1673. In the seventeenth century red hair was considered a blemish. *Red Sheldon*. Frances Sheldon, daughter of Sir Edward Sheldon, was a Maid of Honor to the Queen. *Temple*. Philippa Temple was a Maid of Honor to the Queen; see Appendix, Temple.

51. *Bernard*. Sir Bernard Gascoigne, English by ancestry but a Florentine by birth, had served in the armies of King Charles I. He was an adventurer and a skilled diplomat, recently English Resident at Vienna.

53. *Doll Howard*. Dorothy (c. 1652–1701), elder daughter of William Howard, fourth son of Thomas, Earl of Berkshire, was successively a Maid of Honor to the Duchess of York (Anne Hyde) and to Queen Catherine. In December, 1675, she married Col. James Graham. According to John Evelyn (July 11, 1675) Dorothy was "a most virtuous and excellent creature."

57. *St. Albans*. Henry Jermyn (c. 1604–84), formerly chamberlain to Queen Henrietta Maria (and her reputed lover), was now Lord Chamberlain of the Royal Household. He had been created Earl of St. Albans on April 26, 1660.

59. *Bergo*. Variants: Bargo, Borgo, and Pergo. Vieth glossed Borgo as a town in northern Italy. But surely St. Albans would not take a coach and horses to Italy, nor would he travel so far just for fresh air. Probably his destination was Bergholt, East Suffolk, sixty-one miles from London. St. Albans' country mansion, Rushbrooke Hall, was in Suffolk.

64. *burning*. Papier-maché images of the Pope were regularly burned on November 5, the anniversary of the Gunpowder Plot. For the burning of the dildoes, see Butler's "Dildoides" (MS. Firth C. 15, p. 3) with its MS note, "This poem was occasioned by a parcel of dildos brought from France, hid under other commodities, and being discovered was ordered to be burned." On January 26, 1671, Harry Savile wrote to Lord Rochester that at the custom house "has been lately unfortunately siezed a box of those leather instruments your lordship carried down one of, but these barbarian farmers [of the revenue] voted them prohibited goods, so that they were burned without mercy, notwithstanding that Sedley and I made two journeys into the City in their defense" (*Rochester-Savile Letters*, p. 31).

65. *Killigrew*. Charlotte, daughter of John de Hesse, of Holland, married (as his second wife) on January 26, 1665, Thomas Killigrew (1612–83), wit, playwright, a Groom of the Bedchamber, and Master of the King's Company of Players.

70. *Knight*. Mary Knight, a famous singer and a minor member of the royal seraglio, had a house in Pall Mall.

71. *Cazzo*. Italian cant name for penis.

89. *Lady Sands*. Probably Lady Lucy Hamilton Sandys, an intimate of Nell Gwyn, and often at Nell's house in Pall Mall. Lady Sandys may have been a daughter of George Kirke by his wife, Anne (Killigrew) (see *Westminster Abbey Registers*, p. 218).

19

LAMPOON

[*March, 1676*]

All the King's mistresses were obvious targets for the Court satirists, but Barbara Palmer, Countess of Castlemaine, was their favorite. On August 30, 1670, Barbara was created Duchess of Cleveland— and mistress emeritus. Thereafter her influence over King Charles waned with the rising star of the new royal mistress, Louise Keroualle, created Duchess of Portsmouth on July 23, 1673.

Early in 1676 it was rumored that the Duchess of Cleveland was going to France, "and saith she intends to put herself into a monastery" (*Hastings MS*, II, 169). Ostensibly she was going for the sake of her sons' education; actually so that she could live with more splendor on her very large income. The immediate occasion for "Lampoon" was her departure; she sailed from Dover on March 13, 1676, with her three sons, forty servants, and a retinue of horses and carriages (*CSPD*, 1676, p. 25). The copy text for "Lampoon" is Harleian MS. 6913, p. 177; see also MS. Don. b. 8, p. 212, and Harleian MS. 6914, p. 17.

Cleveland was doubtless to blame
    On such a he-whore to dote,
Who, wanting both wit and shame,
    Betrayed her with a laced coat.

But lechery so overswayed her,   *5*
    She had no discretion at all;
The cunt that first had raised her
    Was now the cause of her fall.

Churchill's delicate shape
    Her dazzling eyes had struck,   *10*
But her wider cunt did gape
    For a more substantial fuck.

20

Which made her in pattens, they say,
  To the Temple so often to trudge,
Where brawny Wycherley lay,   *15*
  Who performed the part of a drudge.

'Twas bad in such as did know it
  To go about to betray her.
Why might she not fuck with a poet,
  When his Majesty fucks with a player?   *20*

Jermyn should not be forgot,
  Who used to fuck her before;
'Tis hard to say who did not—
  There's Brumwych and thousands more.

The number can never be reckoned;   *25*
  She's fucked with great and small,
From good King Charles the Second
  To honest Jacob Hall.

But now she must travel abroad
  And be forced to frig with the nuns.   *30*
For giving our sovereign lord
  So many good buttered buns.

---

2. *he-whore.* Ensign John Churchill (1650–1722), the future great Duke of Marlborough, became one of the Duchess of Cleveland's lovers in 1670. She is said to
have given him £5,000, with which he bought a £500 annuity from Lord Halifax.
According to one account, King Charles found Churchill hiding in the duchess's closet
and said to him, "Go. You are a rascal, but I forgive you because you do it to
get your bread" (Winston Churchill, *Marlborough*, 1933, I, 61). On July 16, 1672,
the duchess gave birth to a daughter, Barbara, supposedly fathered by Churchill.

4. *laced coat.* A uniform coat decorated with lace or gold braid.

13. *pattens.* Clogs, designed to keep shoes off the wet ground.

14. *the Temple.* William Wycherley, the playwright (1640–1715) became the duch-
ess's lover soon after the production of his first play, *Love in a Wood*, March, 1671.
At the time he may have been living at the Inner Temple, one of the Inns of Court.
In an MS note to Langbaine's *Account of the English Dramatic Poets*, 1691, William
Oldys wrote, "The Duchess of Cleveland used to visit Wycherley at his chambers
in the Temple, dressed like a country maid in a straw hat, with pattens on, a basket

or box in her hand, etc." In his MS Commonplace Book (Stratford Shakespeare Library), Sir Francis Fane tells an agreeable anecdote. "The King being jealous of the Duchess of Cleveland, and having intelligence by her maid that she and Mr. Wycherley lay at Mrs. Knight's, the famous singer, in Pall Mall that night, early the next morning went thither and found him muffled in his cloak upon the stair head, and then went into the chamber where he found the duchess on a bed, whom he asked what she made there, who replied it was the beginning of Lent and she retired hither to perform her devotions. The King replied, "Very likely, and that was your confessor I met on the stairs."

20. *a player*. Nell Gwyn.

21. *Jermyn*. Henry Jermyn (1636–1708), nephew of Henry, Earl of St. Albans, was Master of the Horse to the Duke of York, 1660–75. He became Baron Dover of Dover in 1685 and Earl of Dover in 1689 (a title conferred on him by the deposed king, James II). On July 29, 1667, Pepys wrote of Lady Castlemaine, "She is fallen in love with young Jermin, who hath of late lain with her oftener than the King, and is now going to marry my Lady Falmouth; the King he is mad at her entertaining Jermin, and she is mad at Jermin's going to marry from her: so they are all mad; and thus the kingdom is governed!"

24. *Brumwych*. Probably Captain Francis Bromwich, a cousin-german of James, Duke of Ormonde. A noted duelist, he was killed on January 9, 1669, by Mr. Symonds, one of Queen Henrietta Maria's servants (*Bulstrode*, p. 83). Bromwich is not listed elsewhere as one of the duchess's lovers.

28. *Jacob Hall*. A famous ropedancer who usually performed at Bartholomew Fair. He was one of "his Majesty's servants as vaulters and dancers on the rope and other agility of body" (PRO, Lord Chamberlain, 3/25, p. 172). In 1674, Nell Gwyn commissioned John Coques, silversmith, to construct for her a silver bedstead. As a symbol of her triumph over the Duchess of Cleveland, she had him make, among other decorations, a miniature figure of Jacob Hall, "dancing upon a rope of wire work" (Wilson, *Nell Gwyn, Royal Mistress*, p. 169).

30. *frig*. Masturbate.

32. *buttered buns*. Busy prostitutes, over-ridden jades.

22

COLIN

([*Late Summer*,] *1679*)

In the late summer of 1679, the Duchess of Portsmouth, a French-woman and a Roman Catholic, was so frightened by the "Popish Plot" hysteria that she talked of fleeing to France. Our poet imagines her offering for sale her place as chief mistress to King Charles II. Following the model of "sessions" satires, the poet brings a number of disreputable candidates into court to make their bids, with the King acting as judge. Colin (a pastoral name for a shepherd) looks on with cynical amusement. Of course no candidate is successful, and the Duchess of Portsmouth remains as favorite mistress.

"Colin" may be the poem referred to in the following note dated September 11, 1679, "There's a satyr against several named ladies of the Town, which J. Ste[wkesley] has promised to send you, else I would have done it" (*Seventh Report*, p. 475A). The poem is frequently ascribed to Charles, Earl of Dorset.

The copy text is "A Satyr," Add. MS. 27, 407, f. 22, an aggregation collected by Peter Le Neve. The verses are variously entitled "The Duchess of Portsmouth's place exposed to sale," Harleian MS. 7317, p. 102; "A Satyr on Several Women, 1679," Dyce MS. 43, I, 297; "Colon, by Lord Buckhurst, 1679," Harleian MS. 6913, p. 79; "Colon 1679," Add. MS. 23, 722, f.23v; and "A Satyr," in Douce MS. 357, f. 58v; MS. Don. b. 8, p. 598; and Harvard MS. 636F, p. 76. For a modern printed version, see *POAS*, Yale, II, 167.

As Colin drove his sheep along
By Whitehall, there was such a throng
Of early coaches at the gate,
The silly swain was forced to wait.
Chance threw him on Sir Edward Sutton,   5
The jolly knight that rhymes to mutton.

23

"Colin," said he, "this is the day
For which poor England long did pray,
The day that sets our monarch free
From buttered buns and slavery. 10
This hour from French intrigues, 'tis said,
He'll clear his Council and his bed.
Portsmouth, he now vouchsafes to know,
Was the cast miss of Count De Soe,
Each night with her dear as a sessions 15
Of the House, and fuller of petitions,
Which drained him till he was not able
To keep his Council, nor a table;
So that white-staves and grooms and pages
Lived all alike upon board wages. 20
She must retire and sell her place;
Buyers, you see, come in apace."

Silence in the court being once proclaimed,
Up stepped fair Richmond, once so famed.
She offered much, but was refused, 25
And of miscarriages accused.
They said a cunt so used to puke
Could never bear a booby duke;
That Mulgrave, Villiers, and Jack Howe
For one salt duchess were enow; 30
Nor would his Majesty accept her
At thirty, who at eighteen left her.
She blushed and modestly withdrew.
Next Middleton appeared in view,
Who soon was told of Montague, 35
Of baits of Hyde, of clothes from France,
Of armpits, toes, and sufficance,
At which the court set up a laughter;
But then she pleaded for her daughter,
A buxom lass fit for the place 40
Were not her father in disgrace,

24

Whose monstrous chin 'twas thought begun
Her pretty face to over-run;
Besides some strange, incestuous stories
Of Harvey and her long clitoris.   *45*
With those exceptions she's dismissed,
And Morland fair enters the list,
Husband in hand most decently,
And begs at any rate to buy.
She offered jewels of great price   *50*
And dear Sir Samuel's next device,
Whether it be a pump or table,
Glass-house or any other bauble.
But she was told she had been tried
And for good reason laid aside.   *55*
Next in steps pretty Lady Grey,
Offered her lord should nothing say
Against the next Treasurer accused,
So her pretense was not refused.
Rowley enraged bid her begone   *60*
And play her game out with his son;
Or, if she liked an aged carcass,
From Lucy get the noble marquis.
Shrewsbury offered for the place
All she had gotten from his grace;   *65*
She knew his ways and could comply
With all decays of lechery;
Had often licked his amorous sceptre
Until the jaded stallion leapt her;
But long ago had the mishap   *70*
To give the King Dick Talbot's clap.
Though for her all was said that can be
By her lean drudge the Earl of Danby,
She was dismissed with scorn and told
Where a tall page was to be sold.   *75*
Then in came dowdy Mazarin,
That foreign antiquated quean,

Who soon was told the King no more
Would deal with an intriguing whore,
That she already had about her   *80*
Too good an *equipage de foutre*;
Nor was our monarch such a cully
To bear a Moor and swinging bully.
Her grace at this rebuke looked blank
And sneaked away to villain Frank.   *85*
Fair Lichfield, too, her claim put in;
'Twas urged she was too near akin.
She modestly replied, no more
Of kin than Sussex was before;
Besides she had often heard her mother   *90*
Call her the daughter of another.
She did not drivel and had sense,
To which all his had no pretense.
Yet for the present she's put off
And told she was not whore enough.   *95*
Loftus smiled at that exception,
Doubting not of good reception,
Put in her claim, vowing she'd steal
All that her husband won of Neale,
To buy the place, all she could get   *100*
By his long suit with Mr. Pitt.
But from Goliath's size of Gath
Down to the pitch of little Wroth,
The court was told she had lain with all
The roaring roist'rers of Whitehall.   *105*
For which Rowley, lest she grudge,
Gave her the making of a judge.
She bowed and straight bought her six grays
To haunt the Court, the Park, and plays.
In stepped stately Carey Frazier,   *110*
Straight the whole room began to praise her,
As fine as hands or point could make her.
She vowed the King or jail must take 'er.

Rowley replied he was retrenching
And would no more of costly wenching,   *115*
That she was proud and went too gaudy,
Nor could she swear, drink, and talk bawdy,
Virtues requisite for that place
More than youth, wit, or a good face.
Cleveland offered down a million,   *120*
But she was soon told of Chatillon;
At that name she fell a-weeping,
And swore she was undone with keeping,
That Jermyn, Churchill had so drained her
She could not live on the remainder.   *125*
The court said there was no record
Of any to that place restored,
Nor ought the King at these years venture,
When his prime could not content her.
Young Lady Jones stepped up and urged   *130*
She'd give the deed her father forged;
But she was told her family
Were tainted with Presbytery.
She said her mother, with clean heart
And hand, had lately done her part   *135*
In bringing Mazarin to bed,
Nor was't her fault the babe was dead.
Her sister, too, as all men know,
Had fucked as high and married low
As Belasyse or any punk   *140*
Of late with royal seed made drunk.
For her Rowley owned his passion,
But said he stood by declaration,
Engaged no matters of great weight
To pass till after some debate   *145*
In his great Council. So they adjourned,
And Colin to his flock returned,
Swearing there was at every fair
Blither girls than any there.

5. *Sutton.* Sir Edward Sutton, an Irishman knighted by Charles II on June 14, 1660, was a gentleman usher of the Privy Chamber, who played well on the Irish harp (Evelyn, November 17, 1668). On July 30, 1695, Luttrell (III, 506) reported the death of Sir Edward Sutton, "aged near 100 years old."

10. *buttered buns.* Over-ridden prostitutes.

13. *Portsmouth.* Louise Keroualle, Duchess of Portsmouth; see Appendix.

14. *cast miss.* Discarded mistress. *De Soe.* The Comte de Sault, son of the Duc de Lesdiguières, was said to have been Keroualle's lover in France before she came to England. On September 23, 1671, Ralph Montague wrote to Lord Arlington from Paris, "The Conte de Seaux has been sick ever since I came; he pretends it is for love, and some of his friends have been very inquisitive how Mademoiselle de Querualle governs herself in England. I give them an answer that will not conduce much to the Conte's recovery" (*Buccleuch MS*, I, 505).

19. *white-staves.* The wands of office borne by officers of the royal household. On May 26, 1679, King Charles prorogued Parliament and "strictly retrenched his household expenses" (Bryant, *King Charles II*, 1931, p. 289).

24. *Richmond.* Frances Stuart, widowed Duchess of Richmond; see Appendix.

27–28. The couplet, not in the copy text, is from Harleian MS. 6913, p. 80. "Booby duke" seems to have been a favorite term for any of King Charles's illegitimate sons by Barbara, Duchess of Cleveland.

29. *Mulgrave.* John Sheffield, Earl of Mulgrave; see Appendix. *Villiers.* "Villain Frank" Villiers; see Appendix, Villiers (Grandison). *Jack Howe.* John Grubham Howe. For his supposed connection with the Duchess of Richmond in August, 1679, see Appendix, Howe.

32. *left her.* Variant "leapt her."

34. *Middleton.* Mrs. Jane Middleton; see Appendix.

35. *Montague.* Ralph Montague, recently Ambassador to France, was in disgrace in 1679. Formerly one of Mrs. Middleton's lovers, he was an arrant rogue and surprisingly homely.

36. *baits.* Refreshments; light meals. *Hyde.* Lawrence Hyde, second son of Edward, Earl of Clarendon, and later Lord Treasurer and Earl of Rochester.

37. *armpits, toes.* On October 3, 1665, Pepys heard that Mrs. Middleton was "noted for carrying about her body a continued sour base smell, that is very offensive, especially if she be a little hot." *sufficance.* From Harleian MS. 6913, p. 80; The copy text has the meaningless "sustenance." "Sufficance" [Fr.] is conceit. Other variants are "suffocance," "nauseance," and "concupiscence."

39. *her daughter.* In 1678 Jenny Middleton was a candidate for the post of royal mistress (*Rochester-Savile Letters*, p. 56). Ralph Montague had a very heavy chin, but it is unlikely that he was Jenny's father.

44–45. The couplet is from Harleian MS. 6913, p. 80. Lady Anne Harvey, widow of Sir Daniel Harvey (Ambassador to Turkey, 1668–72), was the sister of Ralph Montague. Apparently Lady Harvey was unusual in her sexual equipment. She was a woman of bold and eager spirit, deep in the political intrigues of the day, and famous for her "gallantries." In 1669 she is said to have killed one of her pages, "a young knight of fourteen or fifteen years, and with his own sword," because, she claimed, he tried to attack her. But the rumor was that she stabbed him because "he had boasted of having received some favor from her" (W. Westergaard, *The First Triple Alliance*, 1947, p. 111).

28

47. *Morland.* Anne (Fielding), who died February 20, 1680, was the beautiful third wife of Sir Samuel Morland, a Gentleman of the Privy Chamber and a famous inventor; see Appendix, Morland.

56. *Lady Grey.* Mary (Berkeley), wife of Ford, Lord Grey of Werke; see Appendix.

58. *treasurer.* Variant: "Gainst next the treasurer's accused." Thomas Osborne, Earl of Danby and Lord Treasurer, was impeached by the House of Commons for asking King Louis XIV for money for King Charles. He was sent to the Tower on April 16, 1679, and imprisoned there for five years without a trial. Lord Grey, a strong Whig, was a leader of the anti-Danby forces in the House of Lords.

60. *Rowley.* King Charles was so called after a famous stallion.

61. *his son.* James, Duke of Monmouth, said to be Lady Grey's lover.

63. *Lucy.* Probably Theophila (Berkeley), widow of Sir Kingsmill Lucy and Lady Grey's older sister. The marquis would be Henry Somerset, third Marquis of Worcester, aged fifty. In "A Ballad to the Tune of Cheviot Chace" (see below), Lady Lucy is accused of having once been too free "with the President of Wales," Lord Worcester.

64. *Shrewsbury.* Anna-Maria (Brudenell) Talbot, Countess of Shrewsbury; see Appendix. "His grace" was her former lover, George Villiers, Duke of Buckingham.

66. *his ways.* I.e., the King's tastes and habits. There is no evidence that the King was once Lady Shrewsbury's lover. The pension he gave her in 1674—£1,600 a year— was for her support after the House of Lords ordered Buckingham and Anna-Maria to separate.

71. *Dick Talbot.* Colonel Richard Talbot (1630–91) was created Earl of Tyrconnel in 1685. Grammont (*Memoirs*, II, 24) implies that he had been one of Lady Shrewsbury's lovers.

73. *Danby.* There is no reason to believe that Lord Danby, a tall, lean man, was ever Lady Shrewsbury's lover. Perhaps the poet meant to suggest that he was her pimp.

76. *Mazarin.* Hortense de Mancini, Duchess Mazarin, came to England in January, 1676. King Charles gave her apartments in Whitehall and £4,000 a year. The Duke of York bought for her Lord Windsor's house in St. James's Park.

77. *quean.* Prostitute. The duchess was notably promiscuous, and King Charles was only one of many bedfellows.

81. *equipage de foutre.* "Foutre" [Fr.] to thrust. In brief, too many lovers.

83. *a Moor.* The Duchess Mazarin's page boy was a Moor (or Turk) named Mustapha. Her "swinging" (powerful) bully may have been Luigi I, the handsome young Prince of Monaco, who had followed her to England. The duchess fell in love with him, and King Charles had to stop her pension to bring her to her senses.

85. *villain Frank.* Francis Villiers, second son of George, fourth Viscount Grandison, was at this time Lieutenant of the Band of Gentleman pensioners. He was called "villain Frank" partly in derision and partly to distinguish him from "bold Frank" Newport.

86. *Lichfield.* Charlotte (Fitzroy), daughter of King Charles and the Duchess of Cleveland, was wife of Henry Lee, Earl of Lichfield.

89. *Sussex.* Anne (Fitzroy), daughter of King Charles and the Duchess of Cleveland, was wife of Thomas Lennard, Earl of Sussex. In the summer of 1678, in France, Lady Sussex was seduced by Ralph Montague. There is no ground for the suggestion of incest with King Charles.

96. *Loftus.* Lucy (Brydges), daughter of George, sixth Lord Chandos, and first wife of Adam Loftus, an Irish squire; see Appendix, Loftus. Lucy died in April, 1681.

99. *Neale.* Thomas Neale was Groom Porter and *ex officio* manager of a gambling casino in his lodgings at Whitehall.

101. *Mr. Pitt.* He was probably Mrs. Loftus's stepfather, George Pitt of Strafieldsea, Hants.; see Appendix, Loftus. A Mr. George Pitt was one of the farmers of the Irish revenue in 1675 (Carte, *Ormonde,* IV, 501).

102. *Goliath.* Colonel Richard Talbot was one of the tallest men in England.

103. *Wroth.* Henry Wroth, a very small man, was page of honor to the King and a cornet in Lord Gerard's regiment of horse. On July 21, 1678, he distinguished himself by abducting Bridget Hyde, step-daughter of a city merchant, Sir Robert Viner. The lady was rescued and Wroth lost all his places but escaped arrest (Browning, *Danby,* I, 288–89).

107. *a judge.* I.e., the privilege of selling a judge's appointment.

110. *Carey Frazier.* Daughter of Sir Alexander Frazier, royal physician; see Appendix. In December, 1677, while the Duchess of Portsmouth was enduring a long illness, a gossip reported that "Mrs. Frazier (the doctor's daughter) and Mrs. Elliott and one or two more strive for the preferment" (*Seventh Report,* p. 469).

112. *point.* Lace. For Carey's finery, see Appendix, Frazier.

120. *Cleveland.* Barbara, Duchess of Cleveland, arrived in England on July 26, 1679, and was back in France by late November. Evelyn saw her on November 6, 1679, at the remarriage of her son, the Duke of Grafton, to Isabella, daughter of the Earl of Arlington.

121. *Chatillon.* Alexis Henry, Marquis de Chatillon, a handsome but penniless young gentleman with whom the duchess had had a liaison in Paris.

124. *Jermyn.* Henry Jermyn, nephew of the Earl of St. Albans, and a famous lover. *Churchill.* John Churchill, the future Duke of Marlborough.

130. *Lady Jones.* Katherine, eldest daughter of Richard Jones, Earl of Ranelagh. On June 5, 1679, a gossip reported, "Much talk there is of a new miss [mistress] at Windsor, daughter of Lord Ranelagh" (*Seventh Report,* p. 472A). Evidently Lady Jones won the competition, but did not displace the Duchess of Portsmouth (see W. D. Christie, *Shaftesbury,* 2 vols., 1871, II, 360). Katherine died unmarried on April 12, 1740.

131. *the deed.* Although Lord Ranelagh's dealings with Ireland as vice-treasurer and one of the farmers of the revenue are shot through with chicanery and deceit, there is no evidence that he ever forged a deed.

134. *her mother.* Katherine's mother, Elizabeth, second daughter of Francis Willoughby, fifth Baron Willoughby of Parham, married Richard Jones on October 28, 1662. I have found nothing about her acting as midwife to the Duchess Mazarin. The duchess had four children by her husband, Armande de la Porte, Duc Mazarin.

138. *her sister.* Lady Ranelagh's sister, Frances, married in 1659 William, third Baron Brereton of Leighlin, in Ireland. Her amatory exploits have not been recorded.

140. *Belasyse.* Susan (Armine) daughter of Sir William Armine of Osgodby, Lincs., married on October 20, 1662, Sir Henry Belasyse, son of John, Lord Belasyse. Sir Henry was slain in a duel with Thomas Porter on July 28, 1667. Susan became the Duke of York's mistress. After the death of his first wife, the Duke wanted to marry Susan, but King Charles forbade the match. In compensation for Susan's loss of

greatness, the King created her in 1674 Baronness Belasyse of Osgodby. A Lady of the Bedchamber to Marie Beatrice, second Duchess of York, Lady Belasyse married, before 1684, one of the King's Grooms, James Fortrey of Chequers. She died January 6, 1713.

146. *his great Council.* The new Privy Council of thirty members announced by the King to Parliament on April 21, 1679, was "great" only in the sense that it was much enlarged.

ON SEVERAL WOMEN ABOUT TOWN

[*Spring, 1680*]

In a linked satire, "A Letter to a Friend. By the Lord R." (Harleian MS. 6913, p. 63), presumably written in the spring of 1680, the entertainment at "Ballock Hall" is referred to:

> But above all I gladly would hear tell
> Some passages of that most decent ball
> Where Irish squire so cunningly contrived
> At his own cost to have his lady swived.

Of course both satires are based on gossip, but there may well be some truth beneath the scurrility. Balls were very popular with the idle rich, and no doubt there were opportunities for hanky-panky at such affairs. Some "gallant meetings" seem to have been deliberately designed for ungallant couplings. For example, on January 19, 1677, a gossip wrote that Lord Purbeck had hired a house in St. James's Fields "for to make a ball to the masqueraders in . . . at which was none but the debauch[ed] men and lewd women, no civil [persons] being there but Lady Buckingham and Mrs. Middleton . . . in masks" (*Rutland MS*, II, 36).

The copy text is Douce MS. 357, f. 57v. In Portland MS. Pw V 43, the satire is called "Queen Street Ballad." In the *Gyldenstolpe MS* (p. 275) it is "A Ballad: to the Tune of an old Man with a Bedfull of Bones" (see Simpson, *Broadside Ballad*, p. 129), and it is so printed in *POAS*, 1716, IV, Pt. 2, p. 17, and *The Poetical Works of Rochester*, 1761, p. 224. For other MS versions see Harleian MS. 6912, p. 59, and Add. MS. 34, 362, f. 115. The author is unknown.

> In a famous street near Whetstones Park,
> Where there's commonly fiddlers so soon as 'tis dark,
> There was a gallant meeting of many a fine spark,
>   With a fa-la-la-la.

A matronly dame with a feathered fan,   *5*
Whose knight did formerly charge Tetuan,
Was thought most fit to lead up the van,
    With a fa-la-la-la.

A decent person of riper years,
As by her want of teeth plainly appears,   *10*
For her wisdom was trusted to bring up the rear,
    With a fa-la-la-la.

This feast was made for a lady of air,
Who from the dunghill was raised to a player,
And at last had the luck to bring Flatfoot an heir,   *15*
    With a fa-la-la-la.

The lady of the house was an upright lass,
Invincible lewdness had adorned her face;
Her husband stood by and looked like an ass,
    With a fa-la-la-la.   *20*

From two doors off as soon as 'twas night,
Came tripping along a damsel bright;
Had she kept better company she was wife for a knight,
    With a fa-la-la-la.

Her partner, though more of a noble race,   *25*
Had his prick been no better than his wit or his face,
Had ne'er been so gracious with that pretty lass,
    With a fa-la-la-la.

There was a bouncing widow with a patch on her nose,
Who loves fucking better the older she grows,   *30*
And has learned of the Tartar to frig with her toes,
    With a fa-la-la-la.

She brought along with her a bonny young maid,
Who at sight of the gallants at first seemed afraid,

As if she had not much been used to the trade,   *35*
    With a fa-la-la-la.

A lusty young fellow they'd each of them got,
That trounced 'em and bounced 'em until they were hot,
Then took 'em aside to do I know not what,
    With a fa-la-la-la.   *40*

A Jew there was to make up the farce,
With a great bag of money and a swinging tarse,
Which was ready to thrust into everyone's arse,
    With a fa-la-la-la.

At first they all wondered what a devil he·meant,   *45*
But he gave the women and men such content
That to his house the next day to dinner they went,
    With a fa-la-la-la.

Where after he had feasted this jolly crew,
Their innocent pastimes they did renew,   *50*
And were fucked up and down, both Christian and Jew,
    With a fa-la-la-la.

Take heed all you husbands and mothers all,
Keep your wives and your daughters from Ballock Hall,
Or 'tis forty to one but they get there a fall,   *55*
    With a fa-la-la-la.

---

1. *a famous street*. MS note, "Loftus House in Queen Street." Queen Street, lined with the mansions of the wealthy, ran from Drury Lane to Lincolns Inn Fields. *Whetstones Park*, a street north of Lincolns Inn Fields, was notorious for its brothels.

5. *A matronly dame*. MS note, "Sir Palmes Fairborne's wife." Margery was the wife of Sir Palmes Fairborne, a soldier who had served for eighteen years at Tangier fighting the Moors and was at this time lieutenant governor of that military outpost. Fairborne had been in England on leave in the summer and winter of 1679–80, and had returned to Tangier in April, 1680. He was slain by a musket shot on October

24, 1680. Lady Fairborne was a friend of Nell Gwyn who in her will left her £50 "to buy a ring" (Peter Cunningham, *The Story of Nell Gwyn*, ed. John Drinkwater, 1927, p. 157).

6. *Tetuan*. A Moorish town near Tangier.

9. *a decent person*. MS note, "Mrs. Jennings." Frances Jennings, widow of Richard Jennings of Sandridge, and mother of Frances, Barbara, and Sarah (future Duchess of Marlborough), was famed as a Court bawd. She too was a friend of Nell Gwyn. In 1680 she was at least fifty years old.

13. *a lady of air*. MS note, "Mrs. Ellen Gwyn." Airy, flighty Nell, the King's cockney mistress, was much courted by those who sought preferment at Court.

15. *Flatfoot*. King Charles II. See "Flatfoot, the Gudgeon Taker," *POAS*, Yale, II, 189. The *heir* was Charles Beauclerc, Earl of Burford and later Duke of St. Albans.

17. *The lady of the house*. MS note, "Loftus." Lucy (Brydges), wife of Adam Loftus, "the Irish squire," had an unsavory reputation. She died in France in April, 1681.

19. *her husband*. Adam Loftus, later Lord Lisburne; see Appendix, Loftus.

22. *a damsel bright*. Conjecturally Olive Porter, daughter of George Porter, Esq. She lived with her mother at 66 Queen Street. Baronne D'Aulnoy (*Memoirs of the Court of England in 1675*, pp. 243–45) asserts that Olive had formed a liaison with William, Lord Cavendish.

25. *her partner*. An MS note in Portland MS. PwV 38 identifies the gentleman as William, Lord Cavendish (see *Gyldenstolpe*, p. 356). In "The Ladies' March," 1681 (see below), is a quatrain:

> Next in place comes Mrs. Porter,
> But fools grow nice, not one would court her;
> This short lived princess owed her fall
> To the Principal of Ballock Hall.

Presumably Cavendish was the "Principal," as if he were head of a school.

29. *a bouncing widow*. MS note, "Mrs. Brownlow." Margaret (Brydges), widow of William Brownlow of Humby, Lincs., was Lucy Loftus's half-sister. In "Satyr" (Harleian MS. 6913, p. 235) she is called "patch Brownlo," probably because she wore a patch to cover a facial blemish.

31. *the Tartar*. John, "Tartar" Cox, who published *The School of Venus*, or *The Ladies' Delight*; see below, note to line 78, "An Essay of Scandal."

41. *a Jew*. Unidentified, but probably "The lustful buggering Jew" of "A Letter to a Friend. By the Lord. R."

54. *Ballock Hall*. This indelicate title for Loftus House is repeated at the end of "An Ironical Satire," 1680 (*POAS*, Yale, II, 200). The poet concludes with the hope that "Mrs. Strafford" (Sarah Stratford, a famous bawd) will "yield to Ballock Hall."

SATIRE ON THE COURT LADIES

([*Spring,*] *1680*)

The author of this shotgun libel seems to have been a confirmed misogynist, more interested in denigrating women in general than in vilifying a few choice specimens. But he was also viciously anti-York and anti-Catholic; it is significant that many of his victims were or had been Roman Catholics. Probably the author was a "Mutineer," a member of the "Country" Party (soon to be known as Whigs), and a bigoted Protestant. References to events late in 1679 tend to place the satire early in 1680.

The copy text is Harleian MS. 7319, p. 87, dated 1680. It is dated 1680 also in MS. Firth, c. 15, p. 78; and in "A Choyce Collection," p. 69. It is undated in Dyce MS. 43, I, 215, and Harleian MS. 6913, p. 137.

Curse on those critics, ignorant and vain,
Who say a satire is too sharp and plain;
Who blame the matchless Dryden's bold essay
Because it spares no vices in its way.
'Tis charity to foes, kindness to's friend.   *5*
The more we love, the more we wish they'd mend.
To purge lewd follies and destructive sins,
Prophets and poets are th'appointed means.
The men of wit and judgment do admire
In useful satire a resistless fire;   *10*
The heavenly lightning church and throne destroys,
While the dim candle only singes flies.
 Speak out, then, Muse, and all the vices tell
With which our countries, Courts, and cities swell.
Though Oglethorpe, bold Lucy, and the Beast   *15*
Are stately pillars of York's interest,

Yet still we'll curse the monster who'd enslave
Our free-born souls and make's own brother's grave.
Though Portsmouth have strong ruffians she can trust
As well to serve her malice as her lust,   20
Yet still she's slavish, prostrate, false and foul,
Destroys our prince's honor, health, and soul.
Though Richmond can complain at council table
That single strength to please her was not able,
Her house and body have a thousand ways   25
To let in fucksters which she still betrays.
These from their wickedness do boldness get,
As blooding mastiffs does their courage whet.
Yet while their infamies do libels crave,
We'll fear nor ruffian, minister, nor brave.   30
    Example from the great the lesser take,
And some grow scandalous for scandal's sake.
While Arundel lies low at Cloris's feet,
Pleased with contempt he is so used to meet,
Or while, content, to his wife's woman sneaks,   35
And there the sweets of a belle-passion takes,
His lady 'mongst a crowd of stallions lies,
Nor is less sparing of her arse than eyes,
Whose glances all that seek 'em may divide,
But mighty lust can't innate malice hide.   40
Dissolute lewdness, falseness, and ill nature
Appear in every look, in every feature.
The common coxcombs which about her buzz,
And which I think (as male) she can't refuse,
Are Lumley beau and Mall Howard's witty Harry,   45
Who lately went to Wales but did not marry.
She suffers these because she'd still be getting,
But Shrewsbury's the man in constant waiting.
From plays to park, thence to Millbank at night,
He scarcely loses smell, and seldom sight;   50
Whenever she removes to country house,
He is as sure packed up as wearing clothes.

37

And thus the industrious cuckold does obtain
Shame and contempt at mighty cost and pain.
    Felton's false sacrifice no virtue proves;   *55*
'Tis not enough t'have once refused to love,
While in a course of lewdness still she lives,
And scarce such pleasure as she scandal gives.
Broughal's her friend and darling of her eye,
The pink of goodness and of modesty;   *60*
She'll either make the bed or hold the door;
Nature has made her better bawd than whore;
Though where she may, both functions she supplies;
When Mrs. Gosnel's cruel, down she lies,
For Mulgrave triumphs in varieties.   *65*
    Albemarle's folly and detested pride
The Bath as well as Court does now deride,
And smart Dumbarton has her virtue tried.
She weakness, but they impudence, betrayed,
Who prostrate under Monmouth's window laid,   *70*
Expressed lewd wishes in soft serenade.
    These are the pretty innocent delights
In which our greatest ladies spend their nights.
These are diversions they'll scarce blush to own,
But blame the nauseous, unjust, censuring Town,   *75*
For why should strangers show a discontent,
Where husbands, mothers, and all friends consent?
Few wives are base, few maidens are betrayed,
But husband is the pimp, and dam the bawd.
Some, portions for their daughter's honor get,   *80*
And they that don't contrive at least permit.
The good man smiles to see his lady pleased,
And hugs the fop by whom his horns are raised,
While, next her lust, the chiefest joy she takes
Is slyly to deride the fool she makes.   *85*
Nor will she to one lover be confined,
But is as surely false as she is kind.
Husbands and lovers all, she makes her prey,

38

And for her ends by turns will all betray.
No ways to vice does this our age produce,   *90*
But women, with less shame than men, do use.
They'll play, they'll drink, talk filth'ly and profane,
With more extravagance than any man.
I blush to think one impious day has seen
Three duchesses roaring drunk on Richmond Green.   *95*
Yet still we sigh, we love, nay, worse, some wed
And bring pollution to a sacred bed.
Most are deceived by whores to others known,
But some are fools enough to take their own.

---

3. *Dryden's bold essay.* Lord Mulgrave's *An Essay upon Satire*, which circulated in manuscript in November, 1679, was at first attributed to Dryden. For a modern edition of the *Satire*, see *POAS*, Yale, I, 396.

15. *Oglethorpe.* In 1680 Theophilus Oglethorpe (1650–1702) of Godalming, Surrey, was lieutenant colonel in the Duke of York's troop of Guards. An ardent Yorkist, and quick with his sword, he was knighted by King James II in 1685, promoted to brigadier general, and made Gentleman of the Horse. About 1681 he married the Duchess of Portsmouth's personal maid, Eleanor Wall (died 1732), daughter of Richard Wall of Tipperary. *Lucy.* Captain Thomas Lucy of Charlecote commanded a troop of the King's Household Guards. His wife, Katherine, was fond of cards and frequented the Duchess of Portsmouth's gaming tables (see A. Fairfax-Lucy, *Charlecote and the Lucys*, 1958). *the Beast.* One of many epithets applied to the Church of Rome (Rev. 13:17). See, for example, "Funeral Tears Upon the Death of Captain William Bedloe," *The Roxburghe Ballads*, ed. J. W. Ebsworth, 8 vols., 1878–96, IV, 169,

> The valiant Bedloe, learned Oates,
> From Popish knives saved all our throats;
> By such a Sword, and such a Gown,
> Soon would the Beast have tumbled down.

19. *Portsmouth.* Louise, Duchess of Portsmouth, was suspected of instigating the attack on Dryden in Rose Alley, December 18, 1679. Luttrell wrote (I, 50), "Mr. John Dryden was sett on in Covent Garden in the evening by three fellowes, who beat him very severely, and on peoples comeing in they run away; 'tis thought to be done by order of the dutchesse of Portsmouth, she being abused in a late libell called an Essay upon Satyr, of which Mr. Dryden is suspected to be the author."

23. *Richmond.* The poet has confused the story. On November 2, 1679, Dorothy, Lady Sunderland, wrote that Frances, Duchess of Richmond, had "complained to the King of the great injury [Jack] Howe had done her in bragging of her favors and letters, when she had never given him cause for either" (Cartwright, *Sacharissa*, p. 219). Lady Richmond had been brought up in France as a Roman Catholic.

33. *Arundel.* Henry Howard, Earl of Arundel (later Duke of Norfolk) had been a Roman Catholic; he turned Protestant in 1679 to save his seat in the House of Lords. *Cloris,* a common pastoral name, cannot be identified.

35. *his wife's woman.* Probably Mall Howard, a distant cousin and Lady Arundel's companion. Mall was a pattern of lechery for the age; see Appendix, Howard.

37. *his wife.* Mary (Mordaunt), Countess of Arundel, was accused of numerous intrigues. In 1700 her husband divorced her for a notorious affair with John Germaine, a Dutch gambler; see Appendix, Norfolk.

45. *Lumley beau.* The line is from Harleian MS. 6913, p. 138. The copy text has "Is Lumley beau; Mall Howard's witty Harry," but clearly there are two men involved. "Lumley beau," a Roman Catholic, was Henry, younger brother of Richard, Viscount Lumley. *Harry.* Henry Wharton, third son of Philip, Lord Wharton, was a scapegrace whose name was frequently linked with that of Mall Howard.

48. *Shrewsbury.* Charles Talbot, Earl of Shrewsbury, a Roman Catholic who turned Protestant in 1681, was said to be Lady Arundel's lover; see Appendix, Shrewsbury.

49. *Millbank.* Lady Arundel's father, Henry Mordaunt, Earl of Peterborough, had leased a house on the Millbank, Chelsea, just beyond the horse ferry to Lambeth. The building was known as either "Millbank" or "Peterborough House."

51. *country house.* Lady Arundel retired frequently to her family's country house, Drayton, Northants.

55. *Felton.* Perhaps Lady Betty Felton's "false sacrifice" involved her rivalry with Lady Arundel for the affections of Lord Shrewsbury; see Appendix, Felton.

59. *Broughal.* On February 6, 1665, Mary, daughter of Richard Sackvile, fifth Earl of Dorset, married Roger Boyle (1646–82), who was styled Lord Broghill until he inherited as second Earl of Orrery on October 18, 1679. Properly, then, his wife should have been called Lady Orrery, but the name Broghill (or Broughal) seems to have lingered. See, for example, "Rochester's Farewell" (*POAS,* Yale, II, 224), written in the summer of 1680, in which the Duchess Mazarin's three intimates are listed as "Sussex, Broghill, Betty Felton." Lady Broghill, a malicious, quarrelsome woman, separated from her husband in 1675, leaving him in Ireland while she attended the English Court. See *Calendar of Orrery Papers,* passim.

64. *Gosnel.* Perhaps Winifred Gosnel, formerly an actress and once maid to Mrs. Samuel Pepys. From "In Defense of Satire" (*POAS,* Yale, I, 369) we learn that "Grandio" (the Earl of Mulgrave) "Is caught with Gosnell, that old hag, abed."

66. *Albemarle.* In 1669, Elizabeth (1654–1734), daughter of William Cavendish, Duke of Newcastle, married Christopher Monck, second Duke of Albemarle. A capricious, unstable young woman, eventually she lost her mind.

68. *Dumbarton.* George Douglas (c. 1635–92), Earl of Dumbarton in Scotland, was brought up in France as a Roman Catholic and served with distinction in the French army. When he returned to England, he refused to take the necessary oaths and was barred from military command until 1685, when James II appointed him colonel of the Royal Regiment of Foot. He married Anne, daughter of Robert Wheatley of Bracknell, Berks., and sister of Mrs. Katherine Lucy.

70. *Monmouth.* Handsome James, Duke of Monmouth, the King's favorite natural son, was beloved by many Court ladies.

95. *Three duchesses.* This bacchanalian episode has eluded me.

AN ANSWER TO THE SATIRE ON THE COURT LADIES

(*1680*)

"An Answer" is not truly a reply to the preceding poem, but it may have acquired the name by accidental juxtaposition. The author's aim was to attack a collection of Court half-wits, concentrating on two eccentrics, Jack Howe and Goodwin Wharton. Most of the other men named were minor writers of lampoons. They belong to what Alexander Radcliffe called, in "News from Hell,"

> a scribbling fry,
> Ought to be damned eternally;
> An unleavened tribe, o'th'lower rate,
> Who will be poets spite of Fate.

The superior attitude of our anonymous poet suggests that he may have belonged to the inner circle of Court Truewits.

The copy text, dated 1680, is Harleian MS. 7319, p. 93. The poem is dated 1680 in Firth MS. C. 15, p. 85; Folger MS. m.b. 12, f. 119; and "A Choyce Collection," p. 73. It is undated in Dyce MS. 43, I, 364.

> Since every foolish coxcomb thinks it fit
> To rhyme and rail, though without sense or wit,
> Since piebald poetry's of greatest fame,
> And all must write that can but spell their name,
> We'll keep it up, and those the bays shall bear,   *5*
> Not that write best, but most malicious are.
> The ladies we'll leave out, for few or none
> Shall here bear part but those that least are known;
> For if they're kind, 'tis hard that we should curse,
> Or if they're cruel, 'twill but make 'em worse.   *10*
> Men should of choice their kindness recompense,

41

If only for their own convenience.
There's Dryden, though a devil at his pen,
In all his satires pecks at only men,
And therefore to be praised, for he writes best   *15*
That spares not his own sex to make his jest.
Yet there's Sir George, that honest man ne'er fails,
Always of women writes and always rails;
For which the gods have plagued him to the height,
And for his comfort sent him such a wife!   *20*
A wife that represents all forms, a bitch,
A wizard, wrinkled woman and a witch.
Besides there's some young satyrs ply their pen,
That write of others 'cause none think of them.
There's lisping Mordaunt and beau Henningham,   *25*
Much to be famed for two sharp writing men.
Then for heroic style there's Falkland too;
For smutty jests and downright lies, Jack Howe.
He to this function mightily pretends
And satires those the most he calls his friends.   *30*
So fallen angels, once bereft of bliss,
Envy and pine at others' happiness.
His whole design is to be thought a wit;
Therefore this freedom takes to farther it;
Sends forth his spies; his home-spun sisters too   *35*
Daily inform what their acquaintance do.
Then out himself he packs and scouting goes,
Singles out pairs as he thinks fit, and those
He handles civilly, then frames his jest,
Writes what he sees, feigns and makes out the rest.   *40*
His person too he much admires and strove
Once to be thought renowned for feats of love.
But of his constancy and trust in those,
Churchill reports and Richmond too well knows.
These in their lusts happy might still have been   *45*
Had they not loved, believed, and trusted him.
A face he has much like a skeleton,

Two inches broad and fifteen inches long,
His two cheeks sunk, a visage pale as death,
Adorned with pimples and a stinking breath.   50
His scragged carcass moves with antic grace,
And every limb as awkward as his face.
His poisoned corpse wrapped in a wicker skin,
Dismal without and ten times worse within.

    Then there's another spark, as this as bad,   55
He mends the matter, and you'll think him mad.
There's Goodwin Wharton, by his own pretense
And that large stock of his of impudence,
Can scale the heavens, level all the land,
Search the main ocean and the seas command;   60
Digs underground and finds great treasures there,
With which he builds his castles in the air;
And with a thousand whimsies in his brain
Dives into all his mysteries in vain.
He's a philosopher and argues sore   65
Of things he never read or heard before,
As much impertinent as Baber was,
And takes more pains to make himself an ass.
Sir Samuel Morland often has been named
For projects, and for foolish fancies famed,   70
Yet he sometimes, thought a great blockhead, can
Attain to finish what he once began;
Yet our projector cares but to begin;
He'll never end, 'cause he wont do like him.
So singular he is, what others say   75
He says, though in his own peculiar way.
Peculiar in his ways as well as wit,
Beshits his breeches 'cause we go to shit.
'Cause we for pleasure, profit, and for speed,
Most part from place to place on horses ride,   80
He, to be singular in his own way,
Made a sea horse and gallops on the sea.
'Cause those that run, to be at ease and light,

Use pumps as sitting firmer on and tight,
He, that he might his own invention use,   85
Made a huge, heavy pair of running shoes.
Besides these faculties he has a way
Of gaining ships sunk in the boundless sea,
And this, as all his projects did before,
Loads of disgrace instead of profit bore.   90
By studious search and labor of his brain,
Affecting much a politician's name,
He, still misguided, plays the zealot's part,
Vainly keeps up his too deluding art,
While all his projects signify a fart.   95
A haughty mind he bears, brimfull of pride;
Revenge and malice on his forehead ride.
   There are yet more which here a part might bear,
And in their ways as vain and foolish are.
There's Deincourt, Eland, Isham, Baber, Arp,   100
Men that might bear each their respective part.
There's Parsons, Clifton, and poor Walker too,
Each in his function here we well might show;
Some of them cuckolds, others fools, some slaves;
Some of 'em too not only fools but knaves.   105
To write of these my Muse is yet unfit;
In others' books their famed memoirs are writ.
Let all the wits unanimously strive
Each man his truest character to give;
I'll hold my life and will be bound to say   110
Dyedapping Wharton bears the bays away.

13. *Dryden.* It was generally believed that John Dryden was the author of Mulgrave's "Essay upon Satire," 1679, and "Familiar Epistle to Mr. Julian" ("Thou common shore"), Harleian MS. 7319, p. 80.

17. *Sir George.* It is impossible to say what satires by Sir George Etherege are referred to. In 1678 or 1679, Etherege married Mary Arnold, the rich widow of a lawyer, Edmund Arnold, who died March 27, 1676. The marriage was not happy. See J. W. Nichol, "Dame Mary Etherege," *MLN,* LXIV, 1949.

23. *young satyrs.* Writers of satires. Evidently the poet derived "satire" from Latin "satyrus," a lecherous woodland deity, instead of from "satira" or "satura," a poetical medley.

25. *Mordaunt.* This is one of several references to the fact that Charles, second Viscount Mordaunt (1658–1735) had a pronounced lisp. *Henningham.* Henry Heveningham of Heveningham, Suffolk, a member of Parliament and a minor poet.

27. *Falkland.* Anthony Carey, Viscount Falkland; see Appendix.

28. *Jack Howe.* John Grubham Howe; see Appendix. Howe had five sisters, all of whom were still unmarried in 1680. See "Satyr," Harleian MS. 6913, p. 235,

> The sisters of Jack Howe too I must name,
> In vice as knowing, and as bad in fame;
> For fear of children they all men defy,
> The Seignior [Dildo]'s vigor constantly they try.

44. *Churchill.* Arabella Churchill (1648–1730), a Maid of Honor to Anne, Duchess of York, and mistress to the Duke, by whom she had four children. Some time before 1685 she married Colonel Charles Godfey. *Richmond.* Frances (Stuart), the younger Duchess of Richmond. There is no reason to believe that either lady "loved and trusted" Jack Howe.

57. *Goodwin Wharton.* The second son of Philip, Lord Wharton, a notorious Whig, Goodwin was a maggoty-brained gentleman, whose MS autobiography in the British Museum is a farrago of mystical nonsense.

67. *Baber.* John, son of Sir John Baber, physician, was the author of some mediocre occasional poems.

69. *Morland.* Sir Samuel Morland, a famous inventor; see Appendix.

88. *gaining ships.* On July 7, 1675, a patent was issued to Goodwin Wharton for fourteen years for a new invention "for the buoying up of ships and the more easy landing and lading of goods" (*CSPD*, 1675–76, p. 203).

92. *a politician's name.* In August, 1679, Goodwin Wharton was elected to Parliament from Grinstead, Sussex.

100. *Deincourt.* Robert Leke (1654–1707) was styled Lord Deincourt until June 27, 1681, when he inherited as Earl of Scarsdale. He was captain of the Band of Gentlemen Pensioners from 1677 to 1683. He and others listed here are included in a passage from "An Ironical Satire" (*POAS*, Yale, II, 200),

> There's Arpe, to whom heaven no distinction gave
> From John-an-apes, but that the brute can laugh.
> Deincourt would fain be thought both wit and bully,
> But punk-rid Rowley's not a greater cully,
> Nor tawdry Isham, intimately known
> To all poxed whores and famous rooks in town.

Eland. Henry Savile (1661–87), Lord Eland since July 17, 1679, eldest son of George, Marquis of Halifax, was a dissolute wastrel and a poetaster. *Isham.* Sir Thomas Isham of Lamport, Northants., born March 15, 1656, succeeded to the baronetcy on March 2, 1675. He died on July 26, 1681, as he was on the point of marrying Barbara, daughter of William Chiffinch (*Seventh Report*, p. 478B). *Baber.* John, son of Sir John Baber, physician. *Arp.* Otherwise Arpe, Harpe, Orby, and Orpe; Charles Orby, an officer in the Guards; see Appendix, Arpe.

102. *Parsons.* In February, 1680, Sir John Parsons, Bart., (1656–1704), abducted and married Catherine, sister of Sir William Clifton. Sir John, an officer in the Earl of Oxford's regiment, had an estate of only £400 a year (*Hasting MS*, II, 172). *Clifton.* Sir William Clifton, Bart., (1663–86) of Clifton, Notts., was described as a ne'er-do-well who was overly fond of wine and "very skilful in dissembling" (*Finch MS*, II, 83–84). Clifton failed in various attempts to get a wealthy bride. *poor Walker.* Possibly Sir Edward Walker, Garter King at Arms, a faithful follower of King Charles in exile, but a troublesome pedant in matters of heraldry. "Poor" suggests that he was dead; he died February 20, 1677.

111. *Dyedapping.* A didapper is a grebe, a small water fowl which dives for its food; by extension a man who is flighty, ridiculous, and unpredictable.

BALLAD ON BETTY FELTON

[*Summer, 1680*]

Although libels on King Charles's mistresses, notably Nell Gwyn and the Duchesses of Cleveland and Portsmouth, were common enough, satires attacking only one lesser Court lady at a time were rare. Wanton Lady Betty Felton is frequently mentioned in shotgun libels, and in "Rochester's Farewell," 1680 (*POAS*, Yale, II, 224), she is listed as one of the Duchess Mazarin's three "whores of honor." She seems to have been one of the Duke of Monmouth's many mistresses, and, according to this satire, in 1680 she was sharing her favors between William, Lord Cavendish, and "bold Frank" Newport. Lady Betty, daughter of James Howard, third Earl of Suffolk, was the wife of Thomas Felton, a Groom of the King's Bedchamber (see Appendix, Felton).

The copy text is Dyce MS. I, 37. In Harleian MS. 6913, p. 14, the satire is titled simply "A Ballad."

Of all quality whores, modest Betty for me;
He's an impudent rogue dares lay virtue to thee.
Both of tongue and of tail, there's no female more free;
She's always attended by ballocks and tarse,
Sweet Candish in cunt and bold Frank at her arse.   5

Her Savoy devotion she has lately given o'er,
How could she play saint and refrain from the whore,
When more lewd than e'er Howard was, or Villiers before?
She's always attended, etc.

Her zeal and her lust, both equally known,   10
Just gods will reward with a heavenly crown,
Outshining the mitre of sanctified Joan.
She's always attended, etc.

47

She starts at no runion of lubbardly stallion,
But quickly chastizes all pricks in rebellion,   *15*
And is able to break a whole catso battalion.
She's always attended, etc.

Believe, little Jockey, full nimbly she stirs,
Without the incitement of whip or of spurs;
May Newmarket ne'er want such true mettle [whores].   *20*
She's always attended, etc.

She's a delicate filly, that all men agree,
More able than Dragon, than Darcy, or Gee.
What pity it is she runs resty with thee.
She's always attended with ballocks and tarse,   *25*
Sweet Candish in cunt and bold Frank at her arse.

4. *tarse.* Penis.

5. *Candish.* William, Lord Cavendish (1640–1707). On June 9, 1680, Lady Sunderland wrote that Cavendish's "whole business now is to watch where my Lady Betty Felton goes and to follow her" (Cartwright, *Sacharissa*, p. 262). *bold Frank.* Francis Newport, second son of Francis, Viscount Newport, died unmarried on November 29, 1692.

6. *Savoy.* Probably the church of St. Mary-le-Savoy in Savoy Street.

8. *Howard.* Mall Howard, a pattern for lewdness; *Villiers.* Barbara (Villiers), Duchess of Cleveland.

12. *sanctified Joan.* According to legend, Pope Joan was a nun who dressed as a man and was elected Pope. The allusion may have been brought to the poet's mind by the King's Company's production on May 31, 1680, of Settle's *The Female Prelate, or the History of the Life and Death of Pope Joan.*

14. *runion.* Penis.

16. *catso.* Or cadzo, vulgar Italian for penis.

18. *little Jockey.* Lady Betty's husband, Thomas Felton, was a small man and an excellent horseman.

23. *Dragon,* etc. Famous race horses. Dragon belonged to King Charles II (A. I. Dasent, *Nell Gwynne,* 1924, p. 222).

UTILE DULCE

([*January*,] *1681*)

This shotgun satire may be a joint product of the two men named in the last lines, Viscount Falkland and Jack Howe, or at least of the latter. In Howe's usual slashing style, the poet rails at almost everyone: Whig and Tory, fops, fools, poets, cuckolds, bullies, and jilting whores, from the orange wench to the King's chief mistress, meanwhile giving himself full credit for moral indignation. The title, implying "profit mingled with pleasure," is from Horace's *Ars Poetica*, "Omne tulit punctum qui miscuit utile dulci." What may be, in lines 80–85, a reference to the trial of William Howard, Viscount Stafford, November 30 to December 7, 1680, places the satire not long after that event.

The copy text is Harleian MS. 6913, p. 151. The poem is dated 1681 in Harleian MS. 7319, p. 126; Bodleian MS. Firth c. 15, p. 96; and "A Choyce Collection," p. 82. It is undated in Dyce MS. 43, I, 304, and Douce MS. 357, f. 134v.

Muse, let us change our style and live in peace,
In our soft lines let biting satire cease.
Believe me, 'tis an evil trade to rail;
The angry poet's hopes do often fail,
Instead of bays a cudgel oft does find.   *5*
Some lines, for being praised when they were read,
Were once a cause of Dryden's broken head.
    A tedious elegy may without fear
On Peters' table lie for seven year;
Not Henningham, nor any critic fop,   *10*
Scarce wry-mouthed Tyzard, deigns to take it up.
Bold Wharton hears it read without a frown,
And the author safe, unthreatened, walks the town;
But he that jeers and makes the reader smile,

Whom all find fault with, and yet read him still,   *15*
While giddily without respect he flies,
Even those he pleases makes his enemies.
For who about this spacious town can hear
A knave, a fop, a cuckold's character,
But straight he thinks within his guilty mind   *20*
One (if not all of these) for him designed?
Describe a nauseous, false, and withered whore
(As if there were but she), straight Nelly'll roar.
    Might I as freely, as once Juvenal,
In public at prevailing vices rail?   *25*
What it't to me how Hewitt's cravats sit?
Or that some greater fools think him a wit?
Let Mordaunt copy Sir John Suckling's songs,
Call 'em his own and have 'em set in throngs;
Let Mulgrave be thought handsome, Poulteney brave,   *30*
Bennet sincere and Sund[er]land no knave;
Let Harry Wharton pass in Jermyn Street
For honest, prudent, and a man of wit;
Let circulating pox go round the House
'Till there be'nt left so much as a sound mouse;   *35*
Let Deincourt, Nobbs, and 'foresaid Harry troll,
And sacred ballocks 'bout their fingers roll;
Let Gerard houses fire, Oglethrope fight,
And swear each common health is drunk in spite;
It ne'er shall trouble me. Why then complain?   *40*
Henceforward, Muse, we must correct this vein.
If you must rhyme, let's the great praises sing
Of our most potent, just, and prudent King;
His brother's conduct, wit, and policy,
His gratitude and great sincerity,   *45*
Unmatched by anything but's piety.
Let's tell how true friend he proved to Coleman,
And how unjustly he accused—
In vain I labor; 'tis but losing time;
When I would praise, I cannot find one rhyme.   *50*

Each line I write is empty and constrained;
Th'unwilling pen and paper fly my hand;
But when I rail, from off Parnassus' top
Th'officious Sisters haste to help me up.
Words of themselves do in order drop   55
And smoothly say that St. Johns is a fop;
Or would I of a famous cuckold tell,
My hand inspired straight writes down Arundel;
Of bombast poets which infest the town,
There's Otway, Settle, D'Urfey, Lee, and Crowne;   60
I find a dozen where I seek but one.
Fruitful in mischief, thus my Muse prevails,
Careless of what or who, when once she rails;
Jenkins no more than Mustian she saves,
Nor know I why she should, since both are knaves.   65
    To men of worth a just respect I bear;
Their names are sacred, as their virtues are.
None e'er shall in my loosest satires find
A virtuous woman or an honest friend.
Three creatures in the world I own I hate: 70
A fop, a jilting whore, and flatt'ring cheat.
Whilst thus I scribbling sit, methinks I hear
The men in fury, ladies all o'er fear,
"See, there's the censuring monster! Let's be grave,
He'll libel you if he but hear you laugh."   75
But what of that? Must I alone sit still?
Shall all be mad, and I not dare to smile?
When I see puking Portsmouth can I hold,
Seeming to save what she long since has sold,
Blocked up with bawds in humble manner set,   80
Courting the senators with scraps of meat?
Can I see Deincourt robed, resolved to save
(With his no honor) each conspiring knave,
His wife above with pocky Temple sit,
Consulting to his face where next to meet,   85
Hear him give's vote, and say he's just or wise?

51

I could as soon think he no cuckold is.
When I see ladies in the dead of night,
Crammed up in hackney coach with each a knight,
Scouring from house to house like drunk or mad,   90
Plaguing the Town with noise and serenade,
Force Lower from his bed, which h'has denied
To many patients, though the wretches died;
Or when at Potter's bawdy house, renowned
As any of that quality i'th'town,   95
I hear how ladies bred in godly way
Have oft of late been known to go astray—
With all good manners, I presume t'advise,
Not that they be less merry, but more wise.
But he who undertakes this Town to teach   100
Does modesty to ranting Stamford preach,
Who with more pride her tribe of fools discovers
Than Richmond hides the number of her lovers.
  So long in vain have friendly poets taught
To fly those pleasures which with shame are bought: 105
The orange wench that prostrates at the door
Would be thought chaste, and frowns at the name of whore.
While ladies in the boxes seem at strife
Whose reputation shall have shortest life.
  Just now I hear wise Harry Lumley say,   110
"These satires all diversion do destroy.
Such coxcombs know not, nor deserve the bliss
Which a discreet, kind, faithful mistress gives."
Now all the ladies' pride and chiefest joy
Is to be ogled at the next new play;   115
Fleering about, with softest looks they sit
And give encouragement to all the pit;
Then, filled with hopes, to the box the coxcombs crowd,
Grin and speak powerful nonsense very loud.
There's not a fool so awkward in the nation;   120
Even Chute and St. Johns dare now talk of passion.
Baber's a spark, and Hales a politician.

To strut in'th' pit Southerland leaves his duty;
And Lady Warwick sets up for a beauty.
Love, thus burlesqued, withdraws himself in rage,   *125*
And wondrous seldom's seen on this our stage.
But the young, discreet, the witty and the fair,
He promises shall still his blessings share,
And charged me these his last commands to give
To all who in his favor wish to live: *130*
"Be fond in private, but in public grave;
Avoid a fool, a coxcomb, and a knave;
Be wise as maids which are in cloisters blest;
Come veiled to the world, but naked to the priest.
So Falkland will be forced to burn his pen,   *135*
And peevish Jack will never write again."

7. *Dryden's broken head.* A reference to the beating suffered by John Dryden in Rose Alley, December 18, 1679, supposedly incited by someone reflected on in "An Essay upon Satyr," of which Dryden was suspected to be the author.

9. *Peters' table.* Peters' Coffeehouse in Covent Garden was a well-known Whig resort.

10. *Henningham.* Henry Heveningham of Heveningham, Sussex, wit and satirist.

11. *wry-mouthed Tyzard.* Apparently Henry Lumley, younger brother of Richard, Lord Lumley (see Appendix). In "A Satyr," c. 1680 (Add. MS. 34, 362, p. 131), we are told that "wry-mouthed Lumley does in judgment sit."

12. *bold Wharton.* Thomas and Henry Wharton were notably belligerent, but Thomas, the older brother, seems more likely here.

23. *Nelly.* Nell Gwyn.

26. *Hewitt.* Sneers at Sir George Hewitt's cravats are tiresomely frequent in Court satires.

28. *Mordaunt.* The charge that Charles, Viscount Mordaunt, plagiarized from Suckling is repeated in "To Julian. 1684" (Harleian MS. 7317, p. 181); Mordaunt has proved that he can write "By's making Suckling's songs his own."

30. *Mulgrave.* Because John Sheffield, Earl of Mulgrave, had an overly long nose, he was not considered handsome. *Poulteney.* For the reputed cowardice of John, second son of Sir William Pulteney, see Appendix, Pulteney.

31. *Bennet.* Henry Bennet, Earl of Arlington and Lord Chamberlain. *Sund[er]-land.* Robert Spencer, Earl of Sunderland, was dismissed from his post as Secretary of State on January 24, 1681, for advocating the exclusion of the Duke of York from the succession to the throne.

36. *Deincourt.* Robert Leke, Lord Deincourt, inherited as Earl of Scarsdale on January 27, 1681. *Nobbs.* Probably George Porter, Junior; see Appendix. *troll.* Sing lustily.

38. *Gerard.* Sir Gilbert Gerard, Bart., of Fiskerton, was a fiery Whig, but there is no evidence that he fired houses; perhaps the poet implies that he fired (i.e., stirred up) the House of Commons at its various sessions. *Oglethorpe.* Major Theophilus Oglethorpe was a rabid Tory, apparently ready to fight over so small a matter as a "common health," a toast. On February 17, 1680, he challenged various Whigs who had spoken "words against the Duchess of Portsmouth, but the challenge was refused" (Newdigate Newsletter). On January 10, 1681, Oglethorpe, with Cornet Colt as his second, fought a duel with Captain Richardson and Captain Churchill. Oglethorpe killed the first, and Colt wounded the second. Found guilty of manslaughter, Oglethorpe pleaded his clergy, "asked for the book, read it, and was branded"— with a cold iron, no doubt (*Ormonde MS*, N.S., V, 55; *Middlesex County Records*, IV, 150).

47. *Coleman.* Edward Coleman, the Duchess of York's secretary, was executed on December 3, 1678, for complicity in the Popish Plot. According to Burnet (II, 167), "It was given out at that time, to make the Duke [of York] more odious, that Coleman was kept up from making confessions by the hopes the Duke sent him of a pardon at Tyburn."

56. *St. Johns.* Henry (1652–1742), son of Sir Walter St. John of Lydiard, Wilts. On April 16, 1679, Henry Savile wrote from Paris that Mr. St. John was there "fattening his horses for sale." He concluded, "I have already been asked if, besides not speaking the language, he be not *un peu fol*" (*Rochester-Savile Letters*, p. 67).

58. *Arundel.* Henry Howard, Earl of Arundel, inherited as Duke of Norfolk in 1684; see Appendix, Norfolk.

59. *bombast poets.* Five playwrights: Thomas Otway (1652–85), Elkanah Settle (1648–1724), Thomas D'Urfey (1653–1723), Nathaniel Lee (1640–92), and John Crowne (1640–1712).

64. *Jenkins.* Probably Sir Leoline Jenkins (1623–85), Principal Secretary of State from April, 1680, to April, 1684. *Mustian.* Unidentified.

78. *Portsmouth.* In 1680–81, Louise, Duchess of Portsmouth and the King's chief mistress, was dabbling in politics, partly with the hope that if York was excluded from the succession, her own son by the King, the Duke of Richmond, might be named as the King's heir.

82. *Deincourt.* Robert Leke, Lord Deincourt, was called to the House of Lords on October 22, 1680. On November 30, 1680, William Howard, Viscount Stafford, was tried for conspiring to bring about the death of King Charles. His judges and jury were the members of the House of Lords, all in their robes. His prosecutors represented the House of Commons. On December 7 the peers were asked to give their verdicts as their names were called. Then (wrote Evelyn) "the peer spoken to standing up and laying his right hand upon his heart said 'Guilty,' or 'Not guilty, upon my honor.'" Stafford was convicted by a vote of 55 to 31; he was beheaded on December 29.

84. *his wife.* In February, 1672, Deincourt married Mary, daughter of Sir John Lewis, Bart., of York. She became notorious for her affairs and died February 17, 1684. *Temple.* Probably Sir Richard ("Timber") Temple (1634–97), a Whig member of the House of Commons.

92. *Lower.* Sir Richard Lower (1631–91), a famous London physician.

94. *Potter's.* An "India House," or shop for the sale of goods from India, kept by Mrs. Jane Potter. According to the author of "Satyr," c. 1681 (Harleian MS. 6913, p. 233), the bawdy houses in Whetstones Park were closed because

> De Vett and Potter have usurped the trade,
> With Indy trinkets many cuckolds made,
> And in their stuff love letters oft conveyed.

It was said that Mrs. Potter had a part in arranging Thomas Thynne's ill-fated marriage with Lady Elizabeth Ogle in the autumn of 1681 (see Appendix, Ogle).

101. *Stamford.* At this time Elizabeth (Harvey), the wanton Countess of Stamford, was separated from her husband, Thomas Gray, Earl of Stamford.

103. *Richmond.* Frances, Duchess of Richmond; see Appendix.

106. *the orange wench.* A girl who sold oranges in the theatres and, as a side line, her own delectable person.

108. *boxes.* Side boxes in the theatres.

116. *fleering.* Grinning.

121. *Chute.* Chaloner Chute, a minor wit and courtier.

122. *Baber.* John Baber, a poetaster, son of the Court physician, Sir John Baber. *Hales.* Sir Edward Hales, Bart., of Woodchurch, Kent, became a Roman Catholic in 1685, and by King James II was appointed successively lieutenant of Dover Castle, lieutenant of the Tower, and colonel of a regiment of foot. He joined James in exile and died c. 1695 (Dalton, II, 35).

123. *Southerland.* Probably Hugh Southerland, who in 1678 was commissioned captain in the First Footguards (Dalton, I, 289). See "Satyr," c. 1680 (*POAS*, Yale, II, 206).

> Shall Howe and Brandon politicians prove,
> And Sutherland presume to be in love?

124. *Warwick.* Anne (Montague), elderly widow of Robert Rich, sixth Earl of Warwick (1620–75). She died in July, 1689.

135. *Falkland.* Anthony Carey, Viscount Falkland; see Appendix.

136. *peevish Jack.* John Grubham Howe; see Appendix.

THE LADIES' MARCH

([*Early*] *1681*)

In this blunderbuss of satire, the poet presents a procession of twenty-three Court ladies marching across a stage, as if seeking erotic preferment and applause. The poem vaguely resemble a "sessions" satire, as if the ladies were candidates for the Duchess of Portsmouth's place as chief mistress to King Charles. Both the Duchess of Cleveland (who was living in France) and the Duchess of Portsmouth were omitted from the parade. Perhaps the poet was merely venting his spleen against a collection of known or suspected sinners.

The copy text, dated 1681, is Harleian MS. 7317, p. 28. The poem is dated 1681 in Harleian MS. 7319, p. 138; Dyce MS. 43, I, 312; MS. Don b. 8, p. 683; MS. Firth c. 15, p. 106; and "A Choyce Collection," p. 92. In Add. MS. 34,362, f. 20, it is dated "Feb 10 1681" (i.e., 1681 New Style). Internal evidence suggests that the satire was written early in 1681.

Stamford's countess led the van,
   Tallest of the caravan,
She who ne'er wants white or red,
   Or just pretense to keep her bed.
Lofty Richmond followed after;   *5*
   Richmond scorns to hold her water,
Piqued that Stamford should take place
   For height or lewdness of her grace.
She distills her heavenly dew
   On all that swear they will be true.   *10*
Then came pensive Orrery,
   "Oh, Lindano, why should'st thou die?
'Twas Fourcard killed thee and not I,
   Oh, destructive mercury!"

Behold a dame too old to chancre 'em,   *15*
   Vulgarly called my Lady Ancram,
Lodged in a garret at Whitehall,
   Hard by the Countess of Fingal.
Mazarin for St. Peter's glory
   Frigs King Charles and fucks with Lory.   *20*
Next Lory's dearest treads the stage,
   A hopeful matron for her age;
She whose spring resisted stoutly,
   In her autumn fucks devoutly;
Not improper, ne'ertheless,   *25*
   For Nan Hyde's Nancy's governess.
Middleton, where'er she goes,
   Confirms the scandal of her foes;
Quelled by the fair one's funky hose,
   Even Lory's forced to hold his nose.   *30*
Sailing Temple next comes on,
   Led by Corbet's Brereton,
Temple raised by just degrees
   To Manton's spouse from ale and cheese.
Next in order Richmond's sister,   *35*
   Recipient much of ballocks' glister,
But now her sins are wiped away,
   Godolphin fucks her every day.
Lawson, she who's disappointed,
   Grieves to lose the Lord's Anointed,   *40*
Follows next in the reverend clutches
   Of her old aunt and bawd, the duchess.
The next that followed in the rank
   Was Betty Felton led by Frank,
Betty Felton lewd and pocky,   *45*
   Lord have mercy on her jockey!
Next fair Lady Grey appears,
   Her charming eyes bathed in tears,
In such a pitiful condition
   That most men thought it was her Vision.   *50*

57

Next Berkeley's Harriet greets the eye,
   The females of which family,
By nature or by education,
   All love the act of generation.
She, though you catch the man upon her, 55
   Will swear not guilty upon her honor.
Fanshaw's princess posted after
   To take the place of a king's daughter,
Which royal privilege she got
   By gently stroking Mr. Trott. 60
Now view the lass with riveled belly,
   Some call her Nell, some Mrs. Nelly,
A saint to be admired the more
   Because a Church of England's whore.
A bouncing dame appears and laughs; 65
   Who should it be but Mrs. Crofts?
Though many think her an intruder,
   Appointed bawd to Lady Tudor;
Yet here she plys in hope of luck, sir,
   Still itching though St. Albans fucks her. 70
Old Mrs. Jennings next comes crawling,
   A lady too of Crofts's calling,
Who kindly holds the double clout
   And wipes the face at every bout.
The next that marched was Bellasis, 75
   She who can pox you with a kiss,
Bellasis, as famed for dryness
   As Churchill or his royal highness.
Lo, thy daughter, little Sid,
   She who lately slipped her kid, 80
Sure a hopeful babe 'twill be,
   Soaked in pox and Popery.
Next in place comes Mrs. Porter,
   But fools grow nice, not one would court her.
This short-lived princess owed her fall 85
   To the Principal of Ballock Hall.

The Lady Arundel went by,
  Led by her lover with one eye;
Thus nicely managing her prime,
  She may be duchess in good time.   *90*
Courteous Mall would fain pass by her,
  Lined by duke, lord, knight, and squire,
And eke by her confessing friar.
  All trades help to quench the fire,
Pricks as tall as Sarum spire,   *95*
  Daily plunged into her mire,
All too short to satisfy her.

1. *Stamford.* Elizabeth, buxom Countess of Stamford; see Appendix.

3. *white.* For white (or "whites"), see leucorrhea, a chronic vaginal infection. *red.* Menses, probably menorrhagia.

5. *Richmond.* Frances (Stuart), Duchess of Richmond; see Appendix.

11. *Orrery.* Mary (Sackvile), estranged wife of Roger Boyle (Lord Broghill), now second Earl of Orrery.

12. *Lindano.* Perhaps M. de Lindenau, Envoy Extraordinary from Denmark to England, 1668–72 (Sidney, *Diary*, I, 128). The mercury treatment for venereal disease was sometimes fatal.

15. *Fourcard.* Florente Fourcade, since December 20, 1672, had been chirurgeon in ordinary to King Charles II (PRO, Lord Chamberlain, 5/140, p. 155).

16. *Ancram.* Frances, wife of Charles Kerr, Earl of Ancram, and a Lady of the Bedchamber to the Queen, was considered too old for copulation and its consequent venereal sores.

18. *Fingal.* Margaret, wife of Luke Plunkett, Earl of Fingal, was a Lady in Waiting to the Queen. In March, 1692, she accompanied the Dowager Queen abroad as Groom of the Stole (Luttrell, II, 403).

19. *Mazarin.* For an expanded version see Harleian MS. 6913, p. 166,

> Mazarine pursues the track,
> Swived by tawny, white, and black;
> Mazarine for the church's glory,
> Friggs King Charles and fucks with Lory.

By 1681 the Duchess Mazarin was no longer the King's mistress.

20. *Lory.* Lawrence Hyde, second son of Edward, Earl of Clarendon, in 1663 married his "dearest," Henrietta, daughter of Richard Boyle, Earl of Burlington. Hyde was created Viscount Hyde of Kenilworth on April 23, 1681, and Earl of Rochester on November 29, 1682.

26. *Nan Hyde.* Anne Hyde (1637-71), first wife of James, Duke of York. *Nancy.*

Princess Anne (1664-1714). In November, 1677, Lady Henrietta Hyde succeeded Lady Frances Villiers as governess of the Duke of York's children. John Aubrey's often quoted remark that Lady Denham "was poisoned by the hands of the Countess of Rochester with chocolate" referred not to Anne Wilmot but to Henrietta Hyde, Countess of Rochester. Her sister-in-law, Anne (Hyde), Duchess of York, was also suspected of poisoning her husband's mistress. See Pepys, January 8, 1667, and "Queries from the Protestant coffee-house in Amsterdam," 1682 (*CSPD*, 1682, p. 585). Apparently Lady Denham died of natural causes.

27. *Middleton.* Mrs. Jane Middleton; see Appendix.

29. *funky.* Stinking.

31. *Temple.* Philipa Temple, a Maid of Honor to the Queen.

32. *Brereton.* It is possible that John, fourth Baron Brereton of Leighlin, Ireland (1659–1718) was "keeping" Mary Corbett, an undistinguished actress with the King's Company from 1675 to 1681 (Wilson, *All the King's Ladies*, p. 131).

34. *Manton.* Perhaps Dr. Thomas Manton (1620–77), a famous Presbyterian divine, whose services in private houses were often attended by people "of quality" (*Buccleuch MS*, I, 321). The sneer at Miss Temple ("spouse" is used in the sense of "bride of Christ") suggests that she had attended such "fanatic" meetings.

35. *Richmond's sister.* Sophia (Stuart), wife of Henry Bulkeley, Master of the Household; see Appendix, Bulkeley.

38. *Godolphin.* Sidney Godolphin (1645–1712), a Lord of the Treasury and one of the ministry of "chits" in 1679–81.

39. *Lawson.* Probably Elizabeth, third daughter of Sir John Lawson of Brough, Yorks., by his wife Catherine, sister of "Northern Tom" Howard; see Appendix, Lawson.

42. *old aunt.* Her aunt by marriage, Mary (Villiers), Duchess of Richmond, had married, as her second husband, "Northern Tom" Howard, Miss Lawson's uncle. For the plot to get Miss Lawson as a mistress for Charles II, see "Flatfoot, the Gudgeon Taker," 1680, *POAS*, Yale, II, 190.

44. *Betty Felton.* Notorious Lady Elizabeth (Howard), wife of Thomas Felton, a Groom of the Bedchamber, died on December 14, 1681. *Frank.* Francis, "bold Frank," Newport. *her jockey* was her husband, Thomas Felton, a horseman.

47. *Lady Grey.* Mary (Berkeley), wife of Ford, Lord Grey of Werke. Her "Vision" alludes to *A True Relation of a Strange Apparition which appeared to the Lady Grey*, published c. January, 1681 (Luttrell, I, 64). The apparition warned her that there was danger to the blood royal, but bade her not be concerned because her supposed lover, the Duke of Monmouth, had none of the blood royal in his veins.

51. *Harriet.* Henrietta Berkeley, Lady Grey's younger sister and Lord Grey's secret mistress; see Appendix, Grey.

57. *Fanshawe.* Mary (Walter), half-sister to the Duke of Monmouth and wife of William Fanshaw, a Master of Requests.

60. *Mr. Trott.* Jonathan Trott, said to have been cured of the King's evil by Mrs. Fanshaw's touch. *A True and Wonderful Account of a Cure of the King's Evil by Mrs. Fanshawe, sister to the Duke of Monmouth*, appeared in January, 1681 (Luttrell, I, 64).

62. *Nell.* Nell Gwyn. It is related that in 1681 a Whig mob mistook Nell's coach for that of her Catholic rival, the Duchess of Portsmouth. Nell stuck her head out of the window and said, "Pray, good people, be civil. I am the Protestant whore"

(Wilson, *Nell Gwyn*, p. 240). The amanuensis who copied this poem into Harleian MS. 6913, p. 165, added a vulgar passage:

> Whose cunt, arse, mouth and every hole
> Has served for Rowley's prick's close-stool;
> Torrents flow from Nelly's sluice,
> Only Arundel can produce
> An equal stock of wheyey juice.

66. *Mrs. Crofts.* Catherine Crofts (1637–86) spinster sister of Monmouth's former guardian, Lord Crofts, was guardian of Mary Tudor, daughter of King Charles by Moll Davis, until 1684 (*Seventh Report*, 376B).

67. *though many.* Var. Harleian MS. 6913, "The whores may think."

70. *St. Albans.* Apparently Mrs. Crofts had long been mistress to Henry Jermyn, Earl of St. Albans (c. 1640–January 2, 1684). On February 22, 1684, William Bentinck, in a letter to Henry Sidney, wrote, "Je plains Mrs. Crofts de la mort du Conte de St. Albans et de la perte de sa pupille, c'en est trop à la fois" (Sidney, *Diary*, II, 238).

71. *Mrs. Jennings.* Frances Jennings, widow of Richard Jennings of Sandridge, and a well-known Court bawd.

75. *Bellasis.* Susan (Armine), widow of Sir Henry Belasyse, was once mistress to the Duke of York. In 1674 Susan was created Baroness Belasyse of Osgodby. Her second husband, before 1684, was James Fortrey, a Groom of the Bedchamber. Lady Belasyse died January 6, 1713.

78. *Churchill.* Arabella Churchill, eldest daughter of Sir Winston Churchill and sister of John, the future Duke of Marlborough, had been a Maid of Honor to Anne, Duchess of York. As the Duke of York's mistress, she bore him four bastards. Afterward she married Colonel Charles Godfrey.

79. *thy daughter.* Katherine Sedley (1657–1717), daughter of Sir Charles Sedley ("little Sid"), became about 1678 a Maid of Honor to Marie Beatrice, Duchess of York, and mistress to the Duke, to whom she gave a daughter, Lady Katherine Darnley, born in March, 1679, and a son who was born in August, 1684, and died on April 26, 1685. On January 19, 1686, King James created Katherine Sedley Countess of Dorchester, and, at the behest of his priests, banished her from the Court. On August 20, 1696, she married Sir David Colyear, who became Earl of Portmore. Mrs. Sedley, no beauty, was famed for her caustic wit.

83. *Mrs. Porter.* Probably Olive, daughter of George Porter. Apparently she had an illegitimate child about this time. See "Scandal Saty'd" (Harleian MS. 6913, p. 210).

> Porter 'mongst the lewd rabble may be thrown,
> Her last retreat has fixed her doubtful fame,
> A pocky babe's a mark of double shame.

86. *the Principal.* Perhaps William, Lord Cavendish. See above, "On Several Women about Town," note to line 25.

87. *Lady Arundel.* Mary (Mordaunt), Countess of Arundel; see Appendix, Norfolk. MS. Firth c. 15, p. 106, adds this after line 88.

Who boldly brags of cods anointed,
With balm for Arundel appointed;
He, when the Lily Lass invites,
Undaunted launches into her whites.

88. *her lover.* Charles Talbot, Earl of Shrewsbury, had lost the sight of one eye.

91. *courteous Mall.* Mall Howard, Lady Arundel's companion and cousin by marriage.

95. *Sarum spire.* The spire of Sarum (Salisbury) Cathedral. Variant ending, from Harleian MS. 7319, p. 142, after line 94,

Yet still she burns, or men belie her;
Mall is scratched by every briar,
Hers is no common low desire,
If you wont believe me, try her,
Ask her but once, and she'll retire.
Nay, she'll beg, who can deny her?
Though to plunge into the mire.
Pricks as long as Sarum spire
Most devoutly, daily ply her,
All not enough to satisfy her.
Mall, adieu; you've lost your squire.

AN ESSAY OF SCANDAL

([*Summer,*] *1681*)

In the summer of 1681, King Charles II, denied supplies by all his recent Parliaments, was very poor. Since the dissolution of the Oxford Parliament (March 28, 1681), he had been receiving a modest subsidy from France, but it was hardly enough to cover the bare needs of his government. The writer of "An Essay" chose to blame the King's poverty on his acknowledged mistresses, Portsmouth, Cleveland, and Gwyn, and suggested that the monarch get rid of them and turn to cheaper doxies. He seems to have had little hope that his advice would be followed.

The copy text is Add. MS. 27,407, p. 120. The manuscript, folded as a letter, is from the collection of Peter Le Neve. The satire is dated 1681 in MS. Firth c. 25, p. 102; Douce MS. 357, f. 85; Harleian MS. 6913, p. 159; Harleian MS. 7319, p. 133; and "A Choyce Collection," p. 88.

> Of all the plagues with which this world abounds,
> Our discords causes, wid'ners of our wounds,
> Sure woman is the lewdest can be guessed;
> Through woman, mankind early ills did taste;
> She was the world's first curse, will be the last.   *5*
> To show what woman is, Heav'n make Charles wise;
> Some angel scale the blindness from his eyes.
> Restored by miracle, he may believe,
> And seeing's follies, learn though late to live.
> Why art thou poor, O King? Embezzling cunt,   *10*
> That wide-mouthed, greedy monster, that has done't.
> Thee and three kingdoms have thy drabs destroyed,
> Yet they are still uncured and thou uncloyed.
> Go visit Ports[mouth] fasting if thou dar'st,

(Which well thou may'st, at the poor rate thou far'st)   *15*
She'll with her noisome breath blast ev'n thy face,
Till thou thyself grow uglier than her grace.
Remove that costly dunghill from thy doors;
If thou must have 'em, use cheap, wholesome whores.
Take Temple, who can live on cheese and ale,   *20*
Who never but to bishop yet turned tail;
She's seasoned, fit to bear a double brunt,
In her arse London, Rowley in her cunt.
Bishop and King, choose (handy-dandy) either;
They still club votes, why not club seeds together?   *25*
Else choose Godolphin, whom there's little hurt in;
She'll fuck for clothes, for all she's called a fortune.
Besides, there's Swan and Chevins—fuck 'em, fill 'em,
And Mrs. Villiers, sister of Sir William.
Ram all thy Maids of Honor whilst thou'rt able,   *30*
And make thy barren Queen keep up thy table.
But from her den expel old ulcer quite;
She shines i'th' dark like rotten wood by night,
Dreads pepper, penance, Parliaments, and light.
Once with thy peoples' prayers resolve to join;   *35*
She's all the nation's nuisance, why not thine?
Own to the world her brat's not thine at all,
For father Hamilton shines through him all,
His impudence, his falsehood, and ill nature,
Each inward vice and every outward feature;   *40*
True Hamilton in every act and look,
Yet to record thy blindness made a duke.
   Then next turn N[ell]y out of door,
That hare-brained, wrinkled, stopped-up whore,
Daily struck, stabbed, by half the pricks in town;   *45*
Yet still her stubborn courses come not down
But lie and nourish old diseases there,
Which thou and many thy poor subjects share.
'Twas once indeed with her as 'twas with ore,

Uncoined, she was no public store,   *50*
Only Buckhurst's private whore.
But when that thou in wanton itch
With royal tarse had stamped her breech,
She grew a common, current bitch.
Then for that cub, her son and heir,   *55*
Let him remain in Otway's care
To make him (if that's possible to be)
A viler poet and more dull than he.
So at the next Newmarket meeting
(When thy senate should be sitting),   *60*
Where knaves and fools and courtiers do resort,
And players come from far to make thee sport,
As in thy barn thou shalt in state behold
The Fair Maid of the West, or Girl worth Gold,
Sitting with most majestic grace,   *65*
And she fleering in thy face—
Then, like a monarch as thou art,
Lay thy hand upon thy heart,
Kick her for her lewd cajoling,
And bid her turn to her old trade of strolling.   *70*
    But hectors shall forget to drink,
Mall Hinton have no pox, nor stink,
Lord Sun[derlan]d be honest, Mulgrave civil,
Bishops believe a God, or Devil,
Dryden not mouse a whore, when he can get her,   *75*
Or have his pension paid, that's better.
Mon[mouth] turn again to's duty,
And Tartar Cox be thought a beauty.
No more libels shall be written,
And the Court without a Mitton,   *80*
E'er thou shalt have a friend to tell
Thee, I have here advised thee well.
But how slight soe'er they make it,
The counsel's good, believe and take it.

14. *Portsmouth.* Louise Kerouaile, Duchess of Portsmouth, reigning royal mistress.

20. *Temple.* Philipa Temple, a Maid of Honor to Queen Catherine. For the appointment of three new Maids, "Temple, Anstroder, and Nan Howard," November 13, 1673, see *Williamson Letters*, II, 71.

23. *London.* Henry Compton (1632–1713), sixth son of Spencer, second Earl of Northampton, was Bishop of London from 1675. *Rowley.* King Charles II.

26. *Godolphin.* Elizabeth (1665–83), daughter of Sir John Godolphin, was appointed Maid of Honor to the Queen in December, 1677 (*Rutland MS*, II, 43).

28. *Swan.* "One Mrs. Swan, the daughter of Sir Will Swan of Kent, who is very young and pretty, is to succeed [Dorothy Howard] and be Maid of Honor" (*Bulstrode*, I, 325, December 10, 1675). Cecilia Swan appears as a Maid of Honor to the Queen in the *Calendars of Treasury Books* from 1676 through 1682. *Chevins.* Barbara, daughter of William Chiffinch, Closet Keeper to King Charles II. On December 8, 1681, Barbara, about eighteen, married Sir Edward Villiers ("scabby Ned"), son of the Knight Marshall, Colonel Edward Villiers (*London Marriage Licenses*).

29. *Mrs. Villiers.* Katherine Villiers, a daughter of Colonel Edward Villiers, was Maid of Honor to Queen Catherine from 1680 to 1685. See Newdigate Newsletter, May 20, 1680, "fine Mrs. ffrasier one of the Maids of Honor is lately withdrawn from the Court and Colonel Villliers' daughter sworn in her place." See Appendix, Villiers (Jersey). *Sir William* is probably a mistake for Sir Edward, Katherine's brother. Sir William Villiers of Brokesby (1644–1711), who was in charge of the King's stables, was Katherine's cousin.

32. *old ulcer.* Barbara, Duchess of Cleveland, the King's mistress emeritus. Although the duchess was living in France, almost forgotten by the Court poets, there were rumors in the summer of 1681 that she was returning to live in England (Luttrell, I, 127). She returned on April 12, 1682.

34. *pepper.* Supposed to prevent decay in meat. *penance.* In 1663 the duchess became a Roman Catholic.

38. *father Hamilton.* The gossips whispered that the duchess's son by the King, Henry Fitzroy, created Duke of Grafton in 1675, was actually the son of Colonel James Hamilton, a handsome Groom of the Bedchamber.

43. *Nelly.* Nell Gwyn.

51. *Buckhurst.* Charles Sackvile, Lord Buckhurst, and after August 27, 1677, Earl of Dorset, was Nell's first "keeper" (see Pepys, July 13, 1667).

53. *tarse.* Penis.

55. *that cub.* Nell Gwyn's older son, Charles Beauclerc (1670–1726), Earl of Burford and, after January 5, 1684, Duke of St. Albans. Nell's younger son, James, died in France in June, 1680.

56. *Otway.* Thomas Otway (1652–85), the playwright, was at this time young Burford's tutor.

59. *Newmarket.* On September 8, 1681, King Charles went to the race meetings at Newmarket.

64. *the Fair Maid.* I.e., *The Fair Maid of the West*, or *A Girl Worth Gold*, a play by Thomas Heywood, first produced in 1631.

66. *fleering.* Grinning.

72. *Hinton.* Mall Hinton, a famous cyprian; see Appendix.

73. *Sun[derlan]d.* Robert Spencer, Earl of Sunderland (1641–1702), was First Secretary of State from February 11, 1679, to January 14, 1681. He was dismissed for

having advocated exclusion of the Duke of York, and found himself distrusted by both Whigs and Tories. *Mulgrave*. John Sheffield, Earl of Mulgrave, was commonly accused of arrogance and bad manners.

75. The apparently pointless sneer at John Dryden may have been motivated by anger at a Tory pamphlet, *His Majesty's Declaration Defended*, June, 1681, which was attributed to Dryden (C. E. Ward, *Life of John Dryden*, 1961, pp. 160–64). *mouze*. Ruffle, play with amorously. Dryden was commonly accused of lechery. An MS note to Langbaine's *An Account of the English Dramatick Poets*, 1691 (British Museum), quotes a secondhand version of a story by a drawer at a tavern frequented by Dryden, who "often brought women of the town thither." Peeping through the keyhole, the drawer saw "the most filthy obscenities practised by the old goatish poet and his doxies."

77. *Monmouth*. Since the Duke of Monmouth's return from foreign exile without permission on November 27, 1679, he had been dismissed from all his posts and forbidden the Court.

78. *Tartar Cox*. "Tartar," a sharper. On July 8, 1680, a true bill was returned that "John Coxe *alias* Tartar, late of the said parish, yeoman, an infamous and evil person . . . maliciously and scandalously uttered published and offered for sale a certain most pernicious, wicked and vicious book entitled 'The Schoole of Venus or the Ladies Delight, Reduced into Rules of Practice; being the translation of the French *L'Escole des Filles* in two Dialogues Anno 1680' " (*Middlesex County Records*, IV, 146). On October 24, 1682, *The Loyal Protestant and True Domestic Intelligence* noted the death of Captain John Cox, "commonly called "The Tartar."

80. *Mitton*. Sir John Mitton had long been a Gentleman Usher of the Privy Chamber.

AN HEROIC POEM

[*1681*]

The anonymous author of this most unheroic satire sneers at a brace of friends, attacks a group of leading Whigs, libels a pair of Court officials and a Court bawd, and ends by vilifying a bevy of Maids of Honor. He seems to have been motivated more by spite than by moral or political indignation. Curiously, he has nothing to say against Whig principles, and he carefully ignores the Whig leader, Anthony, Earl of Shaftesbury, now in the Tower awaiting trial for high treason.

The copy text is Harleian MS. 6913, p. 197. The poem is called "A Satyr" in Sloane MS. 655, f. 57; "A New Satyr. 1681" in Dyce MS. 43, II, 560; "Satyr against Whigs" in Add. MS. 21,094, f. 70; and "A Satyr, by Dryden," in Harleian MS. 7317, p. 91. The date is certainly before the death of Lady Betty Felton, December 14, 1681.

Of villains, rebels, cuckolds, pimps and spies,
Cowards and fools, and stormers of dirt pies,
Bawds, panders, whores, even all that would be so,
Stale Maids of Honor that are wooed or woo,
Of scouring drunken drabs, foul, old and pocky,   *5*
That cuckold king, lord, captain, knight or jockey,
I sing. Assist me, Shepherd, as thou'rt true
To sacred scandal. Aid me, Fanshaw, too;
So may thy princess thy King's evil cure,
So may ye drink while Dorset's rents endure.   *10*
    Perkin, shall never I lampoon rehearse
But thou must thrust thyself into my verse?
Begone, for satire's weary of thee grown,
As thou art of the cause thou seem'st to own.
Thy chief deserts were but at best our sport,   *15*

And scandal scorns thee now as does the Court.
   But of all villains Macclesfield's the worst;
The royal cause was always in him cursed.
When gallant, bare-faced rogues forsook it quite,
And openly against their king durst fight,   *20*
He was a vermin that stuck fast to bite;
Put sullen virtue on to cloak his sin,
Scipio without, but Cataline within.
Witness against him Newark, where his pride
And falsehood drew him to the rebels' side;   *25*
Unmoved, he saw's afflicted master's tears,
And heard his plaints, yet still he has his ears.
   A son he has too (Brandon is his name),
For playhouse noises much renowned by fame,
And midnight brawls. Arms, arms is all his joy,   *30*
For 'tis recorded once he slew a boy.
This fat, unwieldy fool would needs be great,
So in the lower senate got a seat,
Where in the government great faults he saw,
For from his sire he loyalty did draw,   *35*
And learned Cox the Tartar taught him law.
   But for a faithful friend give me Bab May,
Who scorns as much to cheat as to betray,
Keeps from his master's friends his bounty close,
But lavishes his weakness to his foes;   *40*
Nay, to deserve a confidence so large,
Still keeps cast shitten Moll at the King's charge.
   But prithee, Fenwick, wherefore art thou grieved?
Thy wants have by preferment been relieved;
Thy lady longed and had her wished delight;   *45*
The King dubbed her a whore and thee a knight,
And none can tell which best deserved the grace:
Thy mighty courage or her lovely face.
   Then for Whig Arran, bless us, who can bear
That jewel hanging at a monarch's ear,   *50*
When so many old gibbets on each road

Stand empty and e'en grieve for want of load?
That shrewd, discerning youth's sent here a spy.
Oh, Hamilton, how great's thy policy!
Who'd guess this son, this certain son of thine,   55
Were fit for less than such a deep design?
Survey his face, you politicians all,
And there behold your meditated fall;
Before him let your vanquished wisdoms bow.
Victorious dullness sits upon his brow,   60
And in each line of his notorious face,
As in its proper indisputed place.
In full defiance to pretense of wit,
In broad Scotch characters, Fool, Fool is writ.
    At thee, old Newport, who can choose but laugh,   65
With thy white wig, white gloves, and thy white staff?
Thou art so neat a vermin we're i'th' dark
How to divide the rascal from the spark.
But dog thou art—Pardon me, oh, you race
Of honest curs if I your worth disgrace,   70
For you, they say, are true and never wrong
The benefactors that have fed you long.
But this vile cur's a scandal to your kind,
Who never missed the crust for which he whined;
With a she wolf of Bedford falsely joined,   75
And whelps begot, destined to many a kick:
Fat turnspit Frank and the starved greyhound Dick.
    Bulkeley, how bear'st thee still that burden, life?
For shame, get rid of that, or of thy wife.
Was it thy choice or thy unlucky chance   80
To attend Godolphin's relict into France?
Of fate by bullet thou hast been bereft,
But yet, what's more thy due, there's halter left.
Make that thy honorable last resort,
And come no more into the grinning Court.   85
    But Poslin, Poslin, how hadst thou pretense
To so much roguery with so little sense?

What devil made thee dote on politics,
Hast thou a head t'riddle all their tricks?
Sure everyone that with his mother lies,   *90*
Though lewd as Oedipus is not so wise.
    Now womankind I challenge if it can
Be half so vile and scandalous as man.
Crofts for her sex advancing first we see,
To claim pre-eminence of infamy;   *95*
With age and ugliness and—what is worst
Of all—with sense enough to know it, cursed.
For wit she has, they say, and sure she has;
How else could she be whore with such a face?
No vulgar sense or parts of common size   *100*
To pimp for so much filthiness suffice.
She now excels in the procuring trade,
The ugliest whore makes the most able' bawd;
For all that's learned b'experience or age,
Examples or advice of matrons sage,   *105*
Of mere necessity to her does come;
Bawding, like charity, begins at home.
From bawd to stateswoman advanced she sits
At helm and vies with any of the Chits.
And who so fit for business of the nation   *110*
As those of this so public a vocation?
Bawding the mind enures and does prepare
For politics as hunting does for war;
Th' intrigues and stratagems of both the same,
The like sincerity in either game.   *115*
So her the factious their chief tool create,
As Charles makes pimps his ministers of state.
    Pert Villiers, red Godolphin, widow Swan
(For such she is since Ossory is gone,
Sacred to fame in Otway's mighty line)   *120*
Shall never, never be profaned in mine;
Never till Dering Villiers does embrace,
His false teeth printing in her falser face;

71

Till Sunderland's love-cant and mein prevail
That now Godolphin's tender heart assail;   *125*
Till a new general shall dote on Swan,
That is, till Birnam Wood reach Dunsinane.
First Temple shall forbear t'admire the back
Of some spread pampered stallion robed in black,
She who so long a fallow land has laid,   *130*
And brought a scandal on the name of Maid,
Who while before the other nymphs she walks,
And with her hanging dugs like dewlaps stalks,
As some milch cow that leads the tender mulls,
Licks up and goads the cods of slouching bulls;   *135*
So, drunk with lust, she rambles up and down
And bellows out, "I'm bulling round the town."
Not Felton's wife was in her youth more lewd,
Or on the rising cud has oft'ner chewed,
Nor Nell so much inverted nature spewed.   *140*

---

2. *dirt pies.* Mock fortifications, probably in reference to the mimic siege of Maestricht staged at Windsor in the summer of 1678. See "In Defense of Satire" (*POAS*, Yale, I, 338),

> Warlike, dirt pies our hero Paris [Monmouth] forms,
> Which desperate Bessus [Armstrong] without armor storms.

7. *Shepherd.* Fleetwood Shepherd; see Appendix.
8. *Fanshaw.* William Fanshaw, Master of Requests. His "princess" in the next line was his wife, Mary. See Appendix.
10. *Dorset.* Charles Sackvile (1643–1706), Earl of Dorset, the Maecenas of Restoration poets.
11. *Perkin.* A derisive term applied to James, Duke of Monmouth (presumably by Nell Gwyn) in allusion to Perkin Warbeck, a pretender to the throne in the reign of Henry VII. Monmouth had returned without permission on November 27, 1679, and when he refused to return to banishment the King forebade him the Court.
17. *Macclesfield.* Charles Gerard, first Earl of Macclesfield, a proud and selfish peer. In October, 1645, King Charles I appointed Lord Belasyse governor of Newark, replacing Sir Richard Willis. Willis's friends, including Prince Rupert and General Gerard, protested, and when their protests were ignored they left the Court, "The King looking out of a window and weeping to see them as they went" (Eliot Warburton, *Prince Rupert and the Cavaliers*, 1849, III, 203–7).

23. *Scipio.* Scipio Africanus (237–183 B.C.), hero of the Second Punic War. *Cataline.* Lucius Sergius Catilina (108–62 B.C.), a famous Roman conspirator. In short Macclesfield (now a leading Whig) looked like a general but was always a conspirator.

27. *his ears.* Ear-cropping was a punishment usually reserved for cheats and libelers.

28. *Brandon.* Charles Gerard, Lord Brandon. On May 17, 1676, he killed a footboy with a blow on the ear; see Appendix, Gerard, Brandon.

29. *playhouse noises.* Probably Brandon was one of the Whig "gentlemen in their cups" who, on February 4, 1680, invaded the Duke's Theatre, "flinging links [torches] at the actors, and using several reproachful speeches against the Duchess of P[ortsmouth] and other persons of honor" (*True News; or Mercurius Anglicanus*, February 2–7, 1680). Again, on February 19, 1680, Lady Sunderland wrote that "The players have been disturbed again by drunken people's jokes" (Cartwright, *Sacharissa*, p. 234).

33. *a seat.* Lord Brandon was elected to Parliament from Lancaster on September 9, 1679, and again on February 22, 1681.

36. *Cox the Tartar.* Captain John Cox, purveyor of pornography. See "An Essay of Scandal," note to line 78.

37. *Bab May.* Baptist May (c. 1627–93), Keeper of the King's Privy Purse. (I have transposed lines 37–40 with lines 43–48, as given in Sloane MS. 655, for continuity of thought.)

40. *weakness.* Var. Sloane MS. 655, "secrets."

42. *Moll.* Moll Davis, actress, and once mistress to the King. The scatological epithet refers to an unfortunate encounter she is said to have had with the King after Nell Gwyn had given her a purgative jalap. In Add. MS. 23,722, f. 15, is a squib entitled "On the King's Chamber Door,"

> Charles, by the grace of God King of Great Britain,
> By little Miss Davis was all beshitten.

43. *Fenwick.* Sir John Fenwick of Fenwick, Northumberland, was knighted in 1677 and inherited as third baronet in 1682. On July 14, 1663, he married Lady Mary Howard, eldest daughter of Charles, Earl of Carlisle. The poet asserts that Fenwick was knighted because his wife was the King's mistress. Fenwick, later an ardent Jacobite, was attainted for high treason and executed January 27, 1697.

49. *Arran.* James Douglas, Lord Arran, son of William, Earl of Selkirke, and grandson of the second Duke of Hamilton in Scotland. Born April 11, 1658, he came to Court in 1679 as a Gentleman of the Bedchamber, and *sub rosa*, a representative of the Scots' interest. In 1694 he became Duke of Hamilton, and in 1712 was killed by Lord Mohun in a duel. This is the gentleman aggrandized by Thackeray in Henry Esmond as the honorable and illustrious Duke of Hamilton.

54. *Hamilton.* William, Earl of Selkirke, was also Duke of Hamilton, for life only.

65. *Newport.* Francis, Baron Newport (1620–1708) was created Viscount Newport of Bradford in 1675 and Earl of Bradford in 1694. He was Comptroller of the King's Household 1668–72, and Treasurer of the Household 1672–87 and 1689–1708. In 1642 he married Lady Diana Russell ("A she wolf of Bedford"), daughter of Francis, fourth Earl of Bedford.

77. *Frank.* Francis ("bold Frank") Newport, second son of Lord Newport, died unmarried November 21, 1692. The epithet "turnspit" refers to the fact that small dogs used in a treadmill to turn a spit usually became very fat. *Dick.* Richard Newport

(1642–1723), first son of Lord Newport and Member of Parliament from Shropshire, married April 20, 1681, Mary, daughter of Sir Thomas Wilbraham. His leanness was well known. When fat Henry Savile complained about being wasted by illness, he described his "taille" as like Dick Newport's (*Rochester-Savile Letters*, p. 61).

78. *Bulkeley.* Henry Bulkeley, Master of the Household. A pass for Bulkeley and one servant to go abroad is listed in *CSPD*, 1681, p. 431, August 27, 1681.

81. *Godolphin's relic.* According to the gossips, Mrs. Sophia Bulkeley was for some years mistress to Sidney Godolphin, a Lord Commissioner of the Treasury. "Relict" suggests that by this time Godolphin had left her.

86. *Poslin.* Apparently a nickname. Writing to his wife on September 28, 1677, Lord Danby wrote, "You must excuse me to my brother because I have scarce time to write this to you, the King just going abroad, and I making myself as good a waiter as Poslin himself" (Browning, *Danby*, II, 40). A marginal note in Sloane. 655 identifies "Poslin" as "Tom Howard," perhaps Lord Thomas, second son of Henry, sixth Duke of Norfolk.

Another candidate is Edward Howard, the poet, fifth son of Thomas, Earl of Berkshire. In the *Gyldenstolpe Manuscript* version of "Julian" (p. 185) appears the line "May Pozling Howard live by poetry." In other versions of the satire "pozling" becomes "puzzling." Edward Howard's more famous brother, Sir Robert, was often referred to as "Sir Poz," because of Shadwell's satiric portrait of him as Sir Positive-at-all in *The Sullen Lovers*, 1668. "Pozling" may be a diminutive of "Poz." As a poet, Edward Howard was heartily despised.

94. *Crofts.* Catherine Crofts (1637–86), spinster sister of William, Lord Crofts, of Little Saxham, Suffolk, who had been guardian to the Duke of Monmouth. Mrs. Crofts had apartments in Whitehall and a pension said to be £1,500 a year. Her function is defined in these lines from "A Satire upon the Mistresses" (Harleian MS. 6913, p. 365),

> Next let us view the cock bawds of the Court,
> Kate Crofts and Knight, contrivers of the sport;
> The one for Shaftesbury, th' other spy for Rome;
> When things move thus, who mayn't pronounce our doom?

Apparently her lodgings were always open to the Whig leaders; see, for example, *Ormonde MS*, N.S., VI, 244. December 3, 1681.

109. *the Chits.* Sidney Godolphin and Lawrence Hyde, two Lords Commissioners of the Treasury, and Robert, Earl of Sunderland, First Secretary of State, formed a triumvirate, satirically called "the Chits" (children), which was, in effect, the ministry from 1679 to 1681.

118. *Villiers.* Katherine Villiers, second daughter to Sir Edward Villiers, was a Maid of Honor to the Queen, 1680–85. *Godolphin.* Elizabeth, daughter of Sir John Godolphin, was appointed Maid of Honor to the Queen in December, 1677 (*Rutland MS*, II, 43). She died at the age of eighteen, and was buried March 17, 1683 (Collins). In the seventeenth century red hair was considered a blemish. *Swan.* Cecilia Swan, a Maid of Honor to the Queen from 1676 to 1685. According to Carte (*Ormonde*, IV, 594), Thomas Butler, the gallant Earl of Ossory, "was deemed not insensible of the charms of a daughter of Sir C [Wm] Swan, with whom he was really in love, and could not help showing it by a change of countenance or some other mark when she was in company." Ossory died July 30, 1680; hence "Widow" Swan.

120. *Otway*. Thomas Otway dedicated a long poem, *The Poet's Complaint of his Muse*, 1680, to Lord Ossory.

122. *Dering*. Charles, second son of Sir Edward Dering of Surrenden, Kent, was a noted duelist. According to "A Faithful Catalogue of Our Most Eminent Ninnies," 1687 (*POAS*, Yale, IV, 200),

> Whoever, like Charles Dering, scorns disgrace,
> Can never want, although he lose his place;
> That toothless murd'rer, to his own reproach,
> Pimps for his sister to maintain a coach.

In 1687 Dering was a Gentleman of the Privy Chamber to King James II. Later he was M.P. for Kent and Auditor of the Exchequer in Ireland.

124. *Sunderland*. Robert Spencer, second Earl of Sunderland (1641–1702), a clever opportunist, was dismissed as Secretary of State on January 24, 1681.

126. *general*. The Earl of Ossory had been general of the English forces in the pay of the Netherlands.

128. *Temple*. Philippa Temple, Maid of Honor to the Queen from c. 1674 to 1692.

134. *mulls*. heifers.

137. *bulling*. Hunting like a bull in heat.

138. *Felton's wife*. Lady Elizabeth, wife of Thomas Felton, died December 14, 1681.

140. *Nell*. Nell Gwyn.

ON THREE LATE MARRIAGES

[*Early 1682*]

All three of the women pilloried here had Court connections. Mall Hinton was the daughter of a Court physician, Sir John Hinton. Elizabeth Barry and Charlotte Butler were well known actresses, dependent on the Court for patronage and protection. In addition, Mrs. Barry had been mistress to John Wilmot, Earl of Rochester, by whom she had a daughter in 1677, and Mrs. Butler, said to be the daughter of a decayed knight, was recommended to the stage by King Charles II himself. All three women had a trade in common, the Oldest Profession. To the best of my knowlege, none of the three distinguished trollops ever married.

The copy text, undated, is Harleian MS. 6913, p. 345. The satire is undated also in Harvard MS. 633, "The Wedding," p. 13. The references to the Russian Court tend to date the poem early in 1682.

Three nymphs as chaste as ever Venus bred,
As fair as ever pressed a nuptial bed,
So innocently pure in all their lives
They ne'er profanely thought of being wives,
Now under Hymen's yoke demurely bow;   5
See what our men of wit and love can do!
But know my pious Muse does blush to tell
How wretched Macarene by incest fell,
And 'tis too sad a story to relate
The truth of Canace's unhappy fate.   10
    First then my serious poem I will crown
With one of most repute about the town,
Nay, ev'n in the Russian Court of great renown.
Fine Mrs. Hinton challenges the place
Due to her birth, her stature, and her face,   15

A wit sufficient with a peevish grace;
All which she strictly maintains to th' height,
As being the daughter of a doughty knight.
A greater champion never lancet drew,
Who more than Samson or Drawcansir slew.   20
But when the hero bowed his head to fate,
He left her neither portion or receipt,
Two trifles that had well become her state.
No nymph more gallants e'er received or scorned,
Nor for whose sake more am'rous youths have burned.   25
Like death she spares no quality nor age,
From gentleman to cit, from lord to page.
And whether 'tis that all her spirits combined
And actuate her body by her mind,
Or else that art to her relief she brings,   30
And from experience her perfection springs,
I boldly dare maintain whene'er she's pleased,
Of all the town she does the feat the best.
But then her humor's insolent and lewd,
As though it were beneath her to be good.   35
Her keeper's self can never swive secure,
And 'tis her greatest pride to make him poor.
But now an honorable spouse she gets;
That is the easiest way of paying debts.
Happy the knight by all the world is thought,   40
Who such a prize from all the lists has got.
So once a British monarch did in vain
Aspire alone to th' empire of the main,
Which gave free trade to all the world before,
And will again when once the land is poor.   45
In the front boxes now she takes her place,
And troth a ladyship becomes her face.
No Richardson nor Peters she'll endure
By different ways her body to secure.
Now cully Arundel has lost his whore,   50
And bully Chevens must unrig no more.

But slattern Betty Barry next appears,
Whom every fop upon the stage admires,
But when he sees her off he hangs his ears.
With mouth and cunt, though both awry before,　　　*55*
Her cursed affectation makes 'em more.
At thirty-eight a very hopeful whore,
The only one o'th'trade that's not profuse,
A policy was taught her by the Jews.
Though still the highest bidder she will choose,　　　*60*
Which makes her all the captain's love forget,
And nauseous St. Johns to her arms admit;
Her fifty shillings a week has raised her price.
Besides her other charming qualities,
As dewlaps hanging down her tawny thighs　　　*65*
And ever moistened with congenial glue,
Just like the bull that fierce Almanzor slew;
Besides an odoriferous perfume,
Which yet, like strength of cordials, may o'ercome.
So, with the gums of all Arabia blessed,　　　*70*
The Phoenix lies dissolving in its nest,
But the predominant sense that strikes the brain
Are the divine effluences of her grain.
And have you got at last a husband? Then
What jubilees will be at Surrenden!　　　*75*
If thou art married, Charles, and truly grieved,
As Barry fain would have it be believed,
For thy own sake this life and follies end;
Thy New Year's gift was sent thee by a friend.
　　But Butler, Oh, thou strumpet termagant!　　　*80*
Can'st thou pretend to husband or gallant?
Even to thy own profession a disgrace,
To set up for a whore with such a face!
Who but an Irish fool would make this choice,
Though slighted Echo nothing but a voice.　　　*85*
Thy goose skin arse and of the chestnut brown
Is tanned by being often exposed to th' sun;

Yet for thy sake do May and Barry strive
Who most shall scorn a father or a wife.
Has Bab for this so oft beguiled the purse   *90*
And groaned beneath a suff'ring nation's curse?
Or is it always Heaven's peculiar care
A knave should have a coxcomb for his heir?
May all my whores such easy husbands meet,
And all my foes such virtuous spouses get.   *95*

8. *Macarene.* See Dryden's translation of "Canace to Macareus," in *Ovid's Epistles*, February, 1680.

13. *th' Russian Court.* On November 24, 1681, John Evelyn witnessed the reception of the Russian Ambassador and his retinue in the Banqueting House. On January 26, 1682, a correspondent wrote that the Russian Ambassador "is soe taken with Moll Hinton that he intends to carry her over with him" to Russia (*Rutland MS*, II, 64). Apparently he changed his mind.

14. *Mrs. Hinton.* Mary ("Moll") Hinton, daughter of the Court physician, Sir John Hinton; see Appendix.

20. *Drawcansir.* The blustering hero of Buckingham's *The Rehearsal*, December, 1671.

36. *swive.* Copulate.

40. *the knight.* Presumably the Russian Ambassador.

42. *a British monarch.* King Edgar (944–75), who is supposed to have called himself *Rex Marium Brittaniae* (see Pepys, April 16, 1665).

48. *Richardson.* Perhaps Sarah Richardson, a well-known midwife (see *House of Lords MS*, III, 59). *Peters.* Probably Charles Peter, or Peters (1648–1705), a chirurgion (*Musgrave's Obituaries*).

50. *cully Arundel.* Henry Howard, Earl of Arundel, son of the sixth Duke of Norfolk, was called "cully" because he was easily duped, especially by his wanton wife, Mary.

51. *bully Chevins.* In 1668 William Chiffinch suceeded his brother Thomas as Page of the King's Bedchamber and Keeper of the Privy Closet. A gross libertine, he was chief pimp to King Charles II.

52. *Barry.* Elizabeth Barry (1658–1713), said to be the daughter of one Robert Barry, a barrister, was the greatest actress of the age, beautiful on-stage, but homely off. According to Anthony Aston, "this fine creature was not handsome, her mouth op'ning most on the right side, which she strove to draw t'other way" (*An Apology for the Life of Mr. Colley Cibber*, "A Brief Supplement," ed. R. W. Lowe, 1889, II, 302).

57. *thirty-eight.* In 1682 Elizabeth Barry was twenty-four.

61. *the captain's love.* According to William Oldys, "Captain" Thomas Otway, the dramatist, was desperately in love with Mrs. Barry, but she refused him, "for she could get bastards with other men, though she would hardly condescend to grant

Otway a kiss, who was as amiable in person and address as the best of them" (MS note to Langbaine's *Account of the English Dramatick Poets*, 1691, British Museum).

62. *St. Johns*. Henry St. John, a foolish and violent rake, inherited as fourth baronet in 1708 and became Viscount St. John in 1716. He was the father of Henry, Viscount Bolingbroke.

63. *fifty shillings*. The usual wage for an actress was thirty to forty shillings a week; see Wilson, *All the King's Ladies*, p. 38.

67. *Almanzor*. The swash-buckling hero of Dryden's *The Conquest of Granada*, December, 1670.

73. *Grain*. Groin?

76. *Charles*. Charles Dering, second son of Sir Edward Dering, of Surrenden, Kent. If he had indeed married Mrs. Barry, there would have been mourning at Surrenden. Charles was a drunken young rake. On April 27, 1682, Charles fought with one Mr. Vaughan on the stage of the Duke's Theatre, and Charles was "dangerously wounded" (*Impartial Protestant Mercury*, May 2, 1682).

80. *Butler*. Charlotte Butler, a handsome brunette actress with the Duke's Company, was famed as a singer. She may have been the "Mrs. Butler" who doubled as Plenty and an African Woman in Crowne's *Calisto*, February, 1675 (Eleanor Boswell, *The Restoration Court Stage*, 1932, p. 198).

85. *Echo*. A beautiful nymph condemned by Juno to lose her voice except to repeat what was said to her. "Slighted" by her beloved, Narcissus, she faded away until there was nothing left of her but her voice.

88. *May and Barry*. See below, "Satire on both Whigs and Tories," 1683,

> While witless cuckold May to sea is gone,
> And left his wife with Barry to fuck on.

A marginal note to this couplet in Harleian MS. 7317, identifies these as "Bab May Sea Capt" and "Sr John Barry." Baptist May (c. 1627–98) was never a sailor. Keeper of the Privy Purse to King Charles II, he died unmarried, leaving a natural son, Charles (under age in 1698), and a nephew, also Charles, an Equerry to Queen Mary (G. Steinman Steinman, *Memoir of Mrs. Myddleton*, 1864, p. 55). He may have had another natural son. One Richard May, a "Sea Capt," was captain of a succession of war ships from 1665 to 1683. On November 18, 1682, he commanded the *Ruby*; he died shortly before September 23, 1683. Sir John Berry had his first sea command in 1665. He was captain of the frigate *Gloucester* bearing the Duke of York to Scotland, when, on May 6, 1682, it struck the Lemon and Oar Sands and sank with the loss of some two hundred lives. On June 15, 1682, Sir John Berry, absolved from blame, was appointed to command the *Henrietta*. He died in February, 1690. See *Catalogue of Pepysian MSS*, ed. J. H. Tanner, 1903, I, 324, 383; and *Finch MS*, p. 186.

SATIRE

([*April*,] *1682*)

A spate of Court libels flooded the town in the spring and summer of 1682. On April 20, Lady Campden wrote, "There are sad lampoons made of all the ladies, but I cannot get a copy of them" (*Rutland MS*, II, 69). If by "sad" she meant "scurrilous," this libel, whose author makes his purpose clear in the first stanza, is an outstanding example. The poet says that he will not waste time on an "exordium," the usual preamble in which a satirist loftily proclaimed his reformatory purposes, and gets down to business at once. No doubt the satire was written between Lady Ogle's return to England on March 15, 1682, and her marriage on May 30; April seems a likely month.

The copy text is Dyce MS. 43, II, p. 571. The satire is dated 1682 also in Harleian MS. 7319, p. 197, but is undated in Harleian MS. 6913, p. 263.

This way of writing I observed by some
Is introduced by an exordium,
But I will leave to make all that ado,
And in plain English tell you who fucks who.

Grafton sets up for ogling and smart answers,   *5*
And lies with all her witty set of dancers;
Her crop-eared lord, who is so brisk and airy,
Is managed by the Countess of Orrery.

Lumley has Fox with nose as red as cherry,
And when they are alone, they are so merry!   *10*
His younger brother, who's so famed for nonsense,
Has fucked, or will fuck, Williams, on my conscience.

Poor Nelly all this while has ne'er a runion,
But folks complain that her breath stinks of onion.
Though she exposed her poor defunct Sir Carr,   *15*
She'd now be glad o'th' brother of Dunbar.

Grey's wife has been so long kept out of town,
I fear she'll lose her so well gained renown;
'Tis a long time since she has had her arse filled,
Her husband is so frighted with this Sarsfield.   *20*

Arundel, who is in lechery so knowing,
Finding that the earl's other eye was going,
Took Hewitt in, who near her cunt did lurk,
On the occasion to fuck journey work,
Being told by Mrs. Jennings there's no doubt   *25*
That purblind eyes can never be swived out.

Harriet will do the thing whate'er it cost her,
But first intends to get the sneaking Foster.
Kate Villiers, as they say, has got the notion
To marry ere she puts her breech in motion.   *30*

Vernon, to say the truth,'s a bouncing wench,
She swears and fucks and all the while's so French!
What pity 'tis Wentworth should want a hero.
Oh, Mulgrave, 'twas not done like cavalero
To tantalize her with your lobcock tarse,   *35*
Then leave her, and but only clap her arse.

Monmouth since Felton's dead is yet in doubt
On whom he shall bestow his single bout.
Jack Gibbons says that Lansdown is the fittest,
But Armstrong swears that Lawson is the prettiest,   *40*
Who, under the pretense to cure her cough,
Is roaring drunk each night with usquebaugh.

To speak of Scarsdale is but loss of paper;
She's called a stinking whore in every satire;
And all the writers have as far as able   *45*
Described the lewdness of Hyde's basset table.

Dy tells her Aubrey, believe't who can,
That woman may conceive without a man;
But when alone she gives her lust no check,
And Sidney 'tis must get the Lord Bulbeck.   *50*

Ogle's returned and will consider further
Who next she'll show her arse to for a murder.
I'll say no more, but only this one thing:
All living creatures fuck, except the King.

5. *Grafton.* Isabella (Bennet), Duchess of Grafton, was married to Henry, Duke of Grafton, when she was a child. In 1682, she was still only fifteen! But at the Court of Charles II sexual precocity was the rule.

7. *lord.* Since Henry, Duke of Grafton, was a sailor, he may have worn his hair cropped short about his ears. Evidently he was dominated by Mary Boyle, Countess of Orrery (see below, "Cheviot Chace").

9. *Lumley.* Presumably Richard, Baron Lumley, was dancing the shaking of the sheets with Elizabeth (Trollope) Fox, wife of Charles Fox, Paymaster General to the Army.

11. *his younger brother.* Henry Lumley, wit and soldier, was regularly accused of a liaison with Susannah, Lady Williams, widow of Sir John Williams.

13. *Nelly.* Nell Gwyn. *a runion.* A penis.

15. *Sir Carr.* Sir Carr Scroope; see Appendix. He had tried to make love to Nell, and in June, 1678, she dismissed him because, as she wrote to Lawrence Hyde, "he tould me he could not live allwayes at this rate & so begune to be a littel uncivil which I could not sufer from an uglye baux garscon" (Wilson, *Nell Gwyn,* p. 288). Sir Carr died in July, 1680,

16. *the brother of Dunbar.* William (1654–18), younger brother of Robert Constable, third Viscount Dunbar, was known as an eager whore-master. See "Satire on the Ladies of Honor" ("A Choyce Collection," p. 197),

> The brother of Dunbar full often does trudge,
> And Wycherley-like acts the part of a drudge.

See also his character in "The Lovers' Session," 1687, below.

17. *Grey's wife.* Mary (Berkeley), wife of Ford, Lord Grey of Werke. According to Lady Dorothy Sunderland (Cartwright, *Sacharissa*, p. 233), Lord Grey finally realized that the Duke of Monmouth was cuckolding him; on January 30, 1680, Grey "carried his wife into Northumberland. . . . He gave her but one night's time to take leave, pack up, and be gone."

20. *Sarsfield.* Luttrell (I, 126, September 9, 1681) has the story: "There [has] been a tall Irishman to be seen in Bartholomew Fair, and the Lord Grey being to see him was pleased to say he would make a swinging evidence; on which one Captain [Patrick] Sarsfield, an Irishman, sent his lordship a challenge, taking it as an affront on his countrymen." Grey reported the challenge, and a week later Sarsfield was taken into custody, but escaped.

21. *Arundel.* Mary (Mordaunt), Countess of Arundel. The earl was her one-eyed lover, Charles Talbot, Earl of Shrewsbury.

23. *Hewitt.* Sir George ("Beau") Hewitt. He was hardly purblind, but he may have had poor sight. The word could also mean slow of understanding.

25. *Jennings.* Mrs. Frances Jennings, Court bawd.

27. *Harriet.* Lady Henrietta Berkeley, Lord Grey's sister-in-law and secretly his mistress. When she ran away from home in August, 1682, it was rumored that she had married "one Forrester, Esq., a gent who hath considerable estate" (Price, *Cold Caleb*, p. 95).

29. *Kate Villiers.* Katherine, second daughter of the Knight Marshall, Sir Edward Villiers, a Maid of Honor to Queen Catherine.

31. *Vernon.* Mary (Kirke), wife of Sir Thomas Vernon of Hodnep, Salop; see Appendix, Kirke.

33. *Wentworth.* Lady Henrietta Wentworth, Maid of Honor to the Duchess of York and secretly the Duke of Monmouth's mistress. For the charge that Lord Mulgrave had preceded Monmouth in Henrietta's favor, see "Scandal Satired," c. 1682 (Harleian MS. 6913, p. 209),

> Wentworth may wish she had thought better on't,
> When she let Mulgrave finger-fuck her cunt;
> He taught her then such tricks for sport in bed,
> That Monmouth was too small for her large maidenhead.

35. *lobcock tarse.* "A large, relaxed penis" (J. S. Farmer and W. E. Henley, *A Dictionary of Slang and Colloquial English, 1921).*

37. *Felton.* Lady Betty Felton died December 12, 1681.

39. *Gibbons.* John Gibbons, a gentleman in the service of the Duke of Monmouth, was one of the two men who captured Count Koningsmarck at Greenwich, after the murder of Thomas Thynne (Luttrell, I, 165). *Lansdowne.* Martha (Osborne), wife of Charles Granville, Lord Lansdowne.

40. *Armstrong.* Sir Thomas Armstrong 1624–84), friend and follower of the Duke of Monmouth. *Lawson.* Probably Elizabeth, third daughter of Sir John Lawson of Brough and disappointed aspirant for the post of mistress to Charles II.

42. *usquebaugh.* Irish whisky.

43. *Scarsdale.* Mary (Lewis) wife of Robert Leke, Earl of Scarsdale (formerly Lord Deincourt). The author of "Satire," c. 1682 (Harleian MS. 6913, p. 233) is more specific. Setting his libel in Lincolns Inn Fields, he wrote,

The famous Scarsdale too is hither come,
But who in rhyme will let her have a room?
The common thought of every dirty pen,
By Lumley left would fain set up again;
Poor nauseous fool a fuckster fain would have
To send like Isham chancred to his grave.

46. *Hyde.* Henrietta (Boyle), wife of Lawrence Hyde, created Viscount Hyde on April 23, 1681. *Basset.* A complicated card game with very high stakes.

47. *Dy.* Diana (Kirke), wife of Aubrey de Vere, Earl of Oxford.

50. *Sidney.* "Handsome" Henry Sidney, fourth son of Robert, Earl of Leicester. *Bulbeck.* I.e., a son to inherit Oxford's estates and titles; Bulbeck was a barony in the Vere family. Oxford died without an heir.

51. *Ogle.* Anne, Lady Ogle, had fled to Holland to escape her second husband, Thomas Thynne, who was murdered on February 12, 1682, by followers of Count Koningsmarck. She returned to England on March 15, 1682, and on May 30 she married the Duke of Somerset; see Appendix, Ogle.

54. *except the King.* Either irony or a sly reference to the fact that the King's chief mistress, the Duchess of Portsmouth, was in France from March 4 to May 29, 1682.

SATIRE TO JULIAN

([*Summer,*] *1682*)

Whenever a satirist lacked a title for his shotgun libel, he addressed it to Captain Julian, "Secretary to the Muses," sometimes as a letter or a set of directions. Here the direction to Julian is a temporary device, soon abandoned. Like any good newsmonger, the poet brings us up to date on the scandals of the Town, inventing a few to fill out his lines. He seems to have been strongly anti-Whig.

The copy text, dated 1682, is Harleian MS. 6913, p. 267. The satire is dated 1682 in Harleian MS. 7319, p. 181, "Directions to Secretary Julian," and in Douce MS. 357, f. 94. "A New Lampoon." It is dated 1680 in MS. Firth c. 15, p. 73, and 1683 in "A Choyce Collection," p. 135. A probable date is early summer of 1682.

> Send forth, dear Julian, all thy books
>   Of scandal, large and wide,
> That every knave that in them looks
>   May see himself described.
> Let all their ladies read their own,   5
>   The men their failings see,
> From Nell to him that heads the throne—
>   Then, hey, boys, up go we!
>
> Let Monmouth see himself put down
>   For being turned out of doors,   10
> And Grafton for an arrant clown,
>   And both for sons of whores.
> Large scragged horns for both their heads,
>   They well applied shall see;
> Dunbar and Darcy stain their beds—   15
>   Then, hey, &c.

Each peer shall see his lordship's name,
  Each Whig shall read his life;
Lord Grey shall find his blazoned fame
  Of pimping for his wife.   *20*
His virtuous lady her rebuke
  In manuscript shall see,
For all her favors to the duke—
  Then, hey, &c.

Mordaunt shall flutter up and down,   *25*
  And every man defy;
Each witty sonnet he shall own,
  And his own lines deny;
Yet ere h'has read two pages o'er,
  His lordship's name he'll see,   *30*
For marrying Mulgrave's painted whore—
  Then, hey, &c.

Let little Tom, great Norfolk's son,
  Look still as sharp as ever;
He now may thrum his spouse's bum,   *35*
  For she's just such another.
A froward, testy thief is he,
  A dirty driveler she,
For which in Julian's books she'll be—
  Then, hey, &c.   *40*

Let Armstrong politicly move,
  And spark about no more;
Let that old fool be still in love
  With Fielding's cast-off whore.
When Madam Gwyn has fluxing been,   *45*
  And cast from Rowley, she
Shall in short time be ripe for him—
  Then, hey, &c.

St. John went down and left the Town
   To marry Madam Greville;   *50*
If this ben't done, he'll shoot his son;
   The lady will be civil.
For by what spell that proud minx fell
   A fortune for to be,
The Devil in Hell could never tell—   *55*
   Then, hey, &c.

When Vernon saw her knight withdrawn
   For Scotland, in a trice
Her love was shown ('cause like her own)
   To purp'ling Hewitt's eyes;   *60*
Though Mrs. Jennings said no doubt
   He never blind would be,
His eyes are neither in nor out—
   Then, hey, &c.

Let 'em alone, dear Whistling John,   *65*
   Ne'er strive 'gainst wind and weather;
Since they've begun, e'en whistle on,
   And leave 'em both together.
For Poultney saw thy spouse withdraw;
   With Candish she was free,   *70*
And though 'twas Lent, yet in it went—
   Then, hey &c.

What's that to thee, O mighty Lee,
   If Scroope fucks Madam Willis?
'Twould foolish be, in change for thee,   *75*
   To swive his nasty Phyllis;
For bugg'ring of a rotten door,
   I'd rather famed be,
Than lay leg o'er that painted whore—
   Then, hey &c.   *80*

Let Lady Annabella's girls
    In lust excel each other;
Let 'em pursue their grandam's rules,
    Being taught by lady mother;
For to that truth our poet gives,   *85*
    My sense seems to agree:
When one bawd dies a greater lives—
    Then, hey &c.

Let Lumley coax his Mistress Fox,
    And help his younger brother;   *90*
Let Goodman pox fair Mrs. Cox,
    And all six flux together.
Let Brandon fight and Foster fright,
    And Candish turncoat be,
And every night I'll sit and write—   *95*
    Then, hey, boys, up go we!

7. *Nell.* Nell Gwyn.

8. *Hey, boys.* The refrain to a popular song, originally by Francis Quarles (Simpson, *Broadside Ballad*, pp. 304–8).

9. *Monmouth.* On December 6, 1681, James, Duke of Monmouth, lost his post as Master of the Horse. On January 21, 1682, he was "forbid to come into Whitehall" (*Hatton*, II, 11, 12).

11. *Grafton.* Henry Fitzroy, Duke of Grafton, son of King Charles by the Duchess of Cleveland.

15. *Dunbar.* Robert Constable (1651–1712), third Viscount Dunbar (Scotland), was a worthless drunkard and bully; see Appendix. *Darcy.* John D'Arcy (1659–89) was the eldest son of Conyers, Lord D'Arcy, and grandson of the Earl of Holderness. In "Satyr of the Town" (Harleian MS. 6913, p. 239) the charge is repeated:

> But by what strange art
> Darcy got Grafton's heart
> Is the wonder of all the Town.

The Duchess of Grafton was Isabella, daughter of Henry Bennet, Earl of Arlington. She was married to young Grafton in 1670, when she was three years old and the groom nine. The couple remarried in November, 1679, and consummated in April, 1681, when the bride was fourteen.

19. *Lord Grey.* Ford, Lord Grey of Werke, a leading Whig, was often accused of condoning a liaison between his wife, Mary (Berkeley) and the Duke of Monmouth; see Appendix, Grey.

25. *Mordaunt.* Charles, second Viscount Mordaunt (1658–1735).

35. *Mulgrave's whore.* Carey Frazier, daughter of Sir Alexander Frazier, royal physician; see Appendix, Frazier. On December 12, 1681, Lady Campden wrote, "My Lord Mordaunt has brought out as well as owned his lady . . . " (*Rutland MS*, II, 62). The charge that Carey had been mistress to John, Earl of Mulgrave, is often repeated.

33. *little Tom.* Lord Thomas Howard (1659–89), second son of Henry, sixth Duke of Norfolk, married in 1681 Mary Elizabeth, heiress of Sir John Savile of Copley, Yorks. There seems to be no particular reason for including Lord Thomas and his new bride in the satire.

35. *thrum.* Play on.

37. *froward.* Wilful.

41. *Armstrong.* Sir Thomas Armstrong (1624–84), soldier of fortune, duelist, and Monmouth's devoted follower, was outlawed for complicity in the Rye House plot, captured in Holland, and executed at Tyburn on June 20, 1684. For his long liaison with Betty Mackerel, see "Sir Thomas Armstrong's Last Farewell," *POAS*, Yale, III, 565–66.

44. *Fielding.* Robert ("Handsome") Fielding was a sharper who made his living by dice and women. His "cast-off whore" seems to have been Betty Mackerel. On November 25, 1705, although he was already married to Mary Wadsworth, a woman of the town, Fielding married the widowed Duchess of Cleveland. On December 6, 1706, Fielding was convicted of bigamy, pleaded his clergy, and escaped punishment. He died, aged 61, on May 12, 1712.

45. *fluxing.* Flowing, one result of the mercury treatment for venereal disease.

49. *St. John.* Henry St. John (1652–1742), a widower, inherited as fourth baronet in 1708 and was created Viscount St. John in 1716. On December 18, 1681, Lady Anne Howe wrote, "Mr. St. Johns is much in love with Mrs. Griffeld. They say he was in the country this summer to waite on her . . . she is very grave and takes no notice at all of him" (*Rutland MS*, II, 63). Anne Greville, daughter of Robert, fourth Lord Brooke, was an heiress, and speculations about her possible marriage were rife in 1682–84. She finally married, in January, 1685, William Pierrepont, Earl of Kingston-upon-Hull (1662–90).

51. *his son.* Henry St. John (1678–1751) became Viscount Bolingbroke in 1712 and Prime Minister in 1714.

57. *Vernon.* Mall (Kirke), wife of Sir Thomas Vernon; see Appendix, Kirke. Possibly Sir Thomas went to Scotland with the Duke of York in May, 1682.

60. *Hewitt.* Sir George Hewitt, a ubiquitous fop.

61. *Jennings.* Mrs. Frances Jennings, widow, a famous Court bawd and mother of Sarah, future Duchess of Marlborough.

65. *Whistling John.* The MS note "Berkley" is supported by lines 28–31 in "Lady Freschvile's Song of the Wives," below. John Berkeley (1650–1712), an officer in the Guards, inherited June 13, 1690, as fourth Viscount Fitzharding. His wife was Barbara, third daughter of Sir Edward Villiers, Knight Marshall.

69. *Poultney.* John Pulteney, second son of Sir William Pulteney of Miskerton, Leicestershire; see Appendix.

70. *Candish.* William, Lord Cavendish; see Appendix, Devonshire. In Lent, of course, good Christians abstained from flesh.

73. *mighty Lee.* Probably Captain Edward Lee of the Royal Regiment of Dragoons (Dalton, I, 255; II, 10, 126). On May 16, 1687, Sir George Etherege wrote from Ratisbon, "Pray . . . send me some news of all my friends, particularly of my Lord Dunbar and of Ned Lee, whose prosperity I have always wished" (*Letters*, p. 118).

74. *Scroope.* Sir Scroope Howe, "Peevish Jack" Howe's older brother. His "nasty Phyllis" seems to have been his wife, Anne (Manners), daughter of the eighth Earl of Rutland. *Madam Willis* was a famous bawd and prostitute, with a house in Lincolns Inn Fields; see Appendix.

82. *Lady Annabella's girls.* Lady Annabella, an illegitimate daughter of Emanuel Scrope, Lord Sunderland (1585–1630), by a maid servant, Martha Janes, had married John Grubham Howe of Langer, Notts. She gave birth to four sons and five daughters, "Lady Annabella's girls"; see Appendix, Howe.

89. *Lumley.* Richard, Baron Lumley. *Fox.* Elizabeth (Trollope) Fox, wife of Charles Fox. Lumley's "younger brother" was Henry Lumley, whose mistress at this time was Susannah, widow of Sir John Williams; see "Satire. 1682," above.

91. *Goodman.* Cardell Goodman, a famous actor. *Mrs. Cox.* Elizabeth Cox, an actress with the King's Company, 1671–76, and, after a long absence, 1681–82. In "The Session of Ladies," 1688, she is referred to as "Lord Lumley's cast player, the famed Mrs. Cox" (see below).

93. *Brandon.* Charles Gerard, Lord Brandon. *Foster.* Unidentified, unless he is the "one Mr. Forester," who, according to Luttrell (I, 215, August, 1682), "hath lately stole the Lord Berkeley's daughter and married her." Variant for Foster, "Barrister," in "A Choyce Collection," p. 139.

94. *Candish.* William, Lord Cavendish, is called a turncoat because he had deserted the Whigs. In October, 1681, Luttrell (I, 132) wrote, "The Lord Cavendish hath kissed his Majesty's hand at Newmarket and is received into favor."

A BALLAD

([*August,*] *1682*)

"A Ballad" is a good example of Restoration *ad hominem* criticism. Safe in his anonymity, the poet derides eight of his fellow scribblers, all well-known writers of libels; the result is personal invective, not literary criticism. With the usual superiority of the courtier, the poet rates "lampooning" above the writing of prologues, probably because he and his fellows valued satiric wit above mere dramatic wit.

Although in manuscript the satire is dated 1683, the last stanza, dealing with the Pulteney-Howard duel, July 8, 1682, gives the impression of immediate contemporary comment. Perhaps the poem was written c. August, 1682.

The copy text, dated 1683, is Harleian MS. 7319, p. 248. The satire is dated 1683 also in MS. Rawl. Poet. 159, f. 54.

> The King, Duke, and state
> Are so libeled of late
> That the authors for Whigs are suspected;
> For women in scandal
> By scribblers are damned all, 5
> To Court and to cunt disaffected.
>
> Some say 'tis the labor
> Of sly Mr. Baber,
> Who's a plaguy sharp writer of satire;
> But for one to say true, 10
> Give the devil his due,
> He's a Tory and can't be a traitor.
>
> His best friend to jeer
> He can hardly forbear,

And that way employed his pen is.   *15*
Once I did hear whisper
A brisk holy sister,
"He's better at that than at tennis."

But most people now
Do lay't on Jack Howe;   *20*
So would I too if he could write better
Than when he was long
On a senseless song
And feigned from Richmond a letter.

Some Falkland have guessed at,   *25*
As doggerel he's best at;
Lampooning's a thing much sublimer.
His prologues are such stuff
As show plain enough
He's a poor detestable rhymer.   *30*

Some Mordaunt will have,
But he is too brave
Of scandal to be a mean railer;
For the world knows he writes
As well as he fights;   *35*
He's a poet as good as a sailor.

Sour Frazier's by nature
A libeling creature,
And should therefore be given to lampooning;
But his wit falling short   *40*
Spoils a good deal of sport,
So for nothing he's fit but buffooning.

Where he mimics and acts,
He basely retracts,

93

Which argues his sweet disposition.   *45*
Though Dorset and Fleet
Set him up for a wit,
They'll ne'er set him up for physician.

Fleet has lived long in town,
Yet has less wit than clown,   *50*
And severest on civil behavior;
But I should not care
If me he could spare,
No more than he did our Savior.

Now from France he is come,   *55*
He teases at home
All the world with his wise observations;
King and Court ridicules,
Swears his Council are fools,
And the French good for nothing but fashions.   *60*

Henningham writes, some say;
Believe it you may,
You that still hear him talk like a parrot.
If fortune he gets,
Beholden to's wits,   *65*
He'll be left then to's footman and chariot.

Will Fanshaw's at leisure
To scribble for pleasure,
Who was sharp on the murder of Denham.
Learn of him, for shame,   *70*
Who in private declaim,
And in public spit out all your venom.

Lampoons are grown tedious
And damnable odious,
And now scarce worth the resenting;   *75*

I'll therefore have done
And stanza add one,
Another lampoon for preventing.

Let Poultney nor Howard
Pass now for a coward,   *80*
But let their fierce challenge be boasted.
They who to the field go
And there nothing do
Deserve ten times more to be posted.

8. *Baber*. John, son of Sir John Baber, royal physician. In July, 1683, young Baber ran away with and married Sir Thomas Draper's daughter. See below, "Satire on both Whigs and Tories."

17. *holy sister*. An ironic name for a prostitute. The entire image is sexual, from "pen is" to "tennis." Court, or royal, tennis was a very complicated game: a player could score points by driving the ball over the net, by bouncing it off the walls of the court, or by driving it into certain openings in the walls.

20. *Jack Howe*. John Grubham Howe, a vicious satirist.

24. *Richmond*. Frances (Stuart), widowed Duchess of Richmond. For the episode of the "letter" see Appendix, Howe.

25. *Falkland*. Anthony Carey, Viscount Falkland (1656–94), Treasurer of the Navy. His only known prologue before this date was to Otway's *The Soldier's Fortune*, March, 1680.

31. *Mordaunt*. Eccentric Charles, Viscount Mordaunt (1658–1735), became famous later as Earl of Peterborough. He had served without distinction in the royal Navy, and in 1681 he was captain of his own ship of war, the *Loyal Mordaunt*. He was brave, but an unsuccessful duelist. On August 1, 1681, he fought a duel with James Douglas, Lord Arran. Arran took a sword thrust through the thigh, and Mordaunt was wounded in the arm and body, "but, it is believed, not mortal" (*Ormonde MS*, N.S., VI, 117).

37. *Frazier*. Charles Frazier, son of Sir Alexander Frazier, royal physician, took his M.A. at Trinity College, Cambridge, in 1674, and was created M.D. by royal mandate in 1678. In 1684 he was admitted as a Fellow in the College of Physicians (William Munk, *The Roll of the Royal College of Physicians of London*, 1878, I, 432). The poet's opinion of Frazier is echoed in "To Julian. 1682" (Harleian MS. 6913, p. 301),

Frazier, the pimp, buffoon, or politician,
Frazier that's anything but a physician.

46. *Dorset*. Charles Sackvile, Earl of Dorset (1643-1706), and his protégés, Charles Frazier and facetious Fleetwood Shepherd, composed a threesome of cronies.

See, for example, "Dorset's Lamentation for Moll Howard's Absence" (Harleian MS. 6913, p. 293), in which Frazier and Shepherd are described as Dorset's pimps.

55. *from France*. Shepherd accompanied his patron, the Earl of Dorset, who went to France for his health in August, 1681. On November 21, 1681, Wood recorded a rumor "that Fleetwood Shepherd was either hanged or broke upon the wheel at Paris for some roguery that he had committed" (*Life and Times*, II, 560). Dorset's party returned to England in mid-February, 1682 (Harris, *Dorset*, pp. 83–86), and apparently Shepherd annoyed his friends by his derogatory comments on the King of France, his Court, and his Council. See Prior, "On Mr. Fleetwood Shephard's Killing the French King," *Dialogues of the Dead*, ed. Waller, 1907, p. 288.

61. *Henningham*. Henry Heveningham was a member of Parliament and later lieutenant of the Band of Gentleman Pensioners. Tom Brown described him as "a tall, thin-gutted mortal" (*Amusements* p. 219). On July 3, 1684, Heveningham married the "fortune" who was hardly deserved by his wit, Frances, the wealthy widow of Charles Henry Kirkhoven, Earl Bellamont. See below, "The Lovers' Session," 1687, stanzas 39–41.

67. *Fanshaw*. William Fanshaw was at leisure to write because in July, 1681, he had been dismissed from his post as a Master of Requests "for talking little less than treason upon all occasions that he can" (*Ormonde MS*, N.S., VI, 98). I have not found his verses on the "murder" of Lady Denham, supposedly poisoned in a cup of chocolate, January 6, 1667.

79. *Pultney*. "On Saturday [July 8, 1682] young Pultney and one Mr. Howard (of what family I know not) met and had an encounter and Howard is killed" (*Seventh Report*, p. 497B). According to Luttrell (I, 205) the fight was on account of "a gentlewoman which the said Mr. Pultney hath married." A third account states that "a Mr. Hayward," who pretended a contract to an heiress Pulteney had married in France, challenged him, but Pulteney refused to fight. However, when the two met near St. James's Square, they drew and fought. Afterward Pulteney fled (*CSPD*, 1682, p. 287). John Pulteney, second son of Sir William Pulteney of Miskerton, Leicestershire, married Lucy Colvile of Northamptonshire. See Appendix, Pulteney.

84. *posted*. To post was to affix in a public place a document accusing an enemy of cowardice.

MRS. NELLY'S COMPLAINT

([*Autumn,*] *1682*)

"Mrs. Nelly's Complaint" is unusual among the Court satires. In form
it is essentially a clever dramatic monologue; in tone it is good-natured,
lacking the usual weapons of obscene and scatological epithets. There
is, of course, a deal of exaggeration; we can be reasonably sure that
Mary Knight and Nell Gwyn did not seduce Charles, Lord Lansdowne,
and William Dutton Colt.

Aspiring courtiers were well aware that the King's mistresses could
help their careers, and occasionally an unscrupulous gentleman "managed" a likely lass, hoping for a *quid pro quo* if the King took her
into his seraglio. It was always safe, and wise, to court a royal mistress
and shower her with extravagant compliments, but it was dangerous
to go to bed with her. Easy-going King Charles had a temper. Probably the poet (Sir George Etherege?) put together a couple of harmless
flirtations observed in the summer of 1682, when the Court was at
Windsor, and turned them into a satiric comment on the ladies of
pleasure.

The copy text, dated 1682, is Harleian MS. 7319, p. 163. The satire
is dated 1682 also in MS. Firth c. 15, p. 129, and "A Choyce Collection," p. 105. It is undated in Harleian MS. 6913, p. 309; and Dyce
MS. 43, I, 407. For a discussion of authorship see *The Poems of
Sir George Etherege*, ed. James Thorpe, 1963, pp. 139–40.

> If Sylla's ghost made bloody Catline start
> And shook the fabric of his marble heart;
> If Samuel's shade could wicked Saul affright,
> When Endor raised him from the depths of night;
> Pity poor Nell, that's haunted by Mall Knight.   5
>   You that have seen me in my youthful age,
> Preferred from stall of turnips to the stage,
> Those sympathetic griefs you did bestow,

And tears to scenic suff'rings once allow,
Employ 'em on my real torments now.   *10*
Knight, cruel Knight, that once lay in my breast,
My constant crony and eternal guest,
Th' applauder of my beauty and my jest—
She, she, that cruel she, to France is fled,
Yet lets me not enjoy my quiet bed;   *15*
Whene'er I lay me down to love or sleep,
She through the op'ning curtains seems to peep,
Dreadful as Gorgon, turning all to stone,
Unpainted and without her plumpers on,
Her eyes and cheeks all hollow, so her voice,   *20*
And this she utters with a dreadful noise:
    "Pug! cruel Pug! with whom so long I lived,
For whom so well I faithfully contrived,
Wherein have I deserved so ill of thee
That thou shouldst part my dearest Colt and me?   *25*
Of brawny blockheads hadst thou not before,
By my industrious care, a numerous store?
Cleveland herself was never crammed with more.
By her when first of Wycherley bereft,
My charming Colt was still a treasure left.   *30*
Nor to my wishes did he disagree;
I ogled him and he would squint at me;
But when his charming limbs the first time pressed
My hectic body, ne'er was bawd so blest!
Lansdowne himself for Colt I did despise,   *35*
Lansdowne, in whom each hour new charms arise,
Lansdowne the gay, the sprightly, and the wise.
    Big with my joys, to thee I still did run,
Declared how oft the sacred act was done;
While, as the melting history I told,   *40*
My twinkling eyes in their old sockets rolled.
All this by faithless thee with craft was heard,
No blush, in sign of kindling lust, appeared;
Blushing's a thing thou'st conquered long ago,

And modesty has always been thy foe.   *45*
If e'er thou affect it, 'tis with awkward grace,
For bawd is always opened in thy face;
Bawd is thy art, thy accomplishment and trade,
For that, not love, thou wert a mistress made.
No hero ever to thy arms was won   *50*
But in some drunken hour, when love was gone,
To wallow, fumble, grunt, and spew upon;
Till my false squinter thou didst lead astray,
And her that too much trusted thee betray."

   Thus I, poor nymph, am plagued and must not rest   *55*
Because in that Adonis Colt I'm blest.
Colt, who for close intrigues was doubtless made,
Whose love was never by his looks betrayed;
For while his melting eyes did mine survey,
They craftily still seemed another way,   *60*
Which when fond Knight, our confidante, did see,
She claimed the homage that was paid to me;
Till to redress the mighty wrong sustained,
I to my God-like Sovereign complained,
And by his justice I my right maintained.   *65*

   Let mountebanks make market houses ring
Of what great feats they've done before the King;
Let learn'd Sir Sam his Windsor engine try;
Before great Charles let quacks and seamen lie;
He ne'er heard swearers till Mall Knight and I.   *70*
Never heard oaths less valued or less true
(And yet, 'tis said, he has paid for swearing too),
Loudlier we swore than plundering dragoons;
S'blood followed s'blood, and zoons succeeded zoons;
Till at the last the bawd's weak forces failed,   *75*
And I by noise and impudence prevailed.

   To France my baffled, squeaking rival's gone,
And Colt and all his eyes are now my own.
Should she pretend to what's so much my due,
She might as well take lovely Duncan too.   *80*

Duncan, by my great sway and power preferred,
For mounting me well first, now mounts the guard.
Help, Church and State, to do a princess right,
Guard me from wrongs and exorcize this spright.
Even now in terror on my bed I lie;
Send Doctor Burnet to me or I die.

1. *Sylla*. Lucius Cornelius Sulla, Roman dictator, 138–78 B.C. *Catline*. Lucius Sergius Catilina, Roman politician and conspirator, 108–62 B.C. Ben Jonson's *Catiline* (1611) opened with a long address by "The Ghost of Sylla" to Catiline. The play was revived on December 18, 1668, and Nell Gwyn, "in an Amazonian habit," delivered the prologue.

4. *Endor*. For the woman who had "a familiar spirit at Endor," see I Sam. 28: 7–20.

5. *Mall Knight*. Mary Knight, Nell's friend and neighbor in Pall Mall, was a famous singer and had important roles in Crowne's masque *Calisto*, February, 1675. Reputedly one of the King's earlier mistresses, she was still the recipient of his bounty; an entry in the Lord Chamberlain's records for March 4, 1678, calls for gifts to her of 125 yards of damask for a bed and £100 for furniture (PRO, L.C. 5/ 42, 89v.). Her age is unknown, but on May 19, 1659, John Evelyn called her "the famous singer, Mrs. Knight." She must have been in her forties in 1682.

14. *to France*. The date of Mrs. Knight's trip to France is unknown, but it must have been fairly late in 1682. On June 15, 1683, a letter from France suggests that the Whigs were trying to find out how money was sent to France for investment in foreign securities. The writer concludes, "Besides, if your lordship pleases to reflect upon a certain Duchess's being sent over here a year ago, and since then Mrs. Knight, and now the Countess Pem[broke], the wonder will not be great how things are managed" (*Hastings MS*, II, 173–74). The Duchess of Portsmouth left London for France on March 3, 1682, and was back in London on July 2, 1682.

19. *plumpers*. According to Mary Evelyn ("The Fop Dictionary," appended to *Mundus Muliebris*, 1690), plumpers were "Certain very thin, round, and light balls, to plump out, and fill up the Cavities of the Cheeks, much us'd by old Court-Countesses."

25. *Colt*. William Dutton Colt (1646–93), probably one of the numerous sons of George Colt of Colt's Hall, Suffolk, was in 1682 Gentleman of the Horse to Prince Rupert (who died on November 29, 1682). Later Colt was in the entourage of George Fitzroy, Duke of Northumberland. He was knighted November 26, 1684.

28. *Cleveland*. Barbara, Duchess of Cleveland; see Appendix.

29. *Wycherley*. William Wycherley, playwright, and once the Duchess of Cleveland's lover. Apparently Mrs. Knight once acted as bawd for the duchess and Wycherley; see above, "Lampoon" [1676], note to line 14.

35. *Lansdowne*. Charles Granville (1661–1701), commonly called Lord Lansdowne, eldest son of John, Earl of Bath, married on May 22, 1678, Martha, fifth daughter of Thomas Osborne, Earl of Danby.

68. *Sir Sam.* The famous inventor, Sir Samuel Morland, constructed at Windsor "a new invention of raising any quantity of water to any height by the help of fire only" (*CSPD*, 1682, p. 579). He tried it out in the summer of 1682, and on December 16 he was granted a patent. At Windsor on June 16, 1683, Evelyn commented on the improvements, particularly "the throwing so huge a quantity of excellent water to the enormous height of the castle for the use of the whole house by an extraordinary invention of Sir Samuel Morland."

70. *swearers.* According to Defoe (*Review*, VIII, 247–48), an admirer of Nell Gwyn was once praising her to the Duchess of Portsmouth for her wit, beauty, repartee, and appearance as a lady of quality. "Yes, madam," said the duchess, "but anybody may know she has been an orange wench by her swearing."

80. *Duncan.* Variant "Duncomb." If the name was indeed Duncan, the reference could be to swashbuckling Duncan Abercromy, who was a lieutenant in Colonel Russell's Regiment of Footguards at this time. Abercromy was sometimes called "Duncombe" (see Appendix). There was also one Stint Duncomb who, in February, 1682, was commissioned a lieutenant in Captain Reresby's company in the First Regiment of Footguards (*CSPD*, 1682, p. 103). However, this gentleman was only twenty-seven in 1682, five years younger than Nell (Chester's *Marriage Licenses*).

86. *Doctor Burnet.* Gilbert Burnet, Chaplain of the Rolls, became known to the ladies of pleasure in the summer of 1679 when he attended Jane Roberts on her deathbed. Mrs. Roberts had been successively mistress to the King and to John Wilmot, Earl of Rochester (Burnet, *History*, 1809, I, xxiii).

101

A BALLAD TO THE TUNE OF CHEVIOT CHACE,
OR WHENAS KING HENRY RULED THIS LAND

([*November,*] *1682*)

"A Ballad" is a double-barreled shotgun libel, one barrel aimed at
the reputations of unmarried ladies about the Court, the other at
rampant widows. With fine unconcern, the poet blasts the innocent
and the guilty alike, and seems to have taken some of his information
from earlier libels. The reference to Mulgrave's affair with Princess
Anne dates the satire as not earlier than October, 1682. For a discussion of the ballad tune "Chevy chace, or whenas King Henry ruled
the land," see Simpson, *Broadside Ballad*, pp. 96–101.

The copy text, dated 1682, is Harleian MS. 7319, p. 170. The satire
is dated 1682 in MS. Firth c. 15, p. 124, but it is undated in Harleian
MS. 6913, p. 275; in Harleian MS. 6914, p. 64; and in Dyce MS.
43, I, 371. It is dated 1683 in "A Choyce Collection," p. 122.

> Come all ye youths that yet are free
> From Hymen's deadly snare;
> Come listen all and learn of me,
> And keep my words with care.
>
> For all of you it much concerns,   *5*
> That would lead quiet lives,
> And have no mind to purchase horns,
> Take heed of London wives.
>
> For it's full true, though it's full sad,
> There's ne'er a lass in town   *10*
> But some or other lusty lad
> Has blown her up and down.

102

And first and foremost Princely Nan
    Heirs both her parents' lust,
And Mulgrave is the happy man   *15*
    By whom our breed is crossed.

And, by the way, she did not care,
    For one amongst the crowd
Who helped to get this purblind peer
    Was of the royal blood.   *20*

Hyde's not yet tapped, but bred at Court,
    And all within those doors,
Where none but knaves and bawds resort,
    Or are, or will be, whores.

No wonder then that Villiers should   *25*
    Consent to beardless Phil;
For one in her place never could
    Refuse the pleasing ill.

To be cashiered his Irish place,
    Ranelagh did so dread,   *30*
He was content to make his peace
    With's daughter's maidenhead.

Great Feversham and Thanet too
    Are out of Wentworth's books,
But somebody has done her due,   *35*
    For she in August looks.

Fine Mrs. Greville, though she's rich,
    She'll bring her husband more
By the annual income of her breech,
    Than all her mother's store.   *40*

There's Betty Cholmley, brisk and gay,
    Has neither wit nor grace;
For Bodmin blindfold knows the way
    To her most secret place.

Her brother, that he may be quits,   *45*
    Firks Bodmin's sister's rump;
Though neither of the lords are wits,
    Yet they in this point jump.

The Howes and Pawlets are enjoyed
    By neighbors in the square;   *50*
Old Bess, their cousin, plays the bawd,
    And sometimes gets their share.

Tall strapping Nan in Drury Lane,
    Whose sire would well make two,
At Porter's meets Sir Harry Fane,   *55*
    And what d'ye think they do?

Old cunning Berkeley's daughter Hen,
    They say was once a maid,
But Foster told me it was gone
    Before he backed the jade.   *60*

From Middleton's and Porter's door,
    You sparks I need not fright;
For your own eyes will teach you more
    Than any man can write.

And sure I now may spare my breath,   *65*
    For since poor Hungerford
Was mercifully stopped by death,
    No man will need Mall Howard.

Escric's daughter's much the best
    That family can show;   *70*
But shun her too, amongst the rest
    That on the stock do grow.

For Buchanan long since did write,
    None good were of that name;
The men, he said, would never fight,   *75*
    And women have no shame.

And thus much shall suffice for such
    As for young virgins go;
The widow's failings should I touch,
    I would a volume grow.   *80*

Now if, being warned, you'll take no care,
    And mind not what I say,
The cuckold crest expect to bear,
    Like Arundel and Grey.

Cheviot Chace. Part II. 1682.

Assist me, Stanhope, while I sing   *85*
    Of widows great and small;
You best intelligence can bring,
    For you debauched 'em all.

We'll first begin with Warwick's praise;
    For she the sport begun,   *90*
And has pursued it all her days
    Till now, from forty-one.

She Loftus once, now Armstrong keeps,
    For Loftus could not agree;

And sometimes Brereton with her sleeps,   *95*
   And so he may for me.

Gray-growing Richmond has just right
   To challenge here a place;
She has maintained with all her might
   The noble whoring cause.   *100*

The nimble Houghton and Jack Howe
   Could not make her one stallion,
Nor Mulgrave nor Dumbarton though
   Each helped by his battalion.

Williams, with her chatted foam,   *105*
   Has chancred half the pit,
And is the only she of whom
   No scandal can be writ.

Of Lumley and of twenty more
   Whom she has soundly poxed,   *110*
I'll nothing say because I hear
   She has of late been fluxed.

Freschvile, though not very fair,
   Has a good jointure got,
And has another sex to spare,   *115*
   Which is not everyone's lot.

Dunbar and Clifford both were mired,
   When first they her essayed;
And since with carrying them she's tired,
   And rides her chambermaid.   *120*

Orrery Grafton likes, but not
   For his wit's sake, but tool's;

106

'Tis strange that Dorset's sister's fate
  Is to be poxed by fools.

And such she always has to spare,   *125*
  Thanks to her gentle mother,
Who very kindly bawds for her,
  As she did for her brother.

Of Lucy, Berkeley's daughter, we
  Have nothing but old tales,   *130*
How she was once a little too free
  With the President of Wales.

Lansdown, that mighty charming wit,
  Among the rest shall go;
For though she be no widow, yet   *135*
  I'm sure she would be so.

Her sister Temple, Brandon's look
  Could ease her of her cares,
If she but tell the way she took
  When she got rid of hers.   *140*

Barrington at last has sent,
  They put her husband going;
With a gay fool she'll be content,
  And need but little wooing.

She much abhors a widow's life,   *145*
  And to be gravely clad;
Sackvile will get her for his wife,
  For he has long been mad.

Herbert and Brownlow, who were cloyed
  With the common sort of wenchers,   *150*

Are in due form of law enjoyed
By barristers and benchers.

Their names and chambers where they live
Would take up too much time;
Next week a perfect list I'll give   *155*
In prose, or else in rhyme.

13. *Princely Nan.* On October 31, 1682, it was reported that John Sheffield, Earl of Mulgrave, had long been making "private addresses" to Princess Anne, and had given her various "songs and letters." Learning of Mulgrave's folly, the Duke of York forbade him the Court, and the King deprived him of all his offices (*Egmont MS*, II, 121; *Le Fleming MS*, p. 189). After this episode the Town nicknamed Mulgrave "King John."

20. *royal blood.* Mulgrave's mother, Elizabeth (Cranfield) died in 1672. The poet is saying that since Mulgrave had a "crowd" of fathers, he was, in effect, "a son of a whore."

21. *Hyde.* The poet was not well informed. Anne, the fifteen-year-old daughter of Lawrence, Viscount Hyde, married James, the young Earl of Ossory, on July 15, 1682 (*Ormond MS*, II, 355). She was a pretty, witty, redhead, who died early in 1685.

25. *Villiers.* Since this section deals only with unmarried women, the poet must have had in mind Katherine Villiers, a Maid of Honor to the Queen. But there were two Katherine Villierses. The author of "Advice, or a Heroic Epistle to Mr. Fr. Villiers," 1683 (see below), better informed, connected "Beardless Phil" with Katherine (Fitzgerald), wife of Edward Villiers, older brother of Frank Villiers of the Grandison family; see Appendix, Villiers (Grandison).

26. *beardless Phil.* Captain Philip Kirke, Colonel Percy Kirke's younger brother and Housekeeper of Whitehall Palace.

30. *Ranelagh.* Richard Jones (1641–1712), Earl of Ranelagh. In 1679 his eldest daughter, Katherine, became, at least for a time, the King's mistress (*Seventh Report*, p. 472A).

33. *Feversham.* Louis de Duras, Earl of Feversham (1641–1709). *Thanet.* Richard Tufton (1640–84) inherited as fifth Earl of Thanet on April 27, 1680.

34. *Wentworth.* Lady Henrietta Wentworth (1660–86) a Maid of Honor to the Duchess of York, was secretly the Duke of Monmouth's mistress. The rumor of her pregnancy was false.

37. *Greville.* Anne, daughter of Fulke Greville, Lord Brooke. In April, 1682, it was rumored that she was to marry Lord Cholmondeley (*Rutland MS*, II, 67, 69). In 1685 she married William, Earl of Kingston.

41. *Betty Cholmley.* Elizabeth, daughter of Robert, Viscount Cholmondeley of Kells. See for another comment on the two ladies, "Satire of the Town," 1682 (Harleian MS. 6913, p. 239):

> Though Greville's going down
> Has undone half the Town,
> We've a blessing as great in her place;
> Betty Cholmley's as good,
> As silly, as proud,
> Though she has not so handsome a face.

45. *Bodmin.* Charles Robartes (1660–1723), styled Viscount Bodmin from 1681 to 1685, when he inherited as Earl of Radnor. He had six sisters!

45. *her brother.* Hugh Cholmondeley (1662–1725) succeeded his father as Viscount Cholmondeley of Kells in May, 1681. He was created Baron Cholmondeley of Witch Malbank, Chester, on April 10, 1689, and Earl of Cholmondeley on December 29, 1706. He died unmarried.

46. *firks.* Literally, beats.

49. *The Howes.* The unmarried sisters of John Grubham Howe had a house in Lincolns Inn Fields Square. Charles Pawlet, Marquis of Winchester, had a mansion near the entrance to the square. He had two unmarried daughters, Lady Mary and Lady Elizabeth. The two families were related through the mothers in each: Mary (second wife of Lord Winchester) and Annabella (wife of John Grubham Howe, Senior), natural daughters of Emanuel Scrope, Earl of Sunderland. Perhaps "old Bess" was Sunderland's third natural daughter, Elizabeth, wife of Thomas Savage, Earl Rivers.

53. *tall strapping Nan.* Perhaps Anne, fifth daughter of Arthur, Earl of Anglesey, whose mansion in Drury Lane was well known.

55. *Porter's.* From 1673 to 1700 Lady Diana Porter lived at 66 Great Queen Street, St. Giles-in-the-Fields (*Survey of London*, V, 1914). *Fane.* Perhaps Sir Henry Vane or Fane of Basildon, Berks. (1661–1706).

57. *Hen.* Henrietta Berkeley. On August 30, 1682, Luttrell (I, 215) reported a rumor that "one Mr. Forester hath lately stole my Lord Berkeley's daughter and married her." On November 23, 1682, Ford, Lord Grey, was tried for abducting Henrietta; see Appendix, Grey.

61. *Middleton's.* Notorious Mrs. Jane Middleton had a house in Charles Street, St. Martin's-in-the-Fields (G. Steinman Steinman, *A Memoir of Mrs. Myddleton*, 1864).

66. *Hungerford.* In 1678, Edward, only son of Sir Edward Hungerford (1632–1711), of Farleigh, Somerset., secretly married Lady Aletha Compton, who died in childbed nine months later (*Rutland MS*, II, 46, 53). Her husband died in September, 1681, aged twenty. Possibly he had turned to Mall Howard after his wife's death.

69. *Escric's daughter.* William, third Baron Howard of Escric, by his wife Frances had six children. Together these two stanzas suggest that Mall Howard, famous trollop, was one of Escric's daughters. Escric, a Whig, turned informer after the discovery of the Rye House Plot of 1683.

73. *Buchanan.* George Buchanan (1506–1582), Scottish humanist, poet, and author of *Rerum Scoticarum Historia*, 1582.

84. *Arundel.* Henry Howard, Earl of Arundel and future Duke of Norfolk. His countess was accused of an affair with Charles Talbot, Earl of Shrewsbury. *Grey.* Ford, Lord Grey of Werke, whose wife was said to be the Duke of Monmouth's mistress.

85. *Stanhope.* Alexander Stanhope (1638–1707), a Gentleman Usher of the Privy Chamber to Queen Catherine, was knighted on July 26, 1683. A son of Philip, first

Earl of Chesterfield, by his second wife, Anne Pakington, Stanhope had married Catherine, daughter of Arnold Burghill of Hereford.

89. *Warwick.* Anne, daughter of Edward Montague, second Earl of Manchester, married, before April, 1668, as his second wife, Robert Rich, Earl of Warwick (1620–75). The poet must have confused her with Warwick's first wife, Elizabeth Ingram, whom he married April 8, 1641 ("from forty-one"). Anne lived until July, 1689.

93. *Loftus.* Adam Loftus (1657–91), an Irish squire; see Appendix. *Armstrong.* Sir Thomas Armstrong (1624–84), swashbuckling soldier and follower of the Duke of Monmouth.

95. *Brereton.* John Brereton (1659–1718) succeeded as fourth Baron Brereton of Leighlin, Ireland, in March, 1680.

97. *Richmond.* Frances Teresa (Stuart), widowed Duchess of Richmond. The allegations here seem to be false.

101. *Houghton.* John Holles (1662–1711), called Lord Houghton until January 16, 1689, when he inherited as Earl of Clare. In 1681, John Dryden dedicated *The Spanish Friar* to him. *Jack Howe.* John Grubham Howe; see Appendix.

103. *Mulgrave.* John, Earl of Mulgrave (1648–1721), was colonel of the "Old Holland" Regiment of Foot. *Dumbarton.* George Douglas (c. 1635–92), created Earl of Dumbarton on March 9, 1675, was a colonel of the First Regiment of Foot.

105. *Williams.* Susannah, daughter of Sir Thomas Skipwith and widow (since 1680) of Sir John Williams, Bart., of Minster Court, Kent. *chatted.* From "chatt," the female pudendum.

106. *chancred.* Given venereal sores or ulcers.

109. *Lumley.* Henry Lumley, younger brother of Richard, Lord Lumley; see Appendix.

112. *fluxed.* Purged by calomel, as part of the usual treatment for venereal disease.

113. *Freschvile.* Anne Charlotte (De Vic), widow of John, Baron Freschvile, and a Lady of the Bedchamber to Princess Anne. In "Satire on the Ladies of Honor," 1686 (Harleian MS. 7319, p. 423) she is called "Hermaphrodite Freschvile."

117. *Dunbar.* Robert Constable, third Viscount Dunbar; see Appendix. *Clifford.* Probably Charles Boyle, Lord Clifford (1639–94), eldest son of Richard, second Earl of Cork.

121. *Orrery.* Mary (Sackvile), sister of Charles, Earl of Dorset, and widow of Roger, second Earl of Orrery, who died on March 29, 1682. *Grafton.* Henry Fitzroy, Duke of Grafton.

126. *her gentle mother.* Frances (Cranfield), Dowager Countess of Dorset, a quarrelsome but eminently respectable matron. The "she" in line 128 squints; perhaps the poet meant that Lady Orrery had acted as procuress for her brother.

129. *Lucy.* Theophila, second daughter of George, Earl of Berkeley, and widow (1679) of Sir Kingsmill Lucy of Nettley, Hants. On November 23, 1682, she married Robert Nelson, a clergyman.

132. *the President of Wales.* Henry Somerset, third Marquis of Worcester (1629–99), was created Duke of Beaufort on December 2, 1682. For an earlier comment on his relations with Lady Lucy, see above, "Colin. 1679," "From Lucy get the noble marquis."

133. *Lansdown.* On May 22, 1678, Martha, fifth daughter of Thomas Osborne, Earl of Danby, married Charles Granville, Lord Lansdowne (1661–1701), son of the Earl of Bath. The marriage was not happy. Late in the summer of 1682 it was rumored

that "Lady Lansdowne has left her lord. . . . They say he will see her no more because of some letters that passed between her and Mr. Leveson Gower" (Browning, *Danby*, I, 351). In "Lampoon on Several Ladies," 1683 (Harleian MS. 7319, p. 270), we are told that, "although she wear not bandore"—a widow's head dress—Lady Lansdowne

> Is now turned off by her lord once more,
> For going to bed to Whig Lewson Gore.

Lady Lansdowne died on September 11, 1689.

137. *sister Temple*. Martha (Osborne), Lady Lansdowne, had neither sister nor sister-in-law named Temple. Perhaps the poet, confused by the family names, was thinking of Lady Lansdowne's distant cousin, Dorothy (Osborne), wife of Sir William Temple. The meaning seems to be that Lady Temple would like to profit from the experience of Anne, Lady Brandon, when she "got rid" of her husband, Charles Gerard, Lord Brandon.

141. *Barrington*. Lady Anne, daughter of Robert Rich, Earl of Warwick, and wife of Thomas Barrington, of Barrington Hall, Sussex. On April 6, 1680, Lady Sunderland reported, "My Lady Anne Balendine ran away from her husband, and left a letter upon her table to say she was gone where she should see more happy days than ever she did with him. Mr. Finch's vigilance in the search of her has brought her back to her house again" (Cartwright, *Sacharissa*, p. 254; *Lady Russell's Letters*, p. 58). Thomas Barrington died on January 31, 1682, aged thirty-eight.

147. *Sackvile*. Colonel Edward Sackvile, formerly Governor of Tangier and a mediocre poet, was usually called "Song" Sackvile to distinguish him from Edward Sackvile, Lord Dorset's younger brother. In 1682, Sackvile was Lieutenant Colonel of the Coldstream Guards (Dalton, I, 274, 294).

149. *Herbert and Brownlow*. Elizabeth, daughter of George, sixth Lord Chandos, and widow of Edward, third Lord Herbert of Cherbury, and her sister Margaret, widow of William Brownlow of Snarford, Lincs. For Lady Herbert's career, see Appendix, Herbert. About 1685, Mrs. Brownlow married little Sir Thomas Skipwith; see Appendix, Skipwith.

THE LADY FRESCHVILE'S SONG OF THE WIVES
TO THE TUNE OF FOUR ABLE PHYSICIANS
ARE LATELY COME TO TOWN

(*1682*)

The opening lines of this satire indicate that it was intended as a sequel to "A Ballad to the Tune of Cheviot Chace." It deals with errant Court wives, most of whom were guilty of indiscretion and some of adultery. By this time the names of a few Court ladies— notably Mrs. Jennings, Lady Stamford, Lady Vernon, Lady Ogle (now Duchess of Somerset), Lady Lansdowne, and Carey, Lady Mordaunt—had become almost obligatory in satires. The satire must have been written very late in 1682. For the second title, from a tune called "The Tunbridge Doctors," see Simpson, *Broadside Ballad*, p. 568.

   The copy text, dated 1682, is Harleian MS. 7319, p. 193. It is dated 1682 in MS. Firth, c. 15, p. 121; it is undated in Dyce MS. 43, I, 392; Douce MS. 357, f. 96v; and Harleian MS. 6913, p. 287.

   You scribblers that write still of widows and maids,
   I fear have not served half your time at your trades.
   We poor innocent virgins have reason to huff,
   When the widows complain you've not said half enough.
               For Jennings does swear   *5*
               She cannot forbear
   To laugh at the fools who said nothing of her.
   Old Freschvile and Stanhope laugh in their sleeves,
   And have sent out a song to say more of the wives.

                        2.

   When Stamford, her mightiness, first went astray,   *10*
   Sh'ad a million of monsters still lay in her way;

For prevention of horns her good lord had in store
All the Harveys and Derings and fifty such more.
      Though some do presage,
      That she did engage   *15*
At once both a lord, an esquire, and a page—
Nay, had not her spouse had the luck for to call,
She had found in her heart to have swived with 'em all.

3.

The young Lady Suffolk, that's newly come in
To the list of the wives, must have time to begin;   *20*
She rallies her feeble old husband and scorns
That we should not ere long wish him joy of his horns.
      Mary Gerrard does stare,
      And fain would prefer
Her ugly damned carcass, but none would have her.   *25*
Good Lord! What a monstrous strange sight it would be,
If a brat should be born 'twixt her husband and she!

4.

No sooner can Berkeley go whistling to play,
But straight, to meet Candish, his wife trips away.
When her business is done, she is scarce gotten in,   *30*
Ere the cuckold, contented, comes whistling again.
      Nay, Vernon and Grey
      Have each their own way
To practice in cuckoldom every day.
Sure they must be ladies well versed in their trades;   *35*
They've been both brought to bed and both married for maids.

5.

Old Macclesfield's daughter, whom Gerard did wed,
All the portion she brought him he wears on his head;

113

With art and much cunning, she's come to a pitch,
Though her eyes cannot kill, yet she wounds with her breech. *40*
      Poor hobbling Dumblane
      With her kindness is slain.
Ev'n Parker and Duncan begin to complain.
Nay, her husband and she never yet could agree,
For he ne'er could abide a thing lewder than he.   *45*

6.

Great titles of honor we all do adore,
And 'twas this very reason made Ogle a whore;
For the name of a duchess had so taken place,
Though she'd lain with the count, yet she married his grace.
      And Albemarle can   *50*
      Dispense with her man,
Though her husband's a duke, let him help't if he can.
Hard fate that poor Fane should of luck be beguiled
To marry the page who had got her with child.

7.

Fair Lansdowne's the likeliest of all to hold out,   *55*
For she grants to her spouse the alternative bout.
Lady Parsons with long-legged Sarsfield does do't,
And none is secure of his nasty but Scroope.
      For Mordaunt has swore
      She once was a whore,   *60*
But swears by her Maker she'll be so no more.
Hey, boys! What a time it would be for the men
If everyone's wife should turn honest again!

---

3. *huff.* Take offense.
5. *Jennings.* Mrs. Frances Jennings, Court bawd.

8. *Freschville.* Anne Charlotte (De Vic), widow of John, Baron Freschville of Stavely, who died in April, 1682. A Lady of the Bedchamber to Princess Anne, she died "at a great age" in 1717 (*Complete Peerage*). *Stanhope.* Probably Catherine (Burghill), wife of Alexander Stanhope, a Gentleman Usher to Queen Catherine.

10. *Stamford.* Elizabeth (Harvey), buxom wife of Thomas Grey, second Earl of Stamford; see Appendix.

13. *Harveys.* The poet's argument seems to be that Lord Stamford kept his wanton wife happy with lovers of her own sex, so that she would avoid the "monsters," i.e., cuckold makers. Lady Stamford's mother, Lady Elizabeth Harvey, was commonly accused of Lesbianism (see "Colin. 1679"). *Derings.* Perhaps one of the daughters of Sir Edward Dering, either Katherine, who married Sir John Percival, or Jane, who never married.

19. *Lady Suffolk.* Anne (Montague) married, as his third wife, c. June 10, 1682, James Howard, Earl of Suffolk. Anne was twenty-two, the earl sixty-two. Contrary to prophecy, the countess proved to be a true and faithful wife (*Portland MS*, III, 374).

23. *Mary Gerard.* Mary (Berkeley), daughter of Charles, Earl of Falmouth, married Gilbert Cosins Gerard on May 2, 1681. She was sixteen, wild, wilful, and "a salacious jilt"; see Appendix, Gerard, G. C.

28. *Berkeley.* John Berkeley (1650–1712), an officer in the Guards, known as "whistling John." In 1677 he had married Barbara Villiers (1656–1708), third daughter of Sir Edward Villiers, Knight Marshall; see Appendix, Villiers (Jersey).

29. *Candish.* William, Lord Cavendish (1640–1707), inherited as fourth Earl of Devonshire in 1684.

32. *Vernon.* Mary (Kirke), wife of Sir Thomas Vernon, a Teller of the Exchequer, had given birth before marriage, with resultant scandal; see Appendix, Kirke. *Grey.* Mary (Berkeley), wife of Ford, Lord Grey of Werke, was married some time in 1674, and her only child, Mary, was christened on May 11, 1675. The poet is embroidering on her supposed affair with Monmouth before her marriage.

37. *Macclesfield's daughter.* Digby Gerard, Baron Gerard of Gerard Bromley (1662–84), married, on September 3, 1678, Elizabeth, nineteen-year-old daughter of Charles Gerard, Earl of Macclesfield. "The portion she brought 'him" was, of course, the mythical horns of a cuckold. Gerard, a very debauched young man, died October 10, 1684 "of a drinking match, and fell down on the spot" at the Rose Tavern in Covent Garden (*Ormonde MS*, VII, 278). His widow survived until January 11, 1700, reputedly lewd and promiscuous.

41. *Dumblane.* Peregrine Osborne, Viscount Dumblane (1659–1729), was second but first surviving son of Thomas, Earl of Danby. Apparently Dumblane's pox was contracted before 1678. In his *Diary* (December 22, 1677), Dr. Lake reported the affliction Lady Danby "groaned under" because her first son, Lord Latimer, "and his lady were sadly diseased with the pox, and did even begin to rot; and the Lord Dumblame (her second son and a very boy) was sent into France to be cured of the same disease." In the reign of good King Charles, a courtier who had never had the pox would be a rarity.

43. *Parker.* Lieutenant John Parker, of the Life Guards, was a bold, enterprising young man, "commonly known by the name of the Town Bull" (Dalton, I, 306); *Le Fleming MS*, p. 276). *Duncan.* Lieutenant Duncan Abercromy of Colonel Russell's Regiment of Foot; see Appendix, Abercromy.

115

45. The line is from Harleian MS. 6913, p. 289. The copy text has "For he ne'er met a female more lewder than she."

47. *Ogle*. Elizabeth (Percy), Lady Ogle, twice widowed, married Charles Seymour, Duke of Somerset, on May 30, 1682, three months after the murder of her second husband, Thomas Thynne, at the instigation of Count Koningsmarck; see Appendix, Ogle. On February 18, 1682, a correspondent wrote, "The discourse of the Town is with great reflection upon my Lady Ogle, whom they represent to have had great intimacy with the count [Koningsmarck] in Holland, before he came over hither" (*Ormonde MS*, N.S., VI, 313).

50. *Albemarle*. Elizabeth (1654–1734), daughter of William Cavendish, Duke of Newcastle, married Christopher Monck, second Duke of Albemarle, in 1669. In spite of the libelers, she seems to have been a faithful wife, but in the summer of 1682 she became mentally disturbed. On April 10, 1683, the Duke of Newcastle told Sir John Reresby that "his daughter, the Duchesse of Albemarle, had received and concealed a love letter, which her lord knew of, which had made her dissemble herself distracted" (*Memoirs*, p. 301). A likely story! In later years Elizabeth was known as "the mad duchess."

53. *Fane*. Also Vane. On April 20, 1682, Lady Campden wrote, "My Lady Katherine Vane is married to one that was her sister Exeter's page when she died, but he was a tall, young, handsome man, though still a page" (*Rutland MS*, II, 69). The page was Conyers D'Arcy, who inherited as Earl of Holderness in 1688. "Sister Exeter" was Mary, sixth daughter of Mildmay Fane, Earl of Westmoreland, and second wife of John Cecil, fourth Earl of Exeter (1628–78). Lady Exeter died in October, 1681.

55. *Lansdowne*. Martha (1664–89), fifth daughter of Thomas Osborne, Earl of Danby, married, on May 22, 1678, Charles Granville, Lord Lansdowne. See note to line 133, "Cheviot Chace," above.

57. *Parsons*. Catherine (Clifton), wife of Sir John Parsons, an intimate of Captain Patrick Sarsfield; see Appendix, Sarsfield.

58. *Scroope*. Sir Scroope Howe, whose "nasty" seems to have been his wife Anne (Manners).

59. *Mordaunt*. Carey (Frazier), wife of Charles, Lord Mordaunt; see Appendix, Frazier.

ADVICE, OR A HEROIC EPISTLE TO MR. FR. VILLIERS
TO AN EXCELLENT NEW TUNE CALLED
A HEALTH TO BETTY

[Early 1683]

Rarely a satirist had the courage to sign his lampoons. Eccentric Sir Roger Martin, of Long Melford, Suffolk (1639–1712), was well known as a libeler. In "Letter to Julian," 1684 (see below), his "Advice" to Frank Villiers is mentioned:

> Some say. his lordship [Mulgrave] had done better
> To answer Roger Martin's letter.

Sir Roger tried his hand at political satire, too. See his "Letter from Sr Roger Martin to the Duke of Monmouth" (Folger MS. m.b. 12, p. 275), beginning " 'Twas a foolish fancy, Jemmy." At least one of his contemporaries attacked him in "To Julian," 1682 (Harleian MS. 6913, p. 301) as a

> long, wire-drawn knight,
> A stalking shadow like a moon-lit night,
> Harsh to the ear and hideous to the sight,
> With hollow jaws, no teeth, and toes turned in,
> A greater monster than from Nile they bring,
> With his gray mares, white wig, and gaudy coach,
> Presumes his lady's woman to debauch

The copy text, undated, is Harleian MS. 7319, p. 278. The libel in undated also in Dyce MS. 43, I, 329. It is dated 1683 in MS. Firth C. 15, p. 151; 1682 in Harleian MS. 6914, p. 59, "Advice in a Letter to Mr. Fr. Villiers"; and 1683/4 in "A Choyce Collection," p. 140 ("Advice to Frank Villiers"). A probable date is early in 1683. For the tune of "A Health to Betty," see Simpson, *Broadside Ballad*, p. 298.

117

Leave off your ogling, Francis,
And mind your sister Nancy's;
  She's quite undone
  If once King John
Should get between her haunches.   *5*

I hear Phil Kirke does thrum, sir,
Your brother's lady's bum, sir.
  'Tis ten to one
  He'll get a son
May stand 'twixt you and home, sir.   *10*

Katy's joy commences
At every fop's pretenses;
  Should dimple bring
  A priest and ring,
She'd lose her little senses.   *15*

My worthy friend her brother
Has got just such another,
  A hopeful imp,
  Whose sire's a pimp,
And a common whore her mother.   *20*

Berkeley ne'er will leave it;
Propose and she'll receive it.
  Jack Darcy knows
  Where 'tis she blows,
And will make affidavit.   *25*

Dear Frank, you ha'n't the art right
To please my Lady Cartwright;
  Yet don't despair,
  For one so fair
In time may play her part right.   *30*

But though her beauty much is,
Contempt's a thing that touches;
    And if she scorn,
    You'd best return
To your old Italian duchess.   *35*

Now to conclude at parting,
All I have writ is certain;
    And so I end,
    Your faithful friend
And servant, Roger Martin.   *40*

---

1. *Francis.* Francis ("villain Frank") Villiers was the foppish second son of George Villiers, fourth Viscount Grandison; see Appendix, Villiers (Grandison).

2. *Nancy.* Anne Villiers, the fifteen-year-old daughter of George Villiers, fourth Viscount Grandison.

4. *King John.* John Sheffield, Earl of Mulgrave, dubbed "King John" after he had tried to woo Princess Anne in October, 1682.

6. *Phil Kirke.* Philip ("beardless Phil") Kirke, Percy Kirke's half-brother, succeeded his father, George, as Housekeeper of Whitehall Palace, October 8, 1679; see Appendix, Kirke.

7. *your brother's lady.* In March, 1677, Edward Villiers, first son and heir of George, fourth Viscount Grandison, married an Irish heiress, Katherine Fitzgerald, who was still childless in 1683. A child born from the adultery of Phil Kirke and Edward's wife would, of course, inherit the Grandison title and estates, shutting out the second son, Francis.

11. *Katy.* Sir Roger skips happily from the Grandison Villierses to a related family. Katherine, second daughter of Sir Edward Villiers, Knight Marshall, became a Maid of Honor to Queen Catherine in 1680; see Appendix, Villiers (Jersey). Unlike most Maids, she seems to have retained her virtue. See above, "Satire. 1682."

> Kate Villiers, as they say, has got the notion
> To marry ere she puts her breech in motion.

13. *dimple.* No doubt recognizable as a timid suitor for Kate Villiers' hand in marriage, perhaps "Spendthrift" Alan Bellingham, of Helsington, Westmoreland. See below, "Letter to Julian," 1684 in which the poet suggests that Bellingham "with his folly and estate" might "oblige the world and marry Kate." It seems that Bellingham had long been wooing Kate, but "when he should wed, he wont come to."

16. *her brother.* In December, 1681, Sir Edward Villiers, eldest son of Sir Edward Villiers, Knight Marshall, married Barbara, daughter of William Chiffinch and his wife Barbara (Nunn). Chiffinch was notorious as the King's pimp, and his wife served as a procuress (A. I. Dasent, *Nell Gwynne*, 1924, pp. 133–35).

21. *Berkeley*. It seems most unlikely that this lady could be Elizabeth (Massingbird), wife of George, first Earl of Berkeley (1627–98). In 1683 she was about fifty years old. According to the author of "The Court Diversion," 1686 (see below), the Court was a place

> Where Berkeley and her youthful lover knock it;
> The jilt is ne'er without a dildo in her pocket;
> Old earl's too short, too small for such a socket.

Perhaps Lady Berkeley suffered for the sins of her daughters: Mary, Lady Grey, Theophila, Lady Lucy, and Henrietta.

23. *Jack Darcy*. John D'Arcy (1659–89), eldest son of Conyers, Lord D'Arcy, and grandson of the Earl of Holderness.

26. *Dear Frank*. Francis Villiers again. The author of "To Capt. Warcup," 1686 (see below) reports that Francis Villiers, "out of awful fear," has followed Lady Carteret fruitlessly for "many a year."

27. *Cartwright* (Carteret). In March, 1675, George Carteret (1667–95), the eight-year-old son of Sir Philip Carteret, "and Sir George Cartwright's grandson," married Grace (1669–1744), the six-year-old daughter of John Granville, Earl of Bath (*Verney Memoirs*, II, 316). On October 19, 1681, young Carteret was created Baron Carteret of Hawnes, Bedford.

34. *best*. The copy text has "better," other versions "best."

35. *old Italian duchess*. Hortense, Duchess Mazarin. In "Colin. 1679" (see above), the duchess was denied a place as chief royal mistress.

> Her grace at this rebuke looked blank
> And sneaked away to villain Frank.

See also the conclusion to "To Mr. Julian," 1679 (*Gyldenstolpe*, p. 185),

> May Betty Mackerell cease to be a whore,
> And villain Frank fuck Mazarin no more.

SATIRE ON BOTH WHIGS AND TORIES

[*July, 1683*]

In March, 1683, a group of violent Whigs conspired to kill King
Charles II and the Duke of York in an ambuscade at the Rye House,
near Ware, when the royal brothers were on their way from Newmarket to London. A fire at Newmarket on March 22 forced the
royal party to leave early, and the plot failed. In June, one conspirator,
overcome by his conscience, confessed everything, and "the Rye
House Plot" came unravelled. Twenty-one Whigs were indicted for
high treason. Most of them escaped; five were executed, and one
committed suicide.

The Rye House Plot seems to have been the immediate occasion
for this satire, but it is not a true political poem. Although the poet
detests Whigs more than Tories, his attitude seems to be "a plague
o' both your houses," and his condemnation is more for folly and
wickedness than for political dissent. Moreover, departing from his
text, he vilifies a variety of nonpolitical sinners, both men and women.

The copy text, Harleian MS. 7319, p. 237, is dated 1682. The satire
is dated 1683 in MS. Firth c. 15, p. 142; in Harleian MS. 7317,
p. 21; and in "A Choyce Collection," p. 126. The earliest possible
date is July 10, 1683, when the Earl of Essex was lodged in the
Tower.

> In vain the fulsome errors of the age
> We strive to mend in satire or on stage.
> Fools will be fools, cullies will be undone,
> Though we still rail, and Nokes and Lee show on.
> Satire may plead, of wholesome counsel boast;   5
> Hardened in vice, their sense of feeling's lost;
> How oft 't has lashed the fop and dull buffoon,
> That nauseous nuisance of the Court and Town,

121

That beastly sink, through which all follies run,
Of whom even satire now is weary grown!   *10*
   No mortal counsel's able to convince
Arran's incorrigible impudence,
Who sooner shall forget his northern tone,
His bawdry or his buggery disown,
Turn loyal, as ne'er he was, to have the lot,   *15*
Of being in manners or in notion Scot.
   Name we the Whigs, we must the num'rous troop,
Like faggots, four for sixpence, bind 'em up;
Fools by the dozen, rascals by the gross,
Knaves, fops, and pardoned rebels, which are worse.   *20*
Show me the man (and lay the traitor by)
We cannot charge with knave or foppery.
Kent slavers, wittol Stamford is a tool,
Armstrong a rogue, Monmouth both knave and fool.
Lovelace a sot, Brandon a gaping traitor,   *25*
And lately married quondam footman's daughter,
Who, by the King enriched from scarce a groat,
Gives it to him who'd gladly cut his throat.
To exercise which talent he begins
With murd'ring boys to end with murd'ring kings.   *30*
Ungrateful blockhead! In thy race accursed;
From thy false sire thou learn'dst those maxims first.
   Incestuous Grey, apostate Colchester,
Where knave and fool together blended are;
From pardoned rebel this, dull cuckold that,   *35*
Set up for politicians in the state.
Thou'dst better bullied on, thou held the door,
Than thus to jilt the nations o'er and o'er,
And pimp for Monmouth as for common whore
To satisfy his beastly lust of power.   *40*
   But thou, dull Essex, who so oft has been
Obliged, enriched, and honored by the King,
What folly, or what madness, drove thee on
Into the hell of cursed rebellion?

Thou, whose blest fortune needed no supply,   *45*
Misled by wife and old Presbytery,
'Gainst God's anointed and that cause art fled
For which thy noble father lost his head.
What pity 'tis thou shouldst degenerate,
And for unequal causes meet an equal fate!   *50*
   Of Newport's dogs, Grayhound, that meagre spark,
Once tried his prowess, but 'twas in the dark.
Fat Turnspit never bites, though oft he bark.
His oft repeated jests do seldom hit,
As dull as the last libel Shadwell writ,   *55*
A teasing cur and only fit to nettle,
But dares no more fall on than Coysh's Settle.
Whene'er the reformation dogs engage
The monarch bull, he leaves 'em to its rage;
Sneaks off with threadbare jest, and swears his quarters   *60*
Shall ne'er increase the noble troop of martyrs.
   The Whartons, who so great a reverence bear
To monarchy, to church, and Common Prayer—
Their sire, 'tis true, as ancient story goes,
In sawpit once did violate his nose;   *65*
But our more hopeful youth, to show their zeals,
In reverend pulpit laid their nasty tails,
Profaned the altar, in the font did spew,
And made their footmen frig in every pew.
We're like to have a hopeful reformation,   *70*
When saints like these shall come to rule the nation!
To name 'em all, with all their villainies,
Their follies, shams, their treasons, blasphemies,
Their fine amours, debauches, claps, and pox,
Would fill a volume like our history Fox.   *75*
Yet they're not fops alone; we've Tories too,
With vices full as numberless, and new.
   How oft has Hewitt's cravat had the lash,
Who looks like puppet in a globe of glass,
So neat, so spruce, so finically set,   *80*

A moving thing without one grain of wit;
With whom as much our satire strives in vain
As love to wound his heart since Marshall's reign.
Sets up for quality, but his luck so ill is,
Mistakes for whore of honor old bawd Willis.   *85*
Thus toils the purblind fop, thus dresses on;
The fool increases but the land is gone.
    How oft has Howe (by Rochester undone,
Who soothed him first into opinion
Of being a wit) been told that he was none?   *90*
But found that art the surest way to glide
Not into's heart but his well shaped backside.
Not Nobs's bum more adoration found,
Though oft 'twas sung, his was more white and round.
    How oft has Baber's foppery been the theme,   *95*
How oft the excrement of every pen!
Till, to complete his wondrous farce of life,
He ended with that lucky jest, a wife;
And, like Sir Martin, spoiling each design,
He cheats himself with his own plot, in fine.   *100*
    Whorewood, whom Butler clapped and made a chiaux,
To save his stake, married, and clapped his spouse;
While witless cuckold May to sea is gone,
And left his wife with Barry to fuck on.
    Lucy, that fool, ne'er thought the proverb o'er   *105*
When drab he married, once and still a whore.
Not all the Howards famous for the guilt
(Throughout the race) of wedding long-kept jilt,
But found some poor excuse for want of charms;
The baggages were humble in their arms.   *110*
His grace's bulker, Esme's kitchen maid,
Phil's player, and Sir Pos's common jade,
Ned's seamstress, Tom's mimic of strolling trade,
Had yet to fool and husband more pretense,
As wanting yet thy doxy's insolence.   *115*

Of Gerard and his spouse, since both accurst,
It scarce can be determined which is worst.
Of all the fops, thou hast pre-eminence;
To all the rest w'allow some commonsense;
But thou'rt a formal, stiff, vain, thoughtless fool,   *120*
Below a property or woman's tool,
Who hast no bauble fit for common use,
And only formed by nature for abuse;
A mere example; when we would agree
To sum up every folly, point out thee.   *125*
Thou thing made up of buttons, coach, and show,
The beasts that draw thee have more sense than thou.
Yet still thou mightst have fooled behind the scenes,
Have combed thy head and set thy cravat strings,
Made love to Slingsby when she played the queen—   *130*
The coxcomb in the crowd had passed unseen;
But thus to wed Falmouth's lewd bastard daughter
Has ridiculed the fop, even to loud laughter.
Be judge if man of all the animals
Has not the shallowest intellectuals,   *135*
Man who was born o'er all to bear a rule,
By wiser woman awed and made a fool.
    Observe that sex and every action scan,
And see how they out-do vain, silly man!
Witness the sisters, so renowned by fame,   *140*
While every satire celebrates their name:
Herbert and Brownlow, whom each muse admires
For noble rules of life and lasting fires,
Whose heat like that in glass houses appears,
And has been kindling almost fifty years,   *145*
And charitably warmed the fools o'th'Town,
Where thousand hearts and pricks are melted down.
Youths of all sorts and sizes thither come
T'allay the heat that rages in her womb;
Young Inns of Court men, merchants spruce and neat,   *150*

125

Captains and gownmen, any that will treat,
With whom they wisely serve their lechery,
Then lay the o'er-drained hoping coxcomb by,
That doted on their fop-call, quality.
Whene'er they married, 'twas to hide the whore,   *155*
And have the liberty to ramble more;
But once the cuckold dead, and jointure got,
The devil's in't if they'll again be yoked.
'Tis this that makes brave Sarsfield sigh in vain,
Whose passion arms the jilt with proud disdain;   *160*
Sarsfield, whose every inch (and he has store)
Deserves a younger, juster, kinder whore.
This renders him the object of our pity,
With little Tom, the brave, the gay, the witty.
Before their nauseous, hideous feet they lie   *165*
And whine and sigh and vow and sing and die.
But sure the devil owes them not the shames
To make 'em marry these experienced dames,
Who so salaciously and lewd have lived,
And have so oft from lord to footman swived.   *170*
  Mark but the lewdness of Gerard's wife,
How well she understands the joys of life!
No sooner wed but she th' uneasy yoke
With all the force of generous lewdness broke,
And every night a new-won lover took,   *175*
Who, having served her pleasure and design,
Supplied her ready wants with man and coin.
Then for new prey, in vizor mask she plies,
And a new fop, new want, new lust supplies;
And when she scours the streets *en cavalière*,   *180*
Stand all frail fops and all frail windows clear!
  But thee, kind Mall, we now had given o'er,
Had not thy bawding quite disgraced the whore;
But when an ale-house keeper's punk thou'lt own,
And put her off a fortune in the town,   *185*
An ugly, awkward, flat-faced dowdy sow,

No humor nor no wit, even less than thou,
Who cheats the world with both, the devil knows how,
Like Ned thou fall'st below thy natural parts,
And with acquired jilting and dull arts   *190*
In vain endeavor'st to entrap our hearts.
For shame, give o'er, dear Mall, to play the bawd;
Thou yet has stock enough thyself to trade.

---

4. *Nokes and Leigh.* James Nokes and Anthony Leigh, popular comedians with the Duke of York's Company, usually played "fools" and "cullies."

12. *Arran.* James Douglas (1658–1713), Lord Arran, heir to the Scots Duke of Hamilton and a Gentleman of the Bedchamber to the King.

23. *Kent.* Anthony Grey (1645–1702), eleventh Earl of Kent. *Stamford.* Thomas Grey (1653–1720), second Earl of Stamford, was called a "wittol" because he knew himself to be a cuckold.

24. *Armstrong.* Sir Thomas Armstrong (1624–84), soldier and follower of the Duke of Monmouth. After the revelation of the Rye House Plot, Armstrong fled to Holland, was outlawed, captured, and illegally brought back to England, where he was hanged without the formality of a trial.

25. *Lovelace.* John, third Baron Lovelace of Hurley (1638–93). *Brandon.* On June 18, 1683, Charles Gerard, Lord Brandon, son of Charles, Earl of Macclesfield, married Anne, daughter of Sir Richard Mason; see Appendix, Gerard, Brandon.

30. *murd'ring boys.* In May, 1676, Lord Brandon struck a footboy with such force that the boy died.

33. *Incestuous Grey.* In June, 1682, Ford, Lord Grey of Werke, seduced his wife's younger sister, Henrietta, daughter of George, Earl of Berkeley. On November 23 Grey was tried for the abduction and convicted, but never punished; see Appendix, Grey. *Colchester.* Richard Savage (1654–1712), Lord Colchester from 1680 to 1694, son of Thomas, third Earl Rivers, was called an "apostate" because in 1680 he changed from the Catholic to the Anglican faith. Grey was widely known as a "dull cuckold." Colchester may be called a "pardoned rebel" because in his youth he had stolen money from his father and had been forgiven. His enemies called Colchester "Tyburn Dick."

41. *Essex.* Arthur Capel, Earl of Essex (1632–83), was sent to the Tower on July 10, 1683, and cut his throat three days later. On July 12, 1683, John Fell, Bishop of Oxford, wrote to Lord Hatton, "One would have thought it impossible that the son of the Lord Capel, after wealth and honor heaped upon him, should design the subversion of the government" (*Hatton*, II, 26). On May 19, 1652, Essex had married Elizabeth, fifth daughter of Algernon Percy, Earl of Northumberland.

48. *noble father.* Arthur, Lord Capel, a royalist in the civil wars, was captured at Colchester, Essex, tried and condemned by the High Court of Justice, and executed March 9, 1649.

51. *Grayhound.* Richard Newport (1661–1723), elder son of Francis, Viscount Newport, Treasurer of the Household, was a tall thin man, hence "Grayhound." He was a Whig member of Parliament.

53. *Fat Turnspit.* Francis ("bold Frank") Newport, second son of Viscount Newport. A dog who turned a roasting spit by walking in a treadmill was likely to grow fat.

55. *Shadwell.* The "last libel" by Thomas Shadwell (1640–92), Whig poet, may be Shadwell's attack on Dryden, *The Medal of John Bayes*, May, 1682.

57. *Coysh's Settle.* Elkanah Settle (1648–1724), Whig poet, was associated with John Coysh, a member of the King's Company of Comedians, in producing plays and drolls for Coysh's traveling company. On November 11, 1682, for example, one Joshua Bowes stated that Settle "designed to carry down one Coish and others to act some plays or drolls at York" (*CSPD*, 1682, p. 536).

62. *The Whartons.* Thomas and Henry, sons of Philip, Lord Wharton, and violent Whigs.

65. *In sawpit.* At the Battle of Edgehill, October 23, 1642, Lord Wharton's regiment of Roundheads was routed. Wharton is said to have taken refuge in a sawpit, a pit dug for the use of sawyers, but often employed as a latrine (Wood, *Athenae Oxonienses*, III, col. 177).

67. *reverend pulpit.* On July 2, 1682, it was reported that two of Lord Wharton's sons had played "a grievous prank in Burford Church" (*Seventh Report*, p. 497B). Their unseemly defecation is the episode referred to by Swift in *The Examiner*, no. 23 and no. 25. See Appendix, Wharton.

68. *spew.* Vomit.

69. *frig.* Masturbate.

75. *history Fox.* An ironic reference to John Foxe's *The Acts and Monuments* ("The Book of Martyrs"), 1563. Lord Wharton had been a Puritan, and his sons, Thomas and Henry, professed Puritanism, but both were wild libertines.

78. *Hewitt.* Sir George Hewitt (1652–89), a pattern of Restoration foppery.

83. *Marshall.* Possibly Rebecca Marshall, leading lady of the King's Company of Comedians, 1663 to 1677.

85. *Willis.* Sue Willis; see Appendix. A "whore of honor" was by birth a lady.

88. *Howe.* "Libelling Jack" Howe; see Appendix. *Rochester.* John Wilmot, the poet Earl of Rochester (1647–80).

93. *Nobs.* Probably George Porter, Junior, often called "Nobs" and accused of unnatural practices.

95. *Baber.* John Baber, son of Sir John Baber, royal physician. On July 6, 1683, a search was made for Mary, daughter of Sir Thomas Draper (a City knight), who was "taken by force" from her father's house (*CSPD*, 1683, p. 59). On July 14 it was reported that "Sir John Baber's son has run away with Sir Thomas Draper's daughter" (*Hatton*, II, 30).

99. *Sir Martin.* The bumbling knight in Dryden's eponymous *Sir Martin Mar-all, or The Feigned Innocence*, 1667.

1,01. *Whorwood.* Brome Whorwood of Halton, Oxon., a Whig M.P., had separated from his wife c. 1674, agreeing to pay her £300 a year alimony. In 1682 she petitioned for help in her extremity, claiming that she had never received more than £200 a year, and nothing at all for the past nine months (*CSPD*, 1682, p. 617). Whorwood died on April 12, 1682, leaving a natural son by his mistress, a servant named Katherine Allen (Wood, *Fasti Oxonienses*, II, 43). *Butler.* Charlotte Butler, a handsome, black-eyed singer and actress. *chiaux.* Chiaus, a dupe or fool.

103. *May*. The three men listed here—Whorwood, May, and Barry (properly Berry)—were linked by a common interest in Charlotte Butler. For May and Berry, see above, "On Three Late Marriages," 1682. Conjecturally, the first was Richard May, the second Sir John Berry; both were captains in the Royal Navy.

105. *Lucy*. Thomas Lucy of Charlecote, captain of a troop of Guards, had married Katherine, daughter of Robert Wheatley of Brecknell, Berks. Captain Lucy was then High Sheriff of Wiltshire. According to "A New Ditty" (Harvard MS. Eng. 633, p. 17),

> Tom Lucy, Lord bless us, sits on a sheriff's bench,
> Hey, ho, langle down ditty;
> Because the jilt cried he has married his wench,
> Without ever a penny of money.

Katherine was fond of cards and frequented the Duchess of Portsmouth's apartments. After her husband's death in November, 1684, she married George Fitzroy, Duke of Northumberland.

108. *all the Howards*. Of the six men listed below I can find only one who had certainly married his "long-kept jilt."

111. *his grace's bulker*. Jane (Bickerton), Duchess of Norfolk, had long been the mistress of Henry Howard, sixth Duke of Norfolk, before she became his second wife (see Evelyn, January 23, 1678). A "bulker" was a whore who plied her trade at night on empty bulks, or stalls, in front of shops. *Esmé*. According to Collins, the wife of Esmé Howard (1645–78), was named "Margaret -----." She died January 11, 1716, aged seventy; perhaps she was his "kitchen-maid."

112. *Phil*. In 1668, Sir Philip Howard, seventh son of the first Earl of Berkshire, had a player, Betty Hall, as his mistress (Pepys, December 19, 1668). According to Collins, Sir Philip married "Mary, daughter to ------Jennings." A Mrs. Jennings was listed by John Downes among Davenant's original eight actresses; after 1672, she was one of those who "by force of love were Erept the Stage" (Downes, *Roscius Anglicanus*, ed. Montague Summers, 1928, pp. 20, 35). Of course there is no evidence that she became Sir Philip's wife. *Sir Poz*. Sir Robert Howard, sixth son of the first Earl of Berkshire, was caricatured on the stage as Sir Positive At-all in Shadwell's *The Sullen Lovers*, 1668. Susanna Uphill, a minor actress with the King's Company, seems to have left the stage about 1675 to become Sir Robert's mistress, but Howard's third wife was Mary Uphill, probably a sister of the actress (Wilson, *All the King's Ladies*, pp. 189–91).

113. *Ned*. According to Collins, Edward Howard, poet and playwright, fifth son of the Earl of Berkshire, "married two wives [in succession, of course] and died without issue." Perhaps one of them was a seamstress. *Tom*. The most likely Tom Howard at this time would be Lord Thomas of Worksop, Notts., who married Mary Elizabeth Savile, an heiress. His *mimic* is unidentified.

116. *Gerard*. Gilbert Cosins Gerard; see Appendix.

130. *Slingsby*. By her second marriage, Mary Lee (Aldridge) became Lady Slingsby, perhaps as wife of Sir Charles Slingsby of Bifrons, near Canterbury. She was a leading actress with the Duke's Company from 1670 to 1685 and played many queenly roles, notably Queen Gertrude in *Hamlet*.

132. *Falmouth's daughter*. Mary (Berkeley), daughter of Charles, Earl of Falmouth, married Gerard on May 2, 1681, at the age of sixteen. Immediately she took

129

the full liberty of the town as a female rake. Gerard divorced her (*a mensa et thoro*) in 1684; see Appendix, Gerard, Gilbert Cosins.

142. *Herbert.* Elizabeth (Brydges), Lady Herbert (1651–1718), widow of Edward, third Lord Herbert of Cherbury; see Appendix, Herbert. *Brownlow*. Margaret (Brydges) Brownlow (1637–1732), Lady Herbert's older sister and widow of William Brownlow of Humby, Lincs.

159. *Sarsfield.* On March 24, 1683, Captain Patrick Sarsfield and his crony Sir John Parsons abducted Elizabeth, Lady Herbert. When she refused to marry Sarsfield, he returned her to London; see Appendix, Sarsfield.

164. *little Tom.* Thomas Skipwith of Metheringham (1652–1710) married Mrs. Margaret Brownlow in 1685. She was fifteen years his senior.

171. *Gerard's wife.* Mary (Berkeley), wife of Gilbert Cosins Gerard.

180. *en cavalière.* Dressed as a man. Apparently Mary and her friends were accustomed to scouring the town in male attire. For a frolic in November, 1683, with serious consequences, see Appendix, Gerard, Gilbert Cosins.

182. *kind Mall.* Mall Howard, famous bawd and whore.

184. *punk.* Prostitute. A marginal note in the copy text identifies her as "Mrs Stacy at the Sugar Loaf in Henrietta Street."

189. *like Ned.* That is, like Ned Howard, poet, author of *The British Princes*, 1669, an opus ridiculed by the Court wits. Here the satirist paraphrases a line from Dorset's "On Mr. Edward Howard" (*POAS*, Yale, I, 339), "Thou writ'st below e'en thy own nat'ral parts."

LETTER TO JULIAN

[Summer, 1684]

The first part of the "Letter" is a sharp attack on several Court poets, centering on the writers of the prologues and the epilogue to Rochester's alteration of Fletcher's *Valentinian*. The revised play was sumptuously produced by the United Company on February 11, 1684, and later printed with a preface by Robert Wolseley. Included also were the prologue for the first day, by Aphra Behn; the anonymous prologue for the second day; a "Prologue intended for Valentinian" (evidently never delivered); and the epilogue, "Written by a person of quality." The second part of the "Letter" is a conventional shotgun libel against some Court ladies. The satire must have been written after Lord Kildare's second marriage, June 12, 1684, and probably before November, 1684, when Lord Cavendish became Earl of Devonshire.

The copy text is Harleian MS. 7319, p. 339. It is undated there as also in Harleian MS. 7317, p. 118, *POAS*, 1705, p. 338, and *POAS*, 1716, II, 135.

> Dear Julian, twice or thrice a year
> I write to help thee in some gear;
> For thou by nonsense liv'st, not wit,
> As carps thrive best where cattle shit.
> But now that province I resign,　　　　　　　5
> And to my successor design,
> Eland, whose pen as nimbly glides
> As his good father changes sides;
> His head's with thought as little vexed,
> Or taking care what should come next.　　　　10
> But he a path much safer treads:
> Poets live when statesmen lose their heads.
> Though truth in prose may be a crime,

131

'Twas never known in any time
That one was hanged for writing rhyme.   *15*
But should some poets be accused
That have the government abused
They'd scarce be by their neck-verse freed;
Some Whigs will write that cannot read.

    But charity bids us suppose   *20*
That Mordaunt is not one of those;
Besides, that he can write 'tis known
By's making Suckling's songs his own.
He to the bays in time may rise
If Etherege will but supervise,   *25*
To make his verse more soft and tame,
That would be without life or flame;
Like the epilogue they jointly writ
To ridicule the well-horned pit,
A jest that Mordaunt well might spare   *30*
Unless he sat to hear it there.

    Jack Howe, thy patron, 's left the town,
But first writ something he dare own,
A prologue lawfully begotten
And full nine months maturely thought on,   *35*
Born with hard labor and much pain;
Wolseley was Doctor Chamberlain;
At length from stuff and rubbish picked,
As bear cubs into shape are licked.
When Wharton, Etherege, and Soame,   *40*
To give it the last strokes were come,
Those critics differed in their doom.
Some were for embers *quenched with pages,*
And some for *mending servants' wages.*
Both ways were tried, but neither took,   *45*
And the fault's laid on Mrs. Cook;
Yet Swan says he admired it 'scaped,
Since 'twas Jack Howe's, without being clapped.

Our old friend Cutts has left the trade;
His muse is grown a very jade.   *50*
Phillis did take him on his word,
And has his destiny so spurred,
Of love and verse he's weary grown,
His pen and passion both laid down;
And to his praise it may be said,   *55*
No love nor songs of late h'has made.
   But Mulgrave will not leave off so,
For to his industry we owe
That we the fate in English see
Of Orpheus and Eurydice.   *60*
And 'tis an honor to the state
When a blue garter will translate,
Who bears the bell without dispute
From D'Urfey, Settle, Creech, or Duke.
I thought 'twould puzzle all the Nine   *65*
To spoil that poem so divine,
But he with pains and care doth show
It may be rendered mean and low,
So much can one great blockhead do.
Some say his lordship had done better   *70*
To answer Roger Martin's letter,
Or give Jack Howe his bellyfull,
Who justly calls him a dull owl
For quoting books he never read,
And basely railing at the dead.   *75*
   Of ladies there's no need to tell,
Since they their own intrigues reveal:
As Norfolk with her prince outlandish,
And Isham with her beau, Lord Candish;
And Grov'ner with Dick Middleton   *80*
(Not Cholm'ley, who 'tis said has none),
How Walcop meets with Cartwright's spouse
At Sadler's, the painter's, house;

133

Or how the modest maid complained
That Talbot had her casement strained   *85*
For what he had before obtained;
How Mordaunt Grafton's virtue tries
More than King John does Ossory's.

But yet a line or two we'll spare
In gratitude to Lord Kildare,   *90*
Whose marrying Lady Betty Jones
For's killing his first wife atones;
A wife she'll be to him alone,
But a meet help to all the Town.

Oh, that kind Fate would order't so   *95*
That Bellingham might do so too,
And with his folly and estate
Oblige the world and marry Kate!
How many then full sail would enter,
That in the port now dare not venture?   *100*
But though he's fop enough to woo,
Present, and treat, and keep ado,
When he should wed, he wont come to.

But these affairs are known to all
That haunt the Park, plays, or Whitehall;   *105*
Besides, my labor I may save,
For an account you'll timely have,
Who are made cuckolds or make love,
From some o'th' authors named above.

---

7. *Eland.* Henry Savile, Lord Eland (1661–87), eldest son of George, Marquis of Halifax.

18. *neck-verse.* A Bible verse read by a convicted felon when he pleaded benefit of clergy.

21. *Mordaunt.* Charles, Viscount Mordaunt (1658–1735). For the charge that he plagiarized Suckling's songs, see above, "Utile Dulce,"

> Let Mordaunt copy Sir John Suckling's songs,
> Call 'em his own, and have 'em set in throngs."

25. *Etherege*. Sir George Etherege (1635–c. 1692). Collaboration between Mordaunt (who lisped) and Etherege is earlier indicated in "A Letter to a Friend," c. 1679 (Harleian MS. 6913, p. 63),

> . . . the lisping lord who lately writ
> With many words and with so little wit
> Hath found more work for his correcting friend,
> Who slyly laughs at what he seems to mend.

28. *the epilogue*. Apparently Mordaunt, assisted by Etherege, wrote the epilogue to Rochester's *Valentinian*, described only as "Written by a Person of Quality." The epilogue sneered at the leading character of the play, Maximus, as

> A cuckold, daring to revenge his shame,
> Surly, ill-natured Roman, wanting wit,
> Angry, when all true Englishmen submit,
> Witness the horns of the well headed pit.

32. *Jack Howe*. According to the satirist, "Libeling Jack" Howe was the author of "Prologue to *Valentinian*, spoken by Mrs. Cook the second Day."

37. *Wolseley*. Robert Wolseley, a poetaster, was the eldest son of Sir Charles Wolseley of Wolseley, Staffordshire. Wolseley wrote à preface to *Valentinian* (published, Term Catalogues, November, 1684), defending Lord Rochester against Lord Mulgrave's charges of obscenity and lack of wit, in his *Essay Upon Satire*, 1679. *Chamberlain*. Dr. Hugh Chamberlain was a famous obstetrician. In short, Wolseley acted as a midwife to bring Howe's prologue to the expectant world.

39. *bear cubs*. According to fable, bear cubs were born shapeless and were licked into shape by their mothers.

40. *Wharton*. Probably Thomas Wharton, eldest son of Philip, Lord Wharton; see Appendix. *Soame*. William Soame (c. 1645–86), of Thurlow, Suffolk, was knighted in 1674 and inherited as baronet February 5, 1684. In 1683 he translated Boileau's *Art of Poetry*. Late in 1684 he was appointed Ambassador to Constantinople but died at Malta on his way to Turkey, June 12, 1686.

43. *some were*. From the "Prologue to Valentinian, Spoken by Mrs. Cook the second Day," "our Author"

> Desired the ladies of maturer ages,
> If some remaining spark their hearts enrages,
> At home to quench their embers with their pages.

46. *Mrs. Cook*. Sarah Cooke, a popular actress with the United Company, from 1677 to 1688.

47. *Swan*. Perhaps Richard Swan, a noted punster; see Dryden's *Letters*, ed. C. E. Ward, p. 137.

49. *Cutts*. John Cutts (1661–1707), second son of Richard Cutts of Arkesden, Essex, became a famous soldier, and on December 12, 1690, he was created Baron Cutts of Gowran. He was also a wit and a writer of songs and occasional verses. See, for example, his "On the Death of the Queen," *POAS*, 1705, pp. 254–55.

57. *Mulgrave*. John Sheffield, Earl of Mulgrave, was responsible for the translation of "Part of Virgil's Fourth Georgick" in Dryden's *Miscellany Poems*, April, 1684.

Mulgrave, A Knight Companion of the Most Noble Order of the Garter, was a mediocre poet and translator.

64. *D'Urfey.* Thomas D'Urfey (1653–1723), playwright and songwriter. *Settle.* Elkanah Settle (1648–1724), playwright. *Creech.* Thomas Creech (1659–1700) was responsible for one translation from Ovid and two from Virgil in Dryden's 1684 *Miscellany.* *Duke.* Richard Duke (1658–1711) translated three odes by Horace, an idyl by Theocritus, and an eclogue by Virgil for the 1684 *Miscellany.*

65. *the Nine.* The Nine Muses, daughters of Jupiter and Mnemosyne.

71. *Roger Martin's letter.* Probably "Advice in a Heroic Epistle to Mr. Fr. Villiers," c. 1683 (see above), with its warning to Frank Villiers to look out for his sister Nancy, pursued by Mulgrave ("King John").

73. *a dull owl.* In the second prologue to *Valentinian* is an obvious reference to Mulgrave, who, in his *Essay Upon Satire* (1679) had attacked the Earl of Rochester for "his want of wit" and for the obscenity of his poems. According to Jack Howe, then,

> No fury's like a libeled blockhead's rage;
> Hence some despised him [Rochester] for his want of wit,
> And others said he too obscenely writ. . . .
> But all weak eyes are hurt by too much light.
> Let then these owls against the eagle preach,
> And blame those flights which they want wing to reach.
> Like Falstaff let 'em conquer heroes dead,
> And praise Greek poets they could never read.

78. *Norfolk.* Mary (Mordaunt), Countess of Arundell, became Duchess of Norfolk on January 11, 1684, when her husband, Henry, inherited as seventh duke. Her lover, the "prince outlandish," was a Dutch gambler, John Germaine, said to be the illegitimate son of William II of Orange (*Hatton*, II, 170).

79. *Isham.* Elizabeth, daughter of Sir Edmund Turner of Stoke Rochford, Lincs., married on July 16, 1683, Sir Justinian Isham of Lamport, Northants. *Candish.* William, Lord Cavendish, inherited as Earl of Devonshire in November, 1684.

80. *Grov'ner.* The only lady who seems to fit here is Mary (Davies), who married Sir Thomas Grosvenor of Eaton, near Chester, October 19, 1677. She was a great heiress; see Charles T. Gatty, *Mary Davies and the Manor of Ebury*, 1929. *Middleton.* Probably Richard Middleton (1655–1716) of Chirk, Denbighshire, who inherited as baronet on February 5, 1684. For his marriage to widowed Frances Whitmore in 1686, see below, "Madam Le Croix."

81. *Cholm'ley.* Hugh Cholmondeley (1662–1725) succeeded in 1681 as third Viscount Cholmondeley of Kells.

82. *Walcop.* Probably Warcup. The best known gentleman of that name was Lenthal Warcup, a captain in the Royal Regiment of Footguards. *Cartwright's spouse.* Grace, daughter of John Granville, Earl of Bath, married on March 18, 1675 (when she was six and the groom was eight) George Carteret (1667–95), son of Sir Philip Carteret. "Questionless," said an observer, "they will carry themselves very gravely and love dearly" (*Verney Memoirs*, II, 316). They did neither. George succeeded to the baronetcy on January 13, 1680, and became Baron Carteret of Hawnes on October 19, 1681.

83. *Sadler.* Thomas Sadler, second son of John Sadler, a Master in Chancery, was a pupil of Lely and became a miniaturist and portrait painter. Possibly he was painting Lady Carteret at the time.

84. *the modest maid.* Unidentified, but obviously a *rara avis.*

85. *Talbot.* Probably John Talbot (1665–86), a frantic libertine, younger brother of Charles, Earl of Shrewsbury.

87. *Grafton.* Isabella (Bennet), wife of Henry Fitzroy, Duke of Grafton, natural son of King Charles II by the Duchess of Cleveland.

88. *King John.* Derisive name for John, Earl of Mulgrave. *Ossory.* Anne (Hyde), who, on July 15, 1682, married James, the young Earl of Ossory, died of a miscarriage in January, 1685, aged eighteen.

90. *Kildare.* John Fitzgerald, Earl of Kildare (1661–1707), lost his first wife on November 24, 1683. "Lady Kildare is dead of the smallpox, which she got with being with her lord who has had it" (*Hatton*, II, 39). As his second wife, Kildare married on June 12, 1684, Elizabeth, a daughter of Richard Jones, Earl of Ranelagh.

96. *Bellingham.* "Spendthrift" Alan Bellingham of Levens, Helsington, Westmoreland, ruined his family by his extravagance and fled abroad to escape his creditors in October, 1688. For the account of a harmless duel between Bellingham and Major Orby (Arpe), December 18, 1683, see Reresby, *Memoirs,* p. 324.

98. *Kate.* Probably Katherine Villiers, a Maid of Honor to Queen Catherine. See above, "Satire. 1682,"

> Kate Villiers, as they say, has got a notion,
> To marry ere she puts her breech in motion.

137

JULIAN'S FAREWELL TO THE MUSES

(*Summer, 1685*)

On May 31, 1684, "Captain" Robert Julian was charged with writing and publishing a libel on King Charles II entitled "Old Rowley the King." He was convicted on November 12 and sentenced to stand in the pillory and to pay a fine of one hundred marks—£66 13s 4d. Unable to pay the fine, he sat in the King's Bench prison until June, 1685, when the judges took pity on his age and decrepitude and released him. His imprisonment drew the attention of the Court poets, who honored him with "A Letter to Julian in Prison" (Dyce MS. 43, II, 637) and the following satire, in which, of course, Julian is the *persona*, not the author. Essentially the poem is a short shotgun libel aimed at six Court poets and five well-known courtesans. The probable date is summer, 1685.

The copy text, dated 1685, is Harleian MS. 7319, p. 389. The satire is dated 1685 in Dyce MS. 43, II, 482; MS. Firth c. 15, p. 169; and "A Choyce Collection," p. 158.

Mine and the poets' plague consume you all,
And all the fools that at your altar fall.
May all the crowd that worship that false flame
Reap nothing thence but penury and shame.
May you all be adorned with bays like me,   5
No laurel crown you, but a pillory!
   Was't not hard measure, say, my Whiggish peers,
Vending your nonsense to expose my ears?
My pocket stuffed with scandal long has been
The house of office to vend out your spleen,   10
The common sink o'th' town, wherein you shit
To carry off your excrements of wit.
Such gallantry has not of late been shown;

138

To save your ears, poor Julian lost his own;
But if you ever catch me at that strain—   *15*
To vend your scurrilous scoundrel stuff again—
May infamy and scandal be my bane.
Though Howe's envenomed pen, whose poison kills,
Should libel all the tribe at Man's and Will's,
Let him his unlicked brat ere it come forth,   *20*
To save a kicking, stifle in the birth.
Let fluxing George his sharp mercurial wit,
Squeezed out in physic, spend again at shit.
Let Eland, one poor thought to bring to life,
First beat his brains, and after that his wife.   *25*
Let haughty Mulgrave own the laureate's rhymes,
And Dryden's back answer for his own crimes.
Poor Julian's off the lay; though every line
Were cudgel proof, it's no concern of mine.
Nay, though inspired with more than Delphic flame,   *30*
My great Maecenas, awful Dorset, came,
And as a mark of his censorious wit
Paid double fees for what himself had writ.
  Let Cleveland to sham Alexander stick,
And Portsmouth pine for want of royal prick.   *35*
Let Richmond rub on still with page and groom,
And Mazarin lodge stallions in her room.
Let Gr[ey] and Exeter win all at play,
And Orrery have not one groat to pay.
Let 'em fuck on and still pursue their game;   *40*
I'll be no more the trumpet of their fame.
Scandal, farewell; I'll take up a new trade,
And safer far by pimping get my bread.

---

1. *the poet's plague*. The pox? Only the first six lines of the satire are directed to the Nine Muses.

10. *house of office*. A privy, usually indoors.

14. *ears*. There is no evidence that Julian lost his ears. Ear-cropping, as punishment for libel, had gone out of style.

18. *Howe*. "Libeling Jack" Howe (1661–1722).

19. *Man's*. Man's Coffee-house, behind Charing Cross, near Scotland Yard, was kept by Alexander Man. *Will's*. Will's Coffee-house, at the corner of Bow and Russell Streets, was kept by Will Urwin.

20. *unlicked*. Shapeless.

22. *fluxing George*. Apparently Sir George Etherege suffered from "the pox." (The Restoration doctors were not aware that there were two venereal diseases.) The usual treatment was sweating, purging with calomel (mercurous chloride), and the application of pure mercury.

24. *Eland*. Henry Savile, Lord Eland (1661–87). His relations with his wife Esther (de Gouvernet) were not happy.

26. *Mulgrave*. The fact that Lord Mulgrave's *An Essay upon Satire* (1679) was thought to be by Dryden, is usually accepted as the cause of Dryden's beating in Rose Street, on December 18, 1679. But see J. H. Wilson, "Rochester, Dryden, and the Rose-Street Affair," *RES*, XV, July, 1939.

31. *Dorset*. Charles Sackville, Earl of Dorset (1643–1706) wrote a number of little satirical lyrics and probably some longer libels. He was also a "Maecenas," a patron of poets.

34. *Cleveland*. Barbara (Villiers), Duchess of Cleveland (1649–1709), formerly mistress to King Charles II, now had as her paramour an actor, Cardell Goodman, famous for his performances as Alexander the Great in Lee's *The Rival Queens*. See J. H. Wilson, *Mr. Goodman, the Player*, 1964, pp. 86 ff.

35. *Portsmouth*. Louise Keroualle, Duchess of Portsmouth (1649–1734), mistress to King Charles II until his death, February 6, 1685, returned to France in August, 1685.

36. *Richmond*. Frances (Stuart), widowed Duchess of Richmond (1647–1702).

37. *Mazarin*. Hortense (Mancini), Duchess Mazarin (1646–99), was considered the most beautiful woman in Europe. Besides King Charles II, she had a legion of lovers.

38. *Gr[ey]*. Since Ford, Lord Grey of Werke, was involved in Monmouth's rebellion, and was in the Tower from July to mid-November, 1685, this must have been Henry Yelverton, Lord Grey of Ruthin (c. 1664–1704). *Exeter*. John Cecil (1648–1700) succeeded as fifth Earl of Exeter in February, 1678.

39. *Orrery*. Mary (Sackville), 1647–1710, widow of Roger Boyle, second Earl of Orrery, was a compulsive gambler. The poet suggests that she paid her gambling losses to Grey and Exeter in bed.

A LETTER TO JULIAN FROM TUNBRIDGE

[*October, 1685*]

King Charles II died on February 6, 1685; his brother was crowned as James II on April 23. The Duke of Monmouth invaded England on June 11, and on July 15 went to the block on Tower Hill. "The Bloody Assizes" took up much of the summer. King James, pressing ahead with his plan to Catholicize England, was rapidly alienating the Protestant lords who had made the reign of Charles so lively— and sinful. Nevertheless, the Court satirists, ignoring politics, religion, and the cruelties of Kirke and Jeffreys, still found material for scandalous libels.

The title of this shotgun libel is not important. Tunbridge Wells was a popular summer resort in Kent, some thirty-four miles from London. Gentry repaired to it in the summer to drink the chalybeate waters of the wells and to enjoy the town's facilities for gaming, dancing, and gallantry. In spite of the title, our poet is clearly writing from London, and only the first part of the satire deals with what "passed last season at the Wells."

The copy text, undated, is Harleian MS. 7319, p. 405. The poem is undated also in Harleian MS. 7317, p. 113, and in Dyce MS. 43, II, 487. Internal evidence places the poem in the early autumn of 1685.

> Dear friend, I fain would try once more
> To help thee clear thy brandy score,
> But London is so empty yet,
> Intelligence is hard to get;
> Yet fame of some adventures tells   5
> That passed last season at the Wells:
> How Rider conquered Bludworth's heart,
> Rider that never uses art,
> I mean with a design to cheat,

141

For 'tis so plain all needs must see't;   *10*
So greasy, does such flavors send
No neighbor can his nose defend.
Each moment with redoubled wounds
That poisoned martyr she confounds.
Her practised looks and sidelong bow   *15*
Has oft caused mirth, we do allow,
But never could give love till now.
In which we her good fortune see
To find a greater fool than she,
A sot so stupid and unheeding   *20*
He takes affectedness for breeding,
Her very singing can admit,
And calls a load of tattling, wit;
Believes all gold in glist'ring Phillis,
And mistakes mercury for lilies;   *25*
So heretofore the Egyptian race
Worshipped a calf with a white face.
The fop in vain has tried all ways
To quench the flame her washes raise;
But were his father now in case,   *30*
Were it no more than London's was—
Good man!—he'd piss it out with ease.
But none received so many vows
As Adam Loftus his fair spouse;
Loftus, the kindest man that lives,   *35*
And blest by Heaven with as kind wives.
No sooner was his first wife gone,
But to a second, fair and young;
Yet though she's much obliged to nature,
Her Irish husband's her best feature.   *40*
In London she met Norfolk's duke;
At Tunbridge Cholmley's letters took,
But waters were a just excuse:
No paper's fitter for that use
Than my Lord Cholmley's *billets doux*.   *45*

Warcup and Whitaker will have it
That Berkeley follows strutt'ring Brathwaite;
'Tis not impossible that he
Should speed with such a fool as she;
Their wits and beauties both agree.   *50*
Yet some that know him much admire
His humble love should e'er aspire
Above a wench that bulks for hire.
Women of quality despise
A man that ogles with sore eyes;   *55*
Keep (my good lord) to your old trade
Of common whore and chambermaid;
There triumph in your boundless joys
O'er jilted footmen or link-boys.
No rival will disturb you there   *60*
Unless that tradesman's ghost appear
You killed so barbarously last year.
    Arran, by some ill planet cursed,
Still aims at what becomes him worst;
Has broke himself and many a shop   *65*
To be esteemed a first-rate fop.
Affecting to appear sublime,
Talks, as he dances, out of time,
And is at length become the sport
Both of the French and English Court.   *70*
He'll quickly to the King's Bench come,
Or (which is worse) to live at home,
If Conway, who has lost her wits,
Don't marry him in her mad fits.
    But for a worthy officer,   *75*
All must give way to Manchester,
Who prudently was pitched upon
To raise men, not to lead 'em on.
Pleased with himself, and pleased alone,
For being born an eldest son.   *80*
Dancing is now his greatest care,

143

Or dogging Lady Cartwright's chair.
The fate which that poor lady rules
Dooms her to have to do with fools,
Which every day itself discovers   *85*
Both in her husband and her lovers.
    Of all our traveled youth, none dare
With Newburgh vie for the *bel air*.
He is so French in all his ways,
Loves dresses, swears *a-la-Francaise*,   *90*
Sings to the spinet and guitar,
Those genteel ways to charm the fair;
And though Sir Edward Villiers's gone,
Is able to support alone
Sir Courtly Nice's character.   *95*
Thus Atlas fell indeed, but Hercules was near.
    Sir Edward, though he hates fatigue,
With much ado has reached The Hague,
The fittest country for him, where
His wit and humor will appear   *100*
As good as any he'll meet there.
Yet that unwholesome foggy air
His fine complexion may impair
Unless his favorite picarre
His master to his old course keeps   *105*
Of a cool clyster ere he sleeps.
    To beauties turn we now our style,
But they're so thin 'tis scarce worth while;
In all the Court 'tis hard to find
One woman that one would wish kind.   *110*
Some Yarburgh's beauty like and say
'Tis glorious as the God of Day;
In this respect 'tis like the sun,
'Tis never at the height till noon,
But then breaks forth with such a light   *115*
Those that she wounds would die outright,
Did not her tongue (which nature made

For tonguing only) lend 'em aid,
And by insipid, dull replies
Release the captives of her eyes.   *120*
   Just so 'tis with her little grace,
Whose charms lie only in her face,
That face, though none can praise too much,
Her shape and understanding's Dutch;
Who else but she would for a lover   *125*
Accept of antiquated Dover,
Long since drained by her husband's mother,
And with him every day repair
In vizor mask to Smithfield Fair,
For which her husband does not care.   *130*
His soul is so extremely thick
His horns don't touch him to the quick.
Nature him for some drudge designed,
And framed his body to his mind:
Strong limbs but weak capacity,   *135*
And Georgeish to the last degree;
Yet treacherous, for all so dull,
Both parent's image to the full.
Thus we see plainly in his grace
And in some others of his race,   *140*
Brains are not needful to be base.
   Here's all this season will afford,
Which for all sorts of trades is hard;
But better times are coming on,
Now everybody flocks to town.   *145*
The winter's like to prove more kind,
For those that write are sure to find
In Betterton's or Trevor's house
Matter much more ridiculous.

7. *Rider*. Probably the wife of William Rider, a minor courtier and racing man, commissioned a captain in the Earl of Oxford's Regiment of Horse in 1685 (Dalton,

145

II, 10). On March 14, 1684, there was a rumor that the Duchess of Portsmouth was out of favor, and that Major Oglethorpe (a commissioner for executing her son's place as Master of the Horse) was "turned out, and Mr. Rider in his place" (Luttrell, I, 303). The rumor was false. *Bludworth.* Sir Thomas Bludworth, son of the Sir Thomas who had been Lord Mayor of London in 1666 (he died May 12, 1682). On February 23, 1685, the younger Sir Thomas was appointed Standard Bearer of the Band of Gentleman Pensioners (*CSPD*, 1685, p. 40), probably by the influence of Lord Chief Justice Jeffreys, who, on June 10, 1679, had married Bludworth's sister Anne, widow of Sir John Jones.

25. *mercury.* Washes of mercury, often used for cosmetic purposes, were dangerous. On April 24, 1686, Henry Savile wrote, "My Lady Henrietta Wentworth is dead, having sacrificed her life to her beauty by painting so beyond measure that the mercury got into her veins and killed her" (*Savile Correspondence*, p. 286).

27. *a calf.* Possibly Hathor, goddess of love and laughter, represented as a woman with a cow's head.

31. *London's.* The allusion is to the great fire of London, September 2–6, 1666, and Lord Mayor Sir Thomas Bludworth, who is said to have boasted that he would put out the fire by the same means that Gulliver used in Lilliput.

34. *Loftus.* Adam Loftus (1657–91), an Irish squire, lost his first wife, Lucy (Brydges) in April, 1681. In May, 1682, Loftus married Dorothy, daughter of Patrick Allen, Esq. See Appendix, Loftus.

41. *Norfolk's duke.* Henry Howard (1655–1701), seventh Duke of Norfolk, was a famous wencher.

42. *Cholmley.* Hugh, third Viscount Cholmondeley (1662–1725).

46. *Warcup.* Captain Lenthal Warcup of the Royal Regiment of Footguards was a well-known courtier and gossip. *Whitaker.* See below, "soft Whitaker" in "The Lovers' Session." Probably this was "Charles Whitacre of New Windsor, gent," who in 1670 was appointed "Foreign Apposer" in the Exchequer Court, with a fee of £40 a year. He held the post for more than thirty years. He seems to have been a man of means: in 1688 he received £1,000 for two houses at Windsor which he had sold to Charles II (*CTB*, 1669–72, pp. 448, 603, 619; *CTB*, 1685–89, p. 1723). Very probably our "Foreign Apposer" was the Charles Whitaker engaged by Tonson, along with a host of other gentlemen, to do translations for *Plutarch's Lives*, 1683–86 (see *The Works of John Dryden*, University of California Press, 1971, XVII, "Life of Plutarch," ed. A. E. W. Maurer, p. 430, note 3).

Whitacre was a friend of Sir George Etherege, yet on April 28, 1687, commenting on Whitacre's changing his lodgings, Etherege wrote, "If he happens into a house with Mr. [John] Crowne, John's songs and Joseph's voice will charm the whole family" (*Letters*, p. 113). Either this was a different Whitacre, or Etherege's memory betrayed him.

47. *Berkeley.* John Berkeley (1660–97) succeeded his brother Charles as third Lord Berkeley of Stratton in 1682. In April, 1685, he was a first lieutenant in the Navy. He is not to be confused with "Whistling John" Berkeley, ten years his senior and an officer in the Guards, who inherited in 1690 as fourth Viscount Fitzharding. *strutt'ring.* Probably "stuttering." *Brathwaite.* Unidentified, but apparently a woman of the town. She is addressed in "A Faithful Catalogue of our Most Eminent Ninnies," 1687 (Harleian MS. 7319, p. 471):

> But why to Ireland, Brathwaite? Will that clime,
> Dost thou imagine, make an easy time?

> That battered fort, which they with ease deceive,
> Pillaged and sacked, to the next foe they leave.

53. *bulks.* A prostitute who plied her trade by night on empty stalls, or bulks, in front of shops, was said to bulk.

59. *link-boys.* Members of "the black-guard" who led pedestrians through the streets by night with flaming links, or torches.

61. *tradesman's ghost.* On April 20, 1684, a Middlesex grand jury brought in a true bill that John, Lord Berkeley, had assaulted Ralph Tonycliffe, gentleman, and had run his rapier into Tonycliffe's belly near the navel (*Middlesex County Records*, IV, 234). On May 12 a pardon was granted to Lord Berkeley for the manslaughter of Ralph Tonycliffe (*CSPD*, 1684–85, p. 13).

63. *Arran.* James Douglas, Lord Arran (1658–1712), the future Scots Duke of Hamilton.

71. *King's Bench.* The King's Bench prison in Southwark. The poet suggests that an even worse fate for Arran would be to "live at home" in Scotland.

73. *Conway.* Ursula (Stawell), nineteen-year-old widow of Edward, Earl of Conway (1623–83), was very rich and much sought after, but there is no evidence that she had lost her wits. On March 18, 1686, she married the Earl of Mulgrave.

76. *Manchester.* Charles Montague (1662–1722) inherited as fourth Earl of Manchester on March 14, 1683. On June 20, 1685, he was commissioned as captain of an independent troop of horse; hence "to raise men." He resigned his commission on December 15, 1685 (Dalton, II, 15).

82. *Cartwright.* Grace (Granville), 1667–1747, wife of George, Baronet Carteret of Hawnes.

88. *Newburgh.* Charles Livingston (c. 1666–94), Earl of Newburgh, was frequently attacked as a pattern of foppery and folly. See "The Complete Fop" (Dyce MS. 43, II, 618),

> If thou wouldst a fop have drawn to the life,
> A coxcomb made up of nonsense and strife,
> That does in one character comprehend all,
> Draw Newburgh the sot come late to Whitehall,
> And then draw him drunk at her Majesty's ball.

93. *Villiers.* Edward Villiers (1656–1711), knighted in 1676, went to Holland in 1677 as Master of the Horse to Princess Mary. He was frequently in England. See Appendix, Villiers (Jersey).

95. *Sir Courtly Nice.* A foolish fop in John Crowne's farce, *Sir Courtly Nice*, Theatre Royal, May, 1685.

103. *his fine complexion.* This is irony; in earlier days Villiers was called "scabby Ned."

104. *picarre.* From Spanish *picaro*, a rogue or servant.

106. *clyster.* An enema.

111. *Yarburgh.* Henrietta Yarborough, one of Queen Marie's Maids of Honor, was a daughter of Sir Thomas Yarborough, of Snaiths, Yorkshire, by Henrietta Maria (Blague), once Maid of Honor to Queen Catherine. On December 9, 1686, Henrietta was granted £2,000 as a marriage portion (*CTB*, 1685–89, p. 1054) and dismissed. Evidently there had been a scandal. On January 25, 1687, Thomas Maule wrote to

Etherege, "poor Robin Sayers . . . has blown . . . Mrs. Yarburgh into the north, there to lead apes in hell [the fabled consequence of dying an old maid]; for she has left the Court, and her Court portion is paid without any obligation of marrying" (*Letters*, p. 274). Eventually she married Sir Marmaduke Wyvill, Bart. (Mark Noble, *Biographical History*, 1806, I, 360).

121. *her little grace*. Isabella (Bennet), wife of Henry Fitzroy, Duke of Grafton, was the daughter of Henry, Earl of Arlington, and Isabella, a daughter of Lewis of Nassau, Lord Beverwaert and Count of Nassau. The duchess was "counted the finest woman in town" (*Rutland MS*, II, 99).

126. *Dover*. Henry Jermyn, once one of the Duchess of Cleveland's lovers, was created Baron Dover of Dover in May, 1685.

129. *Smithfield Fair*. Bartholomew Fair, held annually in Smithfield, East London, for two weeks beginning August 23. It was famous for its booths, drolls, rope dancers, puppet shows, Merry Andrews, and music and gambling houses.

132. *horns*. The mythical horns of a cuckold.

136. *Georgeish*. I.e., Henry, Duke of Grafton, physically powerful, is as stupid as his younger brother, George, Duke of Northumberland.

148. *Betterton's*. In the autumn of 1682 the King's and the Duke's Companies of players had merged, and the famous actor Thomas Betterton was manager of the new United Company. *Trevor's*. Sir John Trevor was speaker of the House of Commons. The new Commons, which first met on May 19, 1685, was adjourned on July 2, to meet again on November 9, and was adjourned again on November 20. Usually members came to London a week or two before the session.

THE COURT DIVERSION

[*January, 1686*]

In the winter of 1685–86, the priest-ridden Court of gloomy King James II settled down to dullness and mediocrity. King James worked steadily at his plans for Catholicizing England. Unhappy Queen Marie, once a blithe spirit, withdrew to a life of religious devotion. In general libertines were frowned upon and light ladies (even the King's mistress, Katherine Sedley) were discountenanced. Libelers still found subjects for satire—including the King—but they had to search farther and dig deeper into the affairs of the day. There were sinners aplenty, but they were less open in their sinning.

The satire must have been written between December 17, 1685, when Lord Ranelagh got Fox's place as Paymaster General, and February 2, 1686, when the Duke of Grafton killed Jack Talbot in a duel. The copy text, undated, is MS. English Poet. d. 152, f. 74. The satire is also undated in Harleian MS. 7319, p. 385.

> Before you're at one tedious page's end,
> Dear bought will be the scandal that I send;
> But, since you'll venture, my part is to give
> A true, though dull, description how we live.
> We have at Court the players twice a week,   5
> Who never fail to play the King asleep.
> How sweet a sight it is I need not tell;
> For all he does, you know, becomes him well.
> At all these games a friend of yours presides,
> Who strikes, knaps dice, makes bargains, and besides   10
> A thousand gifts too long for me to name,
> And scarce a courtier without the same.
> To add more splendor to the Court, a ball
> Calls twice a month the coxcombs to Whitehall,
> Where deep-mouthed booby blockhead's sure to bring   15

149

His little changeling duchess to the ring
To contract a past pox with uncle King.
There Lady Arran, pocky, pale, and lean,
Makes Clifford start at deceased Lady Jane,
Ogling and begging, till she proves at last   *20*
Sweet Mulgrave modest and Jack Talbot chaste.
   Talbot, a youth of so dilate a name,
To let our country 'scape his brighter fame,
In France he was the Town and Court's salt-bitch;
Each page and footman knew him by his breech;   *25*
Till of both sides and tongue he was so free,
H'was banished Sodom for debauchery.
Then, with a pimp's high character, he comes—
Ambitious youth!—with letters of Vendôme's;
Where Portsmouth's whispers began to be thought   *30*
About himself, when 'twas the news he brought.
Mistaken pleasures are his chase all day,
And scorns all reason in a common way;
A convert now, Papist i'th'late King's life,
Buggers the husband to persuade the wife;   *35*
Thrusts that long prick in good Lord Mulgrave's hand,
Which he refused the King's miss of the land.
Thy mother, Jack, would have thought such a prick
Of better use than every page's trick.
   Devonshire, a coxcomb of more low degree,   *40*
At eight and forty, every day we see,
With stinking breath, high shoulders, French grimace,
In fifty postures, ogling each new face,
Declaring love; and love is a fine jest
Without w'are able to perform the rest.   *45*
   Hewitt, whose figure is the jest of pages,
Tells you of nothing but how many stages
Last night he made; derides and laughs at plays,
Where tittle-tattle fool steals all he says.
   Cholmley, a fool yet of a lower sort.   *50*
Dogging with Radnor is the blockhead's sport,

150

Minding who ogles who, and where
Good father Ranelagh brings his daughter fair
To meet a Treasurer with a squirrel face.
Crofts makes the swap 'twixt whore and Fox's place.   *55*
Fine times indeed would young men have in town,
If naught but money bags could throw a countess down!
    Where Lady Lichfield with her new poxed charms
Holds the religious monarch in her arms;
Where Nancy Villiers makes her weak-back stripling   *60*
    shake,
But long prick makes up for a long weak back;
Where Grafton meets her hare-brained buccaneer,
And gets at home a beating from her dear;
Where Berkeley and her youthful lover knock it;
The jilt is ne'er without a dildo in her pocket;   *65*
Old earl's too short, too small for such a socket.
    Poets are next the scandal of our age,
And D'Urfey is the dullest of the stage.
Parsons and Baber, in the same degree,
Excel in melting elegy.   *70*
Falkland might write, could he be brought to moil,
But the degenerate wretch disdains to toil;
Gives votes as if he took the country's part,
But is, I fear, an atheist in his heart.

---

5. *the players.* If by "players" the poet meant "actors," he was mistaken. Theater records show that during the winter of 1685–86 plays were performed at Whitehall not oftener than once a week (Allardyce Nicoll, *A History of English Drama*, 1952, I, 350). Perhaps he meant "gamesters"; see "At all these games."

9. *a friend.* Perhaps either of two well-known professional gamblers, John Germaine or Thomas Bourchier.

10. *strikes.* Throws dice. *knaps.* Throws dice so that one die will not roll upon the table, a favorite trick of sharpers. *makes bargains.* Probably the sharper engages at very favorable odds to share another player's bet.

15. *booby blockhead.* Henry Fitzroy, Duke of Grafton.

16. *changeling duchess.* Isabella (Bennet), Duchess of Grafton, was a small woman, accused of frequently changing her lovers. It was rumored that King James was in

love with his niece by marriage. In "A Faithful Catalogue of our most Eminent Ninnies. 1687" (Harleian MS. 7319, p. 471) are these lines addressed to "sacred James,"

> Poor Sidley's fall, even her own sex deplore,
> Who with so small temptation turned thy whore.
> But Grafton bravely does revenge her fate,
> And says thou court'st her thirty years too late.

18. *Lady Arran*. Dorothy (Ferrers), second wife of Richard Butler, Earl of Arran. When Arran died in Dublin, on January 26, 1686, his widow showed no signs of grief (*Ellis Correspondence*, I, 35).

19. *Clifford*. Lady Jane (Seymour), wife of Charles Boyle, styled Lord Clifford (1639–94), died on November 23, 1679. Clifford was the son of Richard, Earl of Cork. Presumably the sight of Lady Arran reminded Clifford of his deceased wife.

21. *Mulgrave*. John Sheffield, Earl of Mulgrave, now Lord Chamberlain. The adjectives are ironic. *Talbot*. John Talbot (1665–86), second son of Francis, Earl of Shrewsbury by his wife, notorious Anna Maria (Brudenell). On February 2, 1686, Talbot was killed by the Duke of Grafton in a duel, "having given the Duke of Grafton very unhandsome and provoking language" (*Downshire MS*, I, Pt. 1, 115). It was later remembered that Talbot had danced in a shroud at an entertainment given by the Earl of Devonshire on January 12, 1686, and that he was "foretold that he should be killed by a tall black man before he was twenty-one years old" (*Portland MS*, II, 394). Grafton was tall and "black," i.e., brunet.

29. *Vendôme*. Phillipe de Vendome, Grand Prior of France, visited England in the summer of 1683 and made ardent love to Louise, Duchess of Portsmouth, "the King's miss of the land." In November, 1683, King Charles gave him forty-eight hours to leave England. (According to a *chronique scandaleuse*, *The Life of Francelia*, 1734, King Charles caught the pair in bed together.) Vendôme went to Holland and thence to Paris, where, presumably, he gave his letters to Talbot, who brought them to England c. 1684.

34. *a convert*. Young Talbot was brought up in the Roman Catholic faith. Unreasonably, he was a Catholic in the reign of King Charles, and now, in the reign of Catholic King James, he becomes a convert to Protestantism.

38. *Thy mother*. Anna Maria, Countess of Shrewsbury; see Appendix, Shrewsbury.

40. *Devonshire*. William, Lord Cavendish (1640–1707) inherited as fourth Earl of Devonshire in November, 1684.

46. *Hewitt*. Foppish Sir George Hewitt (1652–89).

47. *stages*. Properly stops on a journey, or the distances between stops on a journey. Perhaps the word is used here as a cant term for orgasms. See "A Lampoon," MS. Don. b. 8, p. 485,

> Anstruther all men she comes near she engages,
> And rides them all freely their several stages,
> But she'll fall at last to footmen and pages,
> Which nobody can deny.

50. *Cholmley*. Hugh, third Viscount Cholmondeley of Kells (1662–1725).

51. *Dogging*. Following secretly, shadowing. *Radnor*. Charles Robartes, Lord Bodmin (1660–1723), inherited as Earl of Radnor on July 17, 1685.

53. *Ranelagh*. Richard Jones, Earl of Ranelagh (1641–1712). His "daughter fair" was Elizabeth, who married John Fitzgerald, eighteenth Earl of Kildare, on June 12, 1684. The poet's account is probably no more than idle gossip.

54. *a Treasurer*. Lawrence Hyde, Earl of Rochester, became Lord Treasurer on February 17, 1685. He was not handsome, but "squirrel face" was slanderous.

56. *Crofts*. Catherine Crofts (1637–86) a famous Court bawd. *Fox*. Charles Fox, son of Sir Stephen Fox, had been Paymaster of the Forces. Along with a number of other officials, Fox was dismissed because he voted in Parliament against the King's demand for funds for a standing army. On December 17, 1685, a warrant was recorded "for the Earl of Ranelagh to be Paymaster of the Forces" (*Downshire MS*, I, Pt. 1, 75; *Rutland MS*, II, 96). The poet's argument is that Ranelagh gave his daughter to Rochester as a bribe.

58. *Lichfield*. Charlotte (Fitzroy), Countess of Lichfield (1664–1718), King James's niece.

60. *Nancy Villiers*. Anne, seventeen-year-old daughter of George, fourth Viscount Grandison. Perhaps her *stripling* was young Edward Rumbold, whom she married in April, 1687.

62. *Grafton*. Isabella (Bennet), Duchess of Grafton. Her *buccaneer* was Charles, Viscount Mordaunt, a swashbuckler who had spent two years at sea as a volunteer in the wars with Algiers.

64. *Berkeley*. Elizabeth (Massingbird), Countess of Berkeley. According to "Advice in a Heroic Epistle to Mr. Fr. Villiers" (see above), her *youthful lover* was John D'Arcy, grandson of the Earl of Holderness and lieutenant-colonel of a troop of horse (Dalton, II, 8).

66. *old earl*. George, Earl of Berkeley (1627–98), was fifty-eight, old by Restoration standards.

68. *D'Urfey*. Thomas D'Urfey (1653–1723), songwriter and playwright.

69. *Parsons*. Sir John Parsons, Bart. (1656–1704). See below, "Letter to Capt. Warcup," "Parsons sets up for a Pindaric spark." *Baber*. John, the poetaster son of Sir John Baber, royal physician.

71. *Falkland*. Anthony Carey, Viscount Falkland (1656–94); see Appendix.

THE TWO TOM LUCYS

[*April, 1686*]

In mid-March, 1686, the young and impulsive George Fitzroy, Duke of Northumberland, privately married Katherine, the beautiful widow of Captain Thomas Lucy of Charlecote. The new duchess had neither dowry nor rank, and her reputation was not beyond reproach. It was reported that her father was a poulterer near Fleet Bridge; in fact, he was a country gentleman, Robert Wheatley of Bracknell, Berks. King James II was chagrined at his nephew's folly, especially because at the time the King was "in treaty" for a wealthy wife for Northumberland, a daughter of the Duke of Newcastle.

Repenting his folly, Northumberland sought the help of his older brother, Henry, Duke of Grafton, who advised divorce. When they learned that divorce was impossible, the two dukes, on March 22, kidnapped the duchess aboard a barge at Chelsea, took her to Gravesend, and there embarked for Flanders. At Ghent they placed the lady, "a Papist," in a nunnery, and on April 3 they returned to England. On May 18, at the King's order, a yacht was sent for the duchess. She was restored to her native land, acknowledged by her husband, and presented at Court.

The author of the satire, written (c. April) before the duchess returned, used the scandalous affair as the opening for his shotgun libel, and played on it in his title. Northumberland, of course, is the second foolish "Tom Lucy." The copy text is Add. MS. 29,497, pp. 41–43. In Dyce MS. 43, II, 662, the satire is undated and called "Ballad. The Widows and Maids." In Harleian MS. 7319, p. 430, the poem, undated, is called "A New Ballad." In Harleian MS. 6914, p. 109, and Stowe MS. 969, f. 61, it is "Song, to the Old Tune of Taking of Snuff is the Mode at Court," a title repeated in *POAS*, 1705, p. 440. For a recent edition see *POAS*, Yale, IV, 67.

> Young widows and maids
> Now hold up your heads,

There are men to be had for all uses.
But who could presage
That ever one age   *5*
Should be furnished with two Tom Lucys?

No reason I see
Our Goodman should be
So very much angry with her son;
For though her estate   *10*
Be encumbered with debt,
She always was free of her person.

Since his grace would prefer
The poulterer's heir
To the great match his uncle had made him,   *15*
T'were just if the King
Took away his blue string,
And sewed on two to lead him.

That the lady was sent
To a convent in Ghent   *20*
Was the counsel of kidnapper Grafton;
And we may foretell
That all will do well,
Since the rough blockhead governs the soft one.

King John, who once passed   *25*
For a coward, at last
Gave evident proof of his courage;
There's many a one
Scorns pistol and gun,
Would not venture on such a marriage.   *30*

Moll Hinton best knows
Why Newburgh keeps close,
But it need never trouble her conscience;

'Tis duty to clap
That impertinent fop,   *35*
For then the town's free of his nonsense.

For one that loves peace
And would live at his ease,
Northampton the best way has chosen;
Leaves courting the fair   *40*
To his uncle's care,
And the combating part to his cousin.

In Shrewsbury we find
A generous mind
So kindly to live with his mother,   *45*
And never try yet
To revenge the sad fate
Of his father and only brother.

Since fighting we see
With some don't agree,   *50*
A witness the much safer post is,
And though Ford, Lord Grey,
In the field ran away,
He can charge in a court of justice.

'Tis pleasant to hear   *55*
An eminent peer
Make whoring a case of conscience,
When 'tis so well known
His favor begun
By pimping to Portsmouth not long since.   *60*

It is plain case
The countess's disgrace
The Catholic cause advances,
And 'tis also as plain

That Tyrconnel's chief aim   65
Was to bring in his daughter Frances.

That church will dispense
With no heretic wench,
But yet we have this for our comfort:
If the priest at the Court   70
Denies us the sport,
The Chancery allows us a Mountfort.

Thrice fortunate boy
Who can give double joy,
And at every turn be ready,   75
With pleasures in store,
Both behind and before,
To content both my lord and my lady.

6. *Lucy.* Thomas Lucy (1641–84), Captain of a Troop of the Household Guards, had inherited Charlecote in 1677. He died of smallpox in November, 1684.

8. *Goodman.* Barbara, Duchess of Cleveland, the Duke of Northumberland's mother and mistress of a famous actor, Cardell Goodman. The "her" in line 10 refers to the new Duchess of Northumberland.

14. *poulterer.* "The Duke of Northumberland hath lately married Captain Lucy's widow, who was a poulterer's daughter" (Luttrell, I, 373).

17. *blue string.* The ribbon of the Order of the Garter.

24. *the rough blockhead.* Grafton. *the soft one.* Northumberland.

20. *a convent.* "Yesterday morning the Dukes of Grafton and Northumberland took her new grace and carried her on board a yacht, which is to convey her to a convent, much against her will, who was seduced into the snare under the pretense of taking the air and being reconciled to the Duke of Grafton" (*Savile Correspondence,* p. 280, March 23, 1686).

25. *King John.* John, Earl of Mulgrave, was called "fearful Mulgrave" in "Satire," 1680 (*POAS,* Yale, II, 207), and directly accused of cowardice at Tangier, whither he had been sent in June, 1680 ("The Female Laureat," *POAS,* 1716, II, 147).

30. *marriage.* On March 15, 1686, Mulgrave married Ursula (Stawell), the wealthy young widow of Edward, Earl of Conway.

31. *Hinton.* Mall Hinton, a famous prostitute; see Appendix.

32. *Newburgh.* Foppish Charles Livingston, Earl of Newburgh (c. 1662–94).

39. *Northampton.* In December, 1685, George Compton, fourth Earl of Northampton (1664–1727), and his uncle, Henry Compton, Bishop of London, went a-wooing Ursula, widowed Lady Conway. There were some mysterious underhand deal-

ings between Lord Mulgrave and the lady's step-father, Mr. Henry Seymour. The result was "such a riddle as everybody both laughs and wonders at." In February, 1686, Northampton sent Seymour a challenge by his young cousin, Hatton Compton, but Seymour refused to fight. On February 17, Hatton Compton and Edward Seymour's second son "grew very warm, and this morning [February 18] fought near Kentish Town; nobody was killed, but both the principals and one of the seconds wounded" (*Rutland MS*, II, 99, 103, 104; *Downshire MS*, I, Pt. 1, 123).

43. *Shrewsbury*. The father of Charles Talbot, Earl of Shrewsbury had died as the result of a duel in 1668 with the Duke of Buckingham. Shrewsbury's brother, John, was slain by the Duke of Grafton in a duel on February 2, 1686.

52. *Ford*. Ford, Lord Grey of Werke, who had a leading part in Monmouth's Rebellion, was accused of.leading his troop of horse in flight at the skirmish of Bridport. After Monmouth's defeat, Grey, to save his own life, appeared as a witness against Lord Brandon Gerard, accused of complicity in the Rye House plot, and against Henry Booth, Lord Delamere, accused as one of Monmouth's accomplices. Gerard was convicted but later pardoned. Delamere was acquitted.

55–60. The stanza, not in the copy text, is from Stowe MS. 969, f. 62v.

56. *an eminent peer*. Marginal gloss in *POAS*, 1705, "Sund--land." Robert Spencer, Earl of Sunderland and Secretary of State, took a prominent part in persuading King James II to dismiss his Protestant mistress, Katherine Sedley (he made "whoring a case of conscience"). In earlier years Sunderland had been a sycophant of Louise, Duchess of Portsmouth, mistress of King Charles II.

62. *the countess*. Katherine Sedley, daughter of Sir Charles Sedley, was created Countess of Dorchester on January 19, 1686. On January 26, it was announced that "Mrs. Sedley, Countess of Dorchester, was turned out of Court on Saturday, though she is with child" (*Portland MS*, III, 393). Apparently she went to Ireland in mid-February and returned to London in September, 1686. King James's priests considered her dangerous to their plans for Catholicizing England.

65. *Tyrconnel*. Colonel Richard Talbot (1630–91), created Earl of Tyrconnel on June 20, 1685, was one of the four Catholic lords who tried to persuade King James to dismiss the Countess of Dorchester. The satirist implies that Tyrconnel's purpose was "to bring in" as a new royal mistress, his stepdaughter, Frances, eldest of the three daughters of his second wife, Frances (Jennings), widowed Lady Hamilton. But Tyrconnel seems to have had a more honorable project. On February 23, 1686, it was rumored that there was a design afoot to marry James Fitzjames, King James's son by Arabella Churchill, to Tyrconnel's stepdaughter, Frances (*Ellis Correspondence*, I, 48). The design failed, and eventually Frances married Henry, eighth Viscount Dillon.

68. *dispense with*. Condone by dispensation, pardon.

72. *Mountfort*. In 1686 William Mountfort, popular actor and playwright, was in the service of Lord Chancellor Jeffreys as an entertainer and mimic. See Reresby, *Memoirs*, p. 408. For his supposed bisexual activities, see "Vindication, Part I," (Harleian MS. 7319, p. 453),

> There's a story of late
> That the Chancellor's mate
> Has been fucked and been fucked by player Mountfort;
>   Which though false, yet's as true,
>   My lord gave him his due,
> For he had a small tilt at his bum for it.

TO CAPT. WARCUP

[*June, 1686*]

By the summer of 1686, King James, dominated by Father Edward Petre, S.J., had managed to get rid of many of his old and trusted servants, replacing them with Roman Catholics, noted more for their religious extremism than their administrative abilities. Many of the Protestant courtiers who had made the libertine Court of King Charles II so brilliantly sinful retired to their country estates. Of course there were still secret sinners about the Court of King James, but the satirists, short on gossip and unwilling to turn to political or religious problems, had to content themselves with old tales and scraps of scandal. "To Capt. Warcup" begins with sneers at a group of little poets and proceeds with splenetic attacks on minor members of a staid, dull Court.

The epistolary address "To Capt. Warcup" is merely a variant on the usual "To Julian." Lenthal Warcup, eldest son of Sir Edward Warcup of Northmore, Oxon., was a captain in the Royal Regiment of Footguards. A lieutenant colonel in 1687, he was killed at the Battle of Steinkirk in 1692. Captain Warcup, a lively gossip, is called the "second" scandal monger of the Town, not in succession to Robert Julian (who was out of prison and back in business) but second in importance to Julian.

The copy text is Folger MS. m.b. 12, f. 98. The satire appears also in Harleian MS. 7319, p. 393; in Dyce MS. 43, II, 493; and printed in *POAS*, 1703, p. 143.

Here take this, Warcup, spread this up and down,
Thou second scandal carrier of the Town;
Thy trapstick legs and foolish, puny face
Look as if nature meant thee for the place.
In this vocation should grow greater far   5
Than e'er should do by stratagems of war.

159

Waste not thy time nor hurt thy tender lungs
In going up and down to sing new songs;
But yet in time of Julian's fate beware,
More secret be or you may lose an ear.   *10*
I'll tell thee now where libels may be had,
Who are the benefactors to the trade.

Cholmley has satire for his province chose,
The only way he'll dare attack his foes,
Not in smooth verse, but rough ill-natured prose;   *15*
Laughing at all, which yet may justice seem,
For long we know the Town has laughed at him.
He long has aimed at love yet ne'er could hit,
And now will put ill nature off for wit.
For all his dressing and his foppish train,   *20*
He and his sister ogle still in vain,
The ladies he, and she the cruel men.

And that we may to all due justice render,
Exeter's songs best move the maidens tender;
Yet Lady Bridget doth so cruel prove,   *25*
Six songs a day can't her compassion move.

Never for women was so bad a time,
Falseness in man is grown a common crime,
Which Frazier doth lament in tender rhyme.

Parsons sets up for a Pindaric spark;   *30*
Pindar himself did never write so dark;
So rough his numbers and such rustic sense,
Sarsfield himself scarce knows what 'tis he means.

Baber hath left the panegyric strain,
And now to ballad making turns his brain,   *35*
At which Will Wharton long has toiled in vain.
From that dull fop what could expected be,
The dullest of that senseless family.

160

Sackville wants leisure to attend his muse,
His time's so taken up with those reviews,   *40*
And Skipwith with his grandam of a spouse.

Old Maggot once did write but now has done,
And wisely sets himself to teach his son
Those rules by which he grows a fop complete,
And when he is as old will be as great.   *45*
His neighbor Fenwick with his antic face
This forty years has studied soft grimace,
In ogling Cartwright his delight has placed,
Yet so unhappy does his passion prove,
She takes it all for dotage, not for love.   *50*

While poor Frank Villiers, out of awful fear
And tender love, has followed many a year;
Yet no reward his constant passion claims
But that he may enjoy her in his dreams.
His sister does him service with her friend,   *55*
But Mistress Nancy to her cost doth find
Her feeble charms are by her friend's outshined;
Yet tries by art her comrade to out-do;
Counterfeit beauty still gives way to true.

And yet the meanest beauty boasts a heart;   *60*
Even Swan can wound with her old rusty dart.
Yarborough her wisdom in young Lowther shows,
One fit to make a patient cuckold chose.
South's conquests are too great to be revealed,
And like her pleasures ought to be concealed.   *65*
Next Isham's wife, now Devonshire is gone,
Can brag of senseless Willoughby alone;
For one another made by nature fit,
Her beauty is as nauseous as his wit.

The rest, too mean to have in verse a place,   *70*
Here, as at Court, shall unregarded pass.

161

But to Kildare all beauty sure must yield,
And parks and plays are with her lovers filled.
The mighty Rochester who rules our state
By presents shows he loves at no small rate.   *75*
Her pimping father got young Fox's place
Not by his merit but his daughter's face.
Devonshire's passion all his actions show;
Because he loves her, Montrath does so too.
Scarsdale and Darcy both her captives prove;   *80*
So hard it is to know her and not love.

Disbanded Manchester, when will he go
And in the Spanish Court his dancing show?
He looks already with his formal air
More like a Spanish don than English peer;   *85*
And that he may a well-bred spark become,
Let him take Denmark in his journey home.

There's one more peer we well could wish away,
His own dear cousin, flattering Captain Grey.

The Powis daughters now fill up the Court;   *90*
Doth often Wales such monstrous things bring forth?
It shows some sense when nauseous creatures hide,
But that to show themselves should be their pride
Tells us their wit is worse than their outside.

Twice jilted Cornbury, now thy fortune try;   *95*
The widow Arran ne'er does man deny.
Shrewsbury and twenty more have found her easy;
This is a quality will surely please thee.

King John, who cheating has his business made,
Hath bought the widow o'er Northampton's head;   *100*
This match in heaven was ne'er made, but hell;
All wish them joined, for none wish either well.

Methinks I see the brandy bowl go round,
The drunken countess wallowing on the ground,
With horns instead of bays the hero crowned.   *105*

9. *Julian.* Captain Robert Julian; see Appendix.

13. *Cholmley.* Hugh, third Viscount Cholmondeley of Kells. According to Swift's note to Burnet, he was "good for nothing as far as ever I knew" (*Complete Peerage*).

21. *his sister.* Elizabeth Cholmondeley, who later married John Egerton of Egerton, Chester.

24. *Exeter.* John Cecil (1648–1700), who succeeded as fifth Earl of Exeter on February 1, 1678, seems to have been a wit and a patron of poets. Dryden lived at his home, Burghley House, Northants., while completing his translation of the seventh *Aeneid* in 1697.

25. *Lady Bridget.* Probably Lady Bridget Noel, daughter of Viscount Campden. On February 6, 1686, Charles Bertie wrote, "I wish we could prevail with Lady Bridget to hearken to any fair proposals of marriages, but I cannot say I find any great inclination in her to change her condition upon equal terms" (*Rutland MS*, II, 105). Much to the annoyance of her family, Chaloner Chute of the Vyne bragged of his chances with her, but she refused all offers.

29. *Frazier.* Dr. Charles Frazier, son of Sir Alexander Frazier, Royal Physician, and a companion of Dorset, Fleetwood Shepherd, etc.

30. *Parsons.* Sir John Parsons, Bart. (c. 1656–1704), was appointed in 1684 captain of a troop in the Earl of Oxford's Regiment (Dalton, II, 330).

33. *Sarsfield.* Patrick Sarsfield, colonel of a troop of horse in 1686; see Appendix.

34. *Baber.* John Baber, son of Sir John Baber, usually appears in any list of minor poets without distinction.

36. *Will Wharton.* Younger brother of Thomas and Henry Wharton. He was fatally wounded December 9, 1687, in a duel with a rival poet, Robert Wolseley; see Appendix, Wharton.

39. *Sackvile.* Colonel Edward Sackvile (called "Song" Sackvile to distinguish him from the Earl of Dorset's brother, also Edward Sackvile, who died October 10, 1679). On May 26, 1686, King James set up a military camp on Hounslow Heath, with frequent reviews. Sackvile became a brigadier on July 3, 1685, and a major general on November 2, 1688. He resigned his commission December 19, 1688, and joined King James in exile (Dalton, I, 274).

41. *Skipwith.* Sir Thomas Skipwith had married Margaret, widow of William Brownlow, some fifteen years his senior. See above, "Satire on both Whigs and Tories."

42. *Old Maggot.* The name, which means "whim," may be taken from a character in Shadwell's *A True Widow*, 1679. "Maggot" is marginally identified in *POAS*, 1703, p. 143, as "Griffin," i.e., Edward Griffin, Treasurer of the Chamber to Charles II and James II. Created December 3, 1688, Baron Griffin of Braybrooke, he followed James to France, returned to England later, and died in the Tower on November 10, 1710, aged about eighty. His son James, Tory M.P. for Brackley, was completely undistinguished.

46. *Fenwick*. Sir John Fenwick (c. 1644–97), later famous as a Jacobite conspirator.

48. *Cartwright*. Grace, wife of George, Baron Carteret of Hawnes, appears in many libels, always "in her chair," i.e., her sedan chair.

51. *Frank Villiers*. "Villain Frank," second son of George, fourth Viscount Grandison.

56. *Mistress Nancy*. Anne Villiers, daughter of George, fourth Viscount Grandison; see Appendix, Villiers (Grandison).

61. *Swan*. Cecilia Swan, daughter of Sir Will Swan of Kent and Maid of Honor to Queen Marie was about twenty-seven.

62. *Yarborough*. Henrietta, daughter of Sir Thomas Yarborough, of Snaiths, York, was a Maid of Honor to Queen Marie. See above, "A Letter to Julian from Tunbridge." The implication is that she was in love with "young Lowther," who would be a very complaisant husband—perhaps William Lowther of Swillington, Yorks. (c. 1665–1729), created a baronet on January 6, 1715.

64. *South*. Elizabeth South was a Maid of Honor to Queen Marie.

66. *Isham's wife*. Sir Justinian Isham (1658–1730) succeeded his brother, Sir Thomas, as baronet on July 26, 1681. On July 16, 1683, he married Elizabeth, daughter of Sir Edmund Turner of Stoke Rochfort, Lincs. *Devonshire*. William, Earl of Devonshire, was "gone" from Court because he had been fined £30,000 for striking Colonel Thomas Colepeper in Whitehall.

67. *Willoughby*. Thomas, eleventh Baron Willoughby (1602–92), inherited in 1680; he was eighty-four in 1686!

70–71. I have reordered the lines; in the copy text lines 70–71 follow line 65.

72. *Kildare*. Elizabeth (1665–1758), daughter of Richard Jones, Earl of Ranelagh, married on June 12, 1684 (as his second wife), John Fitzgerald, Earl of Kildare.

74. *Rochester*. Lawrence Hyde, Earl of Rochester (1641–1711), Lord Treasurer.

76. *her pimping father*. In December, 1685, Richard, Lord Ranelagh, succeeded Charles Fox as Paymaster of the Forces, a lucrative post. The daughter whose virtue was supposedly traded for the appointment was Elizabeth, Lady Kildare. See above, "The Court Diversion."

78. *Devonshire*. William Cavendish, third Earl of Devonshire; see Appendix.

79. *Montrath*. Charles Coote (1655–1709), third Earl of Montrath in Ireland.

80. *Scarsdale*. Robert Leake, Earl of Scarsdale; see Appendix. *Darcy*. John D'Arcy (1659–89), colonel of the Second Troop of Horse Guards, a member of Parliament, and grandson of the Earl of Holderness. In 1685 he was turned out of his commission for voting against the Court (*Rutland MS*, II, 97).

82. *Manchester*. On December 15, 1685, Charles Montague, fourth Earl of Manchester, resigned his commission as captain of a troop of horse (Dalton, II, 15). He went abroad in the summer of 1686 (*Downshire MS*, I, 206). See above, "A Letter to Julian from Tunbridge."

89. *Captain Grey*. Henry Yelverton, Lord Grey of Ruthin (1664–1704), was commissioned captain of a troop of horse on June 20, 1685 (Dalton, II, 15).

90. *The Powis daughters*. William Herbert, Baron Powis (1626–96), a Roman Catholic, had been in the Tower from October 25, 1678, to February 18, 1685. He had five daughters: Mary, Frances, Anne, Lucy, and Winifred. The last three were still unmarried in 1686.

95. *Cornbury*. Edward Hyde (1661–1723), son of Lawrence, Earl of Rochester, by his first wife, Theodosia Capell.

96. *Arran*. Dorothy, whose husband, Richard Butler, Earl of Arran, died January 20, 1686.

97. *Shrewsbury*. Charles Talbot, Earl of Shrewsbury; see Appendix.

99. *King John*. John Sheffield, Earl of Mulgrave, on March 11, 1686, married Ursula, Lady Conway; see above, "The Two Tom Lucys." *Northampton*. George Compton, fourth Earl of Northampton.

165

MADAM LE CROIX

[*June, 1686*]

Madam Le Croix was a famous London fortune-teller. On February 16, 1685, Bridget Noel, daughter of Viscount Campden, wrote, "I have been with Madam Le Croy, the great fortune teller. One thing she told me which pleased me much was that I should never have the smallpox" (*Rutland MS*, II, 104). On April 9, 1686, a warrant was issued for apprehending Madam Le Croix "to answer to [Secretary Sunderland] certain matters of misdemeanor whereof she stands accused"—charges not specified (PRO, State Papers 44/336, p. 423).—Four days later Henry Savile was more specific, "Madam de la Croix, the famous fortune teller, is seized in order to sending her away" (*Savile Correspondence*, p. 284). Nothing more is known about her.

Apparently our anonymous poet took advantage of the notoriety of Le Croix's arrest to use her as the *persona* of his shotgun libel, probably written in June, 1686. The satire is practically a summary of all the scandals publicized in the first six months of 1686. According to the doubtful authority of one Tobias Thomas, the comedian Jo Haynes wrote "Madam Le Croix" (*The Life of the Late Famous Comedian, Jo. Haynes*, 1701, p. 47).

The copy text is Add. MS. 21, 094, f. 73. The poem is dated 1686 in MS. Firth c. 16, p. 215; Dyce MS. 43, II, 643; Harleian MS. 7319, p. 496; and "A Choyce Collection," p. 203. It is undated in Douce MS. 357, f. 131; Add. Ms. 29, 497, p. 23; and Add. MS. 27, 408, f. 63. For printed versions see *POAS*, 1705, p. 350, and *POAS*, 1716, II, 152.

> Of all the plagues mankind possess,
> Defend me from the sorceress
> Who draws from lines her calculations
> Instead of squares for demonstrations,
> Such as Le Croix imposes on   5

The credulous, deluded Town,
Who, though they know themselves but fooled,
Pay double fees for being gulled.
So client jilted of his suit
Loses his cause and pays to boot.   *10*
　　In comes a duke, from mighty place
And merit fallen into disgrace.
She views his hand and bids him joy,
Calls him his Excellence Viceroy!
With this high character the bubble   *15*
Is well content and pays her double,
Nor dreams he's banished with his fleet,
A slave, to Patmos or to Crete,
As Richmond to the northern frost,
Or Clarendon to the Irish coast.   *20*
Blinded with pride, senseless of ruin,
So fools embrace their own undoing.
　　Grafton, with jealousy oppressed,
She adds a crescent to his crest;
No planet mount his brow adorns,   *25*
Saturn and Venus turn to horns.
His grace is but an independent,
While Mordaunt rules in the ascendant.
　　Northumberland does next implore
The stars which Lucy cursed before;   *30*
And 'twas his fate, although he made
A cloister of the nuptial bed,
Whence she returned with double charms,
A vestal, to his faithless arms.
St. Albans' duke, who never sought her,   *35*
By the bargain gets Newcastle's daughter;
So says Le Croix, but juster Fate
Dooms him a match at Billingsgate;
Nor will Newcastle his hopes place
In a base, bastard, pippin race.   *40*

167

For Somerset she takes upon her
To sooth him up with Maids of Honor.
"Courage! Thought wit and beauty fail,
Your grace has charms that will prevail;
No virgin but must yield, a martyr   45
T'an idol of the star and garter."
   These, Mulgrave, were the powerful charms
Brought Conway captive to thy arms;
'Twas not thy figure, wit, nor wealth,
It was the star that made the stealth.   50
Shortly she will repent the action;
Thy hopper-arse will cause the fraction.
   Northampton, happier in his choice,
In virgin wedlock placed his joys.
Wisely he shunned that dire intrigue   55
Doomed to be thy eternal plague;
Of all, for better or for worse,
In missing her he 'scaped the curse.
   Grey's little hand she next does prove
Brimfull of luck and heart of love.   60
"The Fates you need no more importune,
This is the very line of fortune.
My lord, you are most sure of Nancy,
If there be truth in necromancy."
   With Eland how shall we demean us?   65
"Bless us! What's here, the mount of Venus?
The table thwarted too; this shows
You'll die a martyr in the cause.
If you would shun this dismal fate,
Go home, my lord, and salivate;   70
Beware of Merucry and such foes;
Compound with Venus for your nose."
   With love and indignation warm,
Cholmly begins to huff and storm,
"I dress and keep an equipage   75
With any coxcomb of the age.

Pray tell me then a reason why
Each tinker has his trull but I."
"Your hand! You need not be so stout,
My lord, your line of love is out.   *80*
Learn then, if you would have success,
More wit and less affectedness."

   With shoulder belt and gaudy feather,
Ten yards of cravat tied together,
Comes Newburgh, by these lines expressed: *85*
"As you'd a narrow 'scape i'th'west,
This demi-circle here declares
You'll meet worse wounds in Venus's wars;
But have a care how you engage
For a new coach and equipage.   *90*
Lavish and love's a double dart,
That breaks your back and this your heart;
So hounds and huntsmen hare o'erpower,
And what those worry these devour."

   But these are not the only fools;   *95*
Le Croix has choice of female gulls,
Who, puffed with pride, do flock in vain,
Blown up ere they discerned the train.

   Thus Lucy into bondage run,
For a great name to be undone;   *100*
Deluded with the hopes of duchess,
She fell into the lion's clutches.
This was Le Croix's bewitching cheat:
Her sacred thirst of being great.
While Grafton, in her duke less blest,   *105*
Is of her buccaneer possessed,
With Shrewsbury, whose love's intent,
And all the rout that nose the scent.

   With withered hand and wrinkled brow,
Cleveland in rage comes next to know   *110*
What desperate tatterdemallion
Should next vouchsafe to be her stallion;

But by the ruins of her face
She's told her charms have lost their grace,
And since she coupled with a stroller,   *115*
Her next admirer must be Jowler.
   Arran, with counterfeited grace
And muffled veil about her face,
Shows to Le Croix her snowy fist,
Who cries, "Six husbands, at the least!"   *120*
And yet there's none; to that lewd damp
No second love dares light a lamp.
   Kildare, a beauty in her bloom,
In vizor steals to know her doom.
"You Gods! A double line of life!   *125*
Madam, you'll make a thundering wife; ·
Great Jove himself, and all the land,
Besides your lord, at your command;
Devon and Mulgrave, Scarsdale, all
Shall captive to your empire fall,   *130*
'Till for a virtuous wife renowned,
Your wittol lord at last is crowned."
   Next comes young Fox's barren bliss;
She reads her fortune in her phiz.
"Besides, I find it in your hand,   *135*
Madam, you must be better manned;
Your brawny spouse's gross infusion
Suits not your airy constitution;
But if an heir you would not want,
Make meagre Darcy your gallant."   *140*
   Fine Lady Cartwright in her chair,
To know her doom does next appear,
Pursued by Fenwick, Frank, and Grey,
Who sigh all night and dog all day;
As beggars dream of golden heaps,   *145*
Each longs, but none the treasure reaps.
   The next, fine Widow Whitmore, she
Is told of gentle Cornbury;

But the sly wight secured the prey,
And flying bore the nymph away.   *150*
   Miss Nancy shall bring up the rear,
Whose fortune is to have a peer,
It't ben't her harder fate to be
Confounded with variety;
So, tired with change, some Courtly Nice   *155*
She makes the last, but the worst choice.
   Why should I tire your patience out
With Warwick and the wrinkled rout,
Hinton or Howard? I could tell ye
Of thousands besides Hughes and Nelly   *160*
Who daily crowd upon the plains
To find out choice of youthful swains;
But all those charms that did kind warmth infuse,
Worn out of date, have chilled my tired muse.

---

3. *lines.* Lines in the hand as compared to the squares of an astrologer's horoscope.

11. *a duke.* MS marginal note, "Albemarle." Christopher Monck, second Duke of Albemarle, was out of favor and employment in 1685, but in April, 1686, King James appointed him Governor of Jamaica. His commission was finally dated November 26, 1686; he sailed on October 5, 1687.

17. *his fleet.* Perhaps the ships *James and Mary* and the *Henry*, which Albemarle and his fellow adventurers had sent out on March 1, 1686, ostensibly for trade but actually to seek sunken treasure in the West Indies. In spite of the poet's claim that Albemarle was "senseless of ruin," in June, 1687, the ships returned to England laden with salvaged Spanish treasure, and Albemarle was richer by some £90,000 (E. F. Ward, *Christopher Monck, Duke of Albemarle*, 1915, pp. 243–52),

19. *Richmond.* Charles Stuart, fourth Duke of Richmond, died in December, 1672, while Ambassador to Denmark.

20. *Clarendon.* In August, 1685, King James appointed his brother-in-law, Henry Hyde, Earl of Clarendon, as Lord Lieutenant of Ireland, replacing the great Duke of Ormonde.

23. *Grafton.* Henry Fitzroy (1665–90), the sailor Duke of Grafton, seems to have had reason to be jealous of his duchess.

24. *a crescent.* The mythical horns of a cuckold.

25. *planet mount.* Elevations in the hand at the bases of the thumb and fingers, at the edge, and in the palm. The palmist identified these areas thus: at the base of the thumb, the Mount of Venus; first finger, Jove or Jupiter; second finger, Saturn; third finger, Sol or Apollo; fourth finger, Mercury; the edge of the hand, Cynthia, the Moon; the hollow of the palm, Mars.

26. *Saturn and Venus.* The mounts of Saturn, denoting wisdom and sobriety, and Venus, denoting love and passion, together form the horns of a cuckold.

28. *Mordaunt.* Charles, Viscount Mordaunt, often cited as the Duchess of Grafton's lover. *Ascendant.* In horoscopy a dominant position.

29. *Northumberland.* Charles Fitzroy, Duke of Northumberland. For his marriage to widowed Katherine Lucy, see Appendix, Northumberland; and see above, "The Two Tom Lucys."

30. *Lucy.* Captain Thomas Lucy, who died in 1684, was cursed by the stars because he was the first husband of wanton Katherine Lucy.

32. *a cloister.* See above, "The Two Tom Lucys."

35. *St. Albans.* Charles Beauclerc, Duke of St. Albans (son of Nell Gwyn by Charles II), married, on April 13, 1694, Diana, daughter of Aubrey De Vere, Earl of Oxford.

36. *Newcastle.* On March 15, 1686, "The King is much concerned at the Duke of Northumberland's marriage, being himself at that time in treaty with the Duke of Newcastle for his daughter" (*Downshire MS*, I, 138). Margaret, third daughter of the Duke of Newcastle, in 1690 married John Holles, fourth Earl of Clare.

38. *Billingsgate.* A London fish market, famous for its fishwives and their coarse language.

40. *pippin race.* John Evelyn once described the Duke of St. Albans as the base son "of Nelly, the comedian and applewoman's daughter" (*Diary*, October 23, 1684).

41. *Somerset.* Charles Seymour, sixth Duke of Somerset (1662–1748), married Lady Elizabeth Ogle on May 30, 1682.

46. *star and garter.* Emblems of the Order of the Garter, to which both Mulgrave and Somerset belonged.

47. *Mulgrave.* On March 18, 1685, John Sheffield, Earl of Mulgrave, married Ursula (Stawell), widowed Lady Conway.

52. *hopper-arse.* Large in the breech.

53. *Northampton.* George Compton, fourth Earl of Northampton, had been a suitor for the hand of wealthy Lady Conway. On May 9, 1686, he married ("virgin wedlock") Jane, youngest daughter of Sir Stephen Fox. At the end of the Douce MS. 357 version of "Madam Le Croix" is the signature "Northamton," as if he were the author of the satire.

55. *dire intrigue.* See above, "The Two Tom Lucys," note to line 39.

59. *Grey.* Not Ford, Lord Grey of Werke, who was finally freed from the Tower on November 12, 1685, and seems to have spent the next two or three years in the country. But Henry Yelverton, Lord Grey of Ruthin (c. 1664–1704), a little man, was much about the Court during the reign of James II. He was not married until July 11, 1689.

63. *Nancy.* Presumably Lord Grey was considering Anne Villiers, a daughter of George, fourth Viscount Grandison, as a possible wife; if so, Le Croix's prediction went awry.

64. *necromancy.* Black magic. Perhaps the poet was trying to think of chiromancy, palmistry.

65. *Eland.* Henry Savile, Lord Eland (1661–87), son of George, Marquis of Halifax, was a trivial poet and a very debauched rake.

66. *Venus.* A well-developed Mount of Venus, at the base of the thumb, indicated strong sexual passion.

67. *the table.* The line of fortune, or table line, thwarted (i.e., crossed) predicted sickness.

70. *salivate.* The mercury treatment for venereal disease produced an excessive flow of saliva.

72. *compound.* Eland is advised to compromise with, or buy off, the goddess of love in order to save his nose, likely to be eaten away by venereal disease.

74. *Cholmly.* Hugh Cholmondeley (1662–1725), third Viscount Cholmondeley of Kells (Ireland), and in 1706 Earl of Cholmondeley, died unmarried.

80. *line of love.* The heart line has come to an end.

85. *Newburgh.* Charles Livingston, Earl of Newburgh (1662–94). In a skirmish between the King's Guards and Monmouth's rebel forces, "My Lord Newburgh [was] shot into the belly" (*Rutland MS*, II, 89, July 27, 1685).

87. *demi-circle.* A half-moon on the head line indicated sickness, here, of course, venereal disease.

96. *gulls.* Dupes, victims.

99. *Lucy.* Katherine, widow of Captain Thomas Lucy, married the Duke of Northumberland in March, 1686.

102. *the lion.* Northumberland's older brother, the brawny Duke of Grafton, who persuaded Northumberland to carry his wife to Flanders and place her in a nunnery. She returned to England in June, 1686.

105. *Grafton.* Isabella (Bennet), Duchess of Grafton.

106. *buccaneer.* Viscount Mordaunt (see above, line 28, and also "The Court Diversion") had spent two years at sea in the wars with Algiers. For his relations with the Duchess of Grafton, see "Tunbridge Satire," 1688 (Stowe MS. 969, f. 43), in which the poet addresses the Duke of Grafton,

> You did your work by halves, my lord,
> When you kidnapped your brother's wife on board.
>   What made you be so blind
>   To leave your own behind,
> Who with her Mordaunt did your absence moan?
> Alas, poor tender heart, she could not weep alone.

107. *Shrewsbury.* Charles Talbot, Earl of Shrewsbury.

110. *Cleveland.* Barbara, Duchess of Cleveland, formerly chief mistress to King Charles II; see Appendix.

115. *a stroller.* The Duchess of Cleveland's current stallion was Cardell Goodman, a distinguished actor, formerly famous as Alexander the Great in Lee's *The Rival Queens*. In April, 1686, while Cleveland's sons were conducting the new Duchess of Northumberland to Flanders, a gossip wrote, "In the meantime, their gracious mother is brought to bed of a son, which the Town has christened Goodman Cleveland" (*Rutland MS*, II, 107). The son was only the wind of rumor.

116. *Jowler.* A popular name for a dog.

117. *Arran.* Dorothy (Ferrers), was the widow of Richard Butler, Earl of Arran, who died on January 27, 1686.

121. *damp.* An explosive gas, fire-damp, in mines.

123. *Kildare.* On June 12, 1684, Elizabeth Jones (1664–1757), second daughter of Richard, Earl of Ranelagh, married, as his second wife, John Fitzgerald, eighteenth Earl of Kildare (1661–1707).

125. *a double line*. A double life line signified long life and good health.

127. *Great Jove*. King James II.

129. *Devon*. William Cavendish, fourth Earl of Devonshire. *Mulgrave*. John Sheffield, third Earl of Mulgrave. *Scarsdale*. Robert Leke, third Earl of Scarsdale.

132. *wittol*. A cuckold who tamely accepts his fate. In short, Lady Kildare's intrigues will be discovered, and Lord Kildare with be crowned with horns.

133. *Fox*. In 1679, Charles Fox (1659–1713), eldest son of Sir John Fox, married Elizabeth Trollope, daughter of Sir John Trollope. Charles was Paymaster General to the Army from 1682 to 1685. According to Evelyn (*Diary*, June 2, 1681), Charles had grown "very fatt." He died childless. See above, "Satire. 1682" and "Satire to Julian," 1682. Mrs. Fox had been mistress to Lord Lumley and, no doubt, to others. On February 26, 1688, Etherege wrote to Charles, Earl of Middleton (Secretary of State), "Be what you please, you can never be more happy than you were in Mrs. Fox's days" (*Letters*, p. 182).

140. *Darcy*. John D'Arcy (1659–89), a notorious wencher, was a grandson of the Earl of Holderness.

141. *Cartwright*. Grace, wife of George, Baron Carteret of Hawnes.

143. *Fenwick*. Sir John Fenwick. *Frank*. "Villain Frank" Villiers. *Grey*. Henry, Lord Grey of Ruthin. Presumably Grey was successful. See "A Supplement to the Session of the Ladies. 1688" (Harleian MS. 7319, p. 572),

> Young Cartwright so fine all along in a chair
> From Island of Jersey came post to the court,
> But she was sent back with a flea in her ear
> For yielding to little Lord Ruthin the fort.

147. *Whitmore*. Frances, daughter of Sir Thomas Whitmore by Frances Brooke, was the widow of William Whitmore of Hackney. A great fortune, she was much sought after, and Edward Hyde, Lord Cornbury (son of Henry, Earl of Clarendon), was a favored suitor (*Rutland MS*, II, 97). The "sly wight," Sir Richard Middleton of Chirk, Denbigh., married her on April 19, 1686 (*Herbert Correspondence*, p. 320).

151. *Miss Nancy*. Anne Villiers. Probably her "peer" was Henry, Lord Grey of Ruthin; see above, line 63.

155. *some Courtly Nice*. The comic fop in Crowne's *Sir Courtly Nice*, 1685, a very popular comedy.

158. *Warwick*. Anne (Montague), widowed Countess of Warwick.

159. *Hinton*. Mall Hinton. *Howard*. Mall Howard, like Mall Hinton a famous trollop.

160. *Hughes*. Margaret ("Peg") Hughes, an actress, had been mistress to Prince Rupert, who died in 1682. By the Prince she had a daughter, Ruperta. Peg died October 1, 1719. *Nelly*. Nell Gwyn.

THE LOVERS' SESSION
IN IMITATION OF SIR JOHN SUCKLING'S
"SESSION OF POETS"

[June, 1687]

"A Session of the Poets," by Sir John Suckling (1609–42), presented Apollo presiding over a gathering of verse writers, each claiming the laurel as his reward for wit. The winner is not a poet but an alderman, Apollo declaring that it is "the best sign/ Of good store of wit to have good store of coin."

"The Lovers' Session," with Venus presiding over a "High Commission Court," follows its famous model in form, but it is nearly three times as long. The poet represents Venus offering as a prize, not the laurel "that had been so long reserved," but a beautiful young prostitute, Mrs. Luck, "long held in reserve." She is to go to the contender who does "least deserve her"—that is, to the man who can prove that he has the smallest store of wit. The satirist gathers together a flock of well-known lackwits and amuses himself at their expense, only obliquely glancing at the social and political problems of the day.

Evidence in stanzas 45–47, dealing with events at Magdalen College, Oxford, suggests that the satire was written in June, 1687. The copy text, Add. MS. 34, 362, p. 154, is dated 1687. The satire is dated 1687 also in Firth MS. c. 25, p. 277; 1687/8 in Harleian MS. 7317, p. 136; 1688 in "A Choyce Collection," p. 256; and undated in Douce MS. 357, f.118; Add. MS. 29, 497, f. 115; and it is badly printed in *POAS*, 1716, II, 156.

> A session of lovers was held t'other day,
> And Venus in person was present they say;
> The best in Christendom, long held in reserve,
> Was now to be his who did least deserve.

175

2.

Therefore the fools of all parties came thither;   *5*
'Twas strange to see how the owls flocked together.
There were fops of breeding and tonies of birth,
Damned oafs of all kinds this fat island brings forth.

3.

Gentle fools of the flute and fools of the pen,
Virtuosos twice married, turned bullies again,   *10*
Dancing fools a vast crowd, and fools learned in arts,
Fops finished in France, with good natural parts.

4.

Familiar dear hearts, who kiss all they salute,
And out of mere dullness with no man dispute,
Who think themselves welcome wherever they come,   *15*
And call all they know, Harry, Jack, Will, and Tom.

5.

Sour fanatics, Christ's wealthy, ill-favored breed,
With strong carnal itches and spiritual pride;
Popish priests in the garb of a lewd lay brother,
Still whoring in couples to absolve one another.   *20*

6.

Time-servers whose hopes all employments devour,
Drunken brutes in the badges of absolute power,
Cits apeing Court fops in debauchery and dress,
And proud, ignorant statesmen, hard of access.

176

7.

Dull blockheads in cassocks, law knaves dyed in   *25*
    grain,
Physicians in cuerpo and clowns in campaign,
Like bees they came swarming at Venus's call;
There was fop of Fop Corner and fop of Fop Hall.

8.

Song Sackvile with all the new beaus at his back,
Lewd rakehelly Spencer by finical Pack,   *30*
Warcup near Newburgh, for they kept no order,
Montrath and Frank Villiers a little farther.

9.

Harry Wharton fresh reeking from Norfolk's lewd Moll,
Sham plot-maker Lumley and Colchester Vol,
Northumberland wrapped in his mother's loved   *35*
    smock,
And Darcy kept lean with old Guy's young hock.

10.

Harsh favored Scarborough with Scarsdale the stinking,
And Bridges created a wit for his drinking,
Soft Whitaker, fop Gerards—both the brothers—
Fop Hewitt, fop Baber, and divers others.   *40*

11.

Devonshire, who all his mistaken life long
Has delighted in show, public meetings, and throng,

177

And at fifty against all reason and rule
Seems resolved to persist in playing the fool,

12.

Ere this strange High Commission Court was well sat,   *45*
Came and knocked, with a lover's concern, at the gate,
And cozening the door keeper with his fop mien,
Without any ticket had like t'have got in.

13.

But Venus, who knew him much better than they,
With a frown like dead Lady Betty's they say,   *50*
Forbid his admittance and told him in short,
'Twas an old fundamental rule of the Court,

14.

Though some the best stored never any would use,
But lived as if Frampton their business did choose,
Though others dressed high and half stared out   *55*
     their eyes,
Not one who had sense must pretend to the prize.

15.

And though his French breeding still floated a-top,
And had taudered his outside over with fop;
Yet plainly appeared to all the world's wonder
The man of true wit and worth that lay under.   *60*

16.

When Mordaunt heard this he leaped up from the throng,
And in whimsical railing full three hours long,

Which gross want of judgment, for Bedlam near fit,
He daily mistakes for abounding in wit,

17.

He excused his intruding and breaking their rules,   *65*
Protesting he did not know they were fools,
But took every member there by his mien
For as hopeful a wit as his pupil Gwin.

18.

This said, he would fain have slipped into the crowd,
But Venus recalled him and told him aloud   *70*
None there to a place had a better pretense,
For just talking not much was the mark of good sense.

19.

That his rambling vein, which for holding out well,
The ablest fanatics' new lights did excel,
Though no man could for wit or for reason approve,   *75*
Might pass with young women for passion or love.

20.

But she bid him beware when his throes did begin,
By his noise not to call the neighborhood in;
For his friends' expectation too oft had been bit
By the loud but false crying out of his wit.   *80*

21.

And therefore,
For a deal of vain love the fair sex did owe him,
As well as for the good of all who should know him,

179

She prayed that the Muses' Lucina would deign
To deliver him of his no jests without pain.   *85*

22.

While Mordaunt's perfections she thus did display,
She perceived little Falkland sneaking away,
And vowed she admired how that frivolous chit
Ever came to pass on the Town for a wit.

23.

His grandfather, honored by all, 'tis confessed,   *90*
Was with wisdom and riches like Solomon blessed,
But he left him nothing, and it was his hard fate
To inherit no more of his wit than estate.

24.

A mimic he is, though a bad one at best,
Still plagued with an impotent itch to a jest;   *95*
In impertinent action he spared no expense;
He had all the ingredients of wit but the sense.

25.

His face oft of laugh and of humor looks full,
But his talk is impertinent, empty and dull,
But if such low buffooning can merit our praise,   *100*
Frank Newport and Jevon and Haynes must have bays.

26.

Or if French memoirs read from Broadstreet to Bow
Can make a man wise, then Falkland is so,
And for full confirmation of all she did say,

She produced his damned prologue to Otway's best   *105*
   play.

27.

Some replied what her majesty said was most true,
Yet to give this vain, ignorant devil his due,
Though he made good judges but indifferent sport,
He was the best fop of a statesman at Court.

28.

But Dorrington now started up in great wrath,   *110*
"What, not Falkland a wit?" "No, sir, by my troth,
Of which for the present clearer proof there needs none
Than his taking your coxcombly worship for one."

29.

The sect of songsters here stirred up sedition,
And in shoals preferred a tumultuous petition,   *115*
Beseeching the court not to think 'em too wise
To raffle their time and estate for the prize,
Alleging,

30.

They used the Muses but as bawds do intrigues,
Caring for 'em no more than for Cromwell or Meggs,   *120*
And that but for their frantic, amorous fits,
They had ne'er took upon 'em the business of wits.

31.

Humbly hoping that sense would not pass for a crime
That was flattened to panegyrical rhyme,

181

And offering good proof from maids, widows, and   *125*
    wives,
Of the inoffensive dullness of their lives,

32.

Proposing at last if the sex were in fears,
They could e'en use their fames as bad as their ears,
That rather than the hopes of their favors they'd quit,
They'd lay by their impudent title to wit.   *130*

33.

But Venus, who all their adventures had learned,
With a gracious smile bid 'em not be concerned,
For that little they had, so void of all charm,
As it did ['em] no good, so 'twould do 'em no harm.

34.

Young Griffin, apparent son of the old,   *135*
In whose *bel air* his booby father is told,
Just image of the pride with which he swells,
And in whom the fullness of his folly dwells,

35.

Not doubting success, first of any did rise
And in arrogant terms first demanded the prize;   *140*
But when told by the court, which his carriage did blame,
He a reason must give for his confident claim,

36.

He pertly replied that truth, reason, and wit
Were three things never asked of his family yet;

182

And though he loved whoring because 'twas a vice,   *145*
He ne'er should be able to pay such a price.

37.

Newburgh was the next stood up to his trial,
Not dreaming that face could e'er meet with denial,
That face which so oft in the circle was praised,
And dissentions among the Queen's virgins had   *150*
   raised.

38.

But the Jewess who still of his purse stood in need,
Had privately ordered the bench to take heed
Not to judge by outsides howe'er likely and fair,
For though stiff in the back he was limber elsewhere.

39.

Harry Henningham thought himself sure of a grant,   *155*
But "Oh, foolish!" cries out villain Frank, "he's all cant.
His mistresses know not—so odd 'tis expressed—
Whether he means to make love or a jest."

40.

"He puts on so many several faces,
Is so full of his frank, familiar grimaces,   *160*
They cannot but think he is acting a part,
And his passion some speech he has gotten by heart."

41.

Besides Lady Bellamont had let the court know
That his person was good for just nothing but show,

183

That his slim, fine Barbary back was too long,   *165*
His stomach too weak, and his hectic too strong.

42.

When Kildare's name was called, all thought he would speed,
And sure he was fool enough to succeed;
But new Rochester straight—Oh, how unlike the first!—
Into terms of a Treasurer's insolence burst.   *170*

43.

And as Venus was going his suit to allow,
On the faith of a cast politician did vow
That of all men living he needed it least,
For his wife's, he knew well, was as good as the best.

44.

Huntington, that his wheaking whey visage might pass,   *175*
Pulled out the best thing that belonged to an ass,
But in Love's court, though one might use such a tool,
They abhorred an inconstant, weathercock fool.

45.

Villain Frank, well informed by a small pocket glass
Of his damned, disagreeable, vermin-like face,   *180*
And knowing what juster pretentions would be,
Brought the bench a mandamus subscribed S.P.

46.

The court on this dangerous practise reflecting,
Cried out, "We'll maintain our old way of electing.

184

Cunts still have been free, nor can any confine 'em,   *185*
Or bring to the beck of their *jus divinum*."

47,

Resolving however to show some respect
To the state whose commands they'd just cause to reject,
Like Maudlins they proved to th'assistants' great joy
Sir Courtly unfit for the courted employ.   *190*

48.

To his shame and confusion, his friends swore point blank
To nun was so spotless a virgin as Frank,
And all, that it's unjust the fair sexes' pride
Should run any risk with a fuckster untried.

49.

The court, though against the strict rule of the laws,   *195*
Declared on that issue they'd put the whole cause;
Had he e'er *rem in re* he should now have the best,
But his guilty silence the scandal confessed.

50.

Here the Exchequer clerks, ere they let him retire,
Told the court 'twas not virtue but want of desire,   *200*
And though he was unable, they'd very good proof
Sister Nancy would for the whole name do enough.

51.

Montrath was in foppery conceived another
Of Whitehall's true breed, Sir Nice's twin brother;

None could tell (so like all their follies do seem)   *205*
Whether he acted Mountfort or Mountfort him.

52.

But all cried at the sound of that Irish name,
His birth was forever a bar to his claim;
No Teague to his love could his blockishness shape;
They had only the gift of murder and rape.   *210*

53.

Harry Lumley, some thought, for an elder beau
By the help of his dress made a pretty good show;
His back too was praised since he first found the trick
To make rammish Williams content with one prick.

54.

But he had a blemish of his blighted look shown,   *215*
Which in beauteous Adonis was never yet known;
The pox that was given him by his own wife
Was likely to last him as long as his life.

55.

When Montague appeared the court gave him a touch
For affecting the wit and the bully so much;   *220*
For the one neither nature had framed him nor art,
And the other was ne'er thought a gentleman's part.

56.

He had faults too, which lost him so much with the fair
As neither his face nor his youth could repair;

They found the raw Templar with half sense accursed,   *225*
Too presuming at last and too bashful at first.

57.

Their eyes were more kindly on Constable cast,
For judging so ill and for prattling so fast;
He slightly skims o'er all that comes in his way,
With as hasty and shallow a fashion as they.   *230*

58.

But though his light humor most women's did hit,
His parts have too near a resemblance of wit;
The court too declared they would first be assured
Whether yet the thrust in his groin was well cured.

59.

Little Rowley was missed, for the Whigs who did know   *235*
His wit nowhere else but in Dutchland would go,
Had there sent him lieger with full reputation
To make jests on the Court for the good of the nation.

60.

But one of his friends swore he'd leave the queen's cause
And turn rebel to love's irresistable laws   *240*
If in all her wide empire she ever did see
A coxcomb so fit for a cully as he.

61.

But politics employed all his time, and 'twas said
Our pert Oxford scholar would ne'er be well bred

Nor brought, so vain is th'unformable elf,   *245*
To admire or mind anything else but himself.

62.

Here the bench in Wem language their anger expressed,
And told his Whig friends they should bid him at least
Get so much sense in his maggoty pate
To use his wife well till he had her estate.   *250*

63.

Feversham, in his Sedgemoor garter and glory,
Proud as the Treasurer and pettish as Lory,
Forgetting how oft he had wrong took his aim,
With a French assurance next put in his claim.

64.

But fifty had brought a defeat of that sort   *255*
As ne'er found forgiveness in Venus's court;
He was never in health, as himself did oft own,
But "ven he did let dat business alone."

65.

Mordaunt would be thought t'have already the best,
But lets his wife's covetous cunt be at rest;   *260*
In vain his invention is still on the tenters,
Don Quixote ne'er went on more luckless adventures.

66.

The damned tedious lies he tells in his own praise,
That supreme adoration he to himself pays,

That contempt of his friends and that unsettled head,   *265*
An aversion in the most forward has bred.

67.

Had it his babbling tongue, St. James's large square
Could punctually tell forth the when and the where,
In the midst of all his vain towering hopes,
He was beaten with his own ladder of ropes.   *270*

68.

Sir James Hayes here his fluent flattery displayed
To the fair, and a thousand fair promises made,
If Falkland might pass a night with her in bed;
But Dapperwit had a trick worth two on't, he said.

69.

The sodomite's hole so his fancy did sway,   *275*
He would fain have used his own wife the wrong way;
But the slattern was restive and vowed she would ne'er
Give any man joy who grudged her a share.

70.

Northumberland now to his trial stood forth,
And pleaded the preference due to his birth.   *280*
"No fool," he said, "sure, howe'er eminent, would
Presume to compare with a fool of the blood."

71.

Appealing besides to his scandalous marriage,
His beautiful face and his dull stupid carriage,

To a soul without sense of true honor or wit,   *285*
If e'er man was formed for a woman so fit.

72.

But his prince-like project to kidnap his wife,
And a lady so free to make pris'ner for life,
Was tyranny to which the sex ne'er would submit,
And an ill-natured fool they liked worse than a wit.   *290*

73.

Grafton, backed by his officers, made an effort
To have the new Venus seen naked in court,
Urging whate'er fame in her favor had spoke,
'Twas unfit men should buy a pig in a poke.

74.

But had she appeared, Duncomb swore by his life   *295*
He had used her as once he did Eland's fair wife.
No sooner was his rude request disallowed,
But on the whole bench he looked big and talked loud.

75.

What his huff speech did mean they were all in suspense;
Some said it was tarpaulin language and sense,   *300*
But this was every tittle the court understood:
It began with G--dam and closed with G--dsblood.

76.

An old ugly lawyer at last did appear,
And brought in black boxes six thousand a year;

190

At which all the assembly murmured, contending   *305*
He had long since passed the age of pretending.

77.

But Venus, reproving 'em, bid him come nigher,
And when he was mounted a little higher,
She gently declared that wealth and estate
Was to catch womankind the infallible bait.   *310*

78.

The powerful temptation none e'er could oppose;
It covers all faults and all virtue bestows;
'Tis a lure which the highest-flown jilts can command,
Makes 'em stoop and brings the wild haggard to hand.

79.

Fifteen it can draw to the arms of three score,   *315*
Procure Apsley a wife and Clifford a whore;
It still carries with it (such philters are in it)
The canonical hour and the critical minute.

80.

'Twas this spell the fair Montague's eyes so put out
She could see neither Suffolk's age nor his gout,   *320*
And in spite of a humor yet worse than his face,
Brought long averse Newport to Herbert's embrace.

81.

This is the charm which yet never did fail
O'er beauty, youth, merit, and wit to prevail;

191

And without a syllable more or less said,   325
To young Luck she put the old fumbler to bed.

82.

Much muttering there was, and some spared not the queen;
In every man's face a displeasure was seen;
Each thought himself by the sentence ill used,
And the partial blindness of Fortune accused,   330

83.

But all cleared up at last; not a fop that was there
But hoped in his turn with the lawyer to share,
And that since for twenty good summers at least
He had left being a man, she would make him a beast.

---

3. *the best.* The best prostitute, in this case Mistress Luck or Luke.

7. *fops.* Foolish dandies. *tonies.* Simpletons, ninnies.

19. *Popish priests.* In his *True Narrative . . . Relating to the Horrid Popish Plot,* 1679, Miles Prance told the story of a French priest who lay with a woman and afterward said Mass. Taxed with his sin, he declared that he had had absolution, that "another French priest and he both lay with her successively at that time, and that they mutually gave each other absolution, which is a notable religious way of whoring."

25. *in cassocks.* Clergymen. *in grain.* Thorough-going knaves.

26. *in cuerpo.* Without cloaks. *campaign.* Country bumpkins in military cloaks.

28. *Fop Corner.* A section of a theatre pit where the fops congregated. *Fop Hall.* Whitehall?

29–32. Compare with Suckling:

> There was Selden, and he sate hard by the chair;
> Wenman not far off, which was very fair;
> Sandys with Townshend, for they kept no order;
> Digby and Shillingsworth a little further.

29. *Song Sackville.* Colonel Edward Sackville had succeeded Sir Palmes Fairborne as Governor of Tangier in 1681. He became a brigadier on July 8, 1685.

30. *Spencer.* Robert, Lord Spencer, eldest son of the Earl of Sunderland, was a noted rake. He died in France on September 5, 1688, of a surfeit of brandy (*Ellis*

Correspondence, II, 165). *Pack*. Symond Pack, a musician and a captain in Princess Anne's Regiment of Foot (Dalton, II, 138), was called "finical" because he was overly fastidious in his choice of whores. On March 13, 1687, Etherege wrote from Ratisbon, "I find a convenience now and then in this Country, but can boast as little success in the pursuit of what I have loved as Captain Pack himself" (*Letters*, p. 101).

31. *Warcup*. Lenthal Warcup, lieutenant-colonel in Grafton's Royal Regiment of Footguards; he was killed at Steinkirk in 1692 (Dalton, I, 220, 315, 324). *Newburgh*. Charles Livingston, Earl of Newburgh (c. 1662–94).

32. *Montrath*. Charles Coote (c. 1655–1709), inherited as third Earl of Mountrath (Ireland) in 1672. *Frank Villiers*. "Villain Frank," see Appendix, Villiers (Grandison).

33. *Wharton*. Colonel Henry Wharton, third son of Philip, Lord Wharton. *lewd Moll*. Possibly the Duke of Norfolk's errant wife, Mary; however, her liaison with the Dutch gambler, John Germaine, was now well established, and she seems to have been true to him. Probably "Moll" is Mall Howard, the duke's cousin, who is frequently referred to as Harry Wharton's mistress. Perhaps there had been a temporary separation. On January 25, 1687, Thomas Maule wrote to Etherege, "he [Harry Wharton] has forsaken Mrs. Mary [Howard] and makes violent love to Mrs. Drumar" (*Letters*, p. 275).

34. *Lumley*. Richard, Viscount Lumley (1650–1721). It is not clear why he is called a "Sham plotmaker." The author of "Scandal Satired," c. 1682 (Harleian MS. 6913, p. 209) asserts that Lumley, "for low dissembling and by bribing high" was "preferred at last and raised to be a spy." Richard was created an English baron on May 21, 1681. *Vol*. Otherwise Vowell or Fowell. The only prominent gentleman by that name in 1687 was Sir John Fowell, Bart. (1665–92), of Fowellscombe, Devon., a Whig who on November 21, 1688, was mentioned as "newly gone to the Pr[ince] of O[range]" (*Hatton Correspondence*, II, 110). Why he was called "Colchester's Vol" is not clear, unless he was a crony of Richard Savage (c. 1660–1712), who was called Lord Colchester until he inherited as fourth Earl Rivers in 1694.

35. *Northumberland*. George Fitzroy (1665–1712), third son of Barbara, Duchess of Cleveland, by Charles II.

36. *Darcy*. Colonel John D'Arcy (1659–89), eldest son of Conyers, Lord D'Arcy. *Guy*. Henry Guy (1631–1711) at this time was Secretary to the Treasury Commission.

37. *Scarborough*. Charles, son of the royal physician, Sir Charles Scarborough, was King James's envoy to Portugal in 1686. *Scarsdale*. Robert Leke, Earl of Scarsdale (1654–1707).

38. *Bridges*. George Rodney Bridges married Anna-Maria, the widowed Countess of Shrewsbury, in 1677, and became a Groom of the Bedchamber. For his drinking, see, on January 7, 1684, the petition of "Crispe Granger, Brewer, against George Bridges, Esq., one and sixty pounds for ale and beer" (PRO, Lord Chamberlain 5/191, p. 120).

39. *Whitaker*. Charles Whitaker, a very minor wit, who had a sinecure as "Foreign Apposer," paying £40 a year. *Fop Gerards*. Charles, Lord Brandon (1659–1701), inherited as second Earl of Macclesfield January 7, 1694. His younger brother, Fitton Gerard (c. 1665–1702), became third Earl of Macclesfield on November 5, 1701.

40. *Hewitt*. Sir George Hewitt, a famous fop. *Baber*. John Baber, poetaster.

41. *Devonshire*. William Cavendish, Earl of Devonshire (1640–1707) was forty-seven.

45. *Court.* A hit at King James, who, on July 15, 1686, appointed an Ecclesiastical Commission, or "Court of High Commission," which was given jurisdiction in cases touching spiritual or ecclesiastical matters.

47. *cozening.* Deceiving.

50. *Lady Betty.* For Devonshire's relations with Lady Betty Felton, see above, "Ballad on Betty Felton," 1680.

53. *best stored.* Those equipped with good sense, but who never used it and left everything to chance, as if they were guided by a famous gambler, Tregonwell Frampton.

58. *taudered.* Decked in tawdry garments.

61. *Mordaunt.* Charles, Viscount Mordaunt (1658–1735).

67. *Gwin.* Francis Gwin, an Irishman, in 1679 became Clerk of the Privy Council; apparently he was Mordaunt's protégé.

74. *fanatics' new lights.* Mordaunt liked "to preach in Coffee Houses and public places." See Appendix.

87. *Falkland.* Anthony Carey, Viscount Falkland (1656–94), Treasurer of the Navy; see Appendix.

90. *grandfather.* Lucius Carey, second Viscount Falkland (1610–43), a distinguished scholar, soldier, and poet.

101. *Frank Newport.* "Bold Frank," second son of Francis, Viscount Newport. *Jevon and Haynes.* Thomas Jevon and Joseph Haynes, two popular comedians.

105. *prologue.* To Otway's *The Soldier's Fortune*, March, 1680.

110. *Dorrington.* James Doddington, or Dorrington, a cornet in Plymouth's Regiment of Horse, December 12, 1686. He was slain at the Battle of the Boyne.

120. *Cromwell or Meggs.* Jenny Cromwell and Mary Meggs, two famous bawds. Mary Meggs ("Orange Moll") was fruitwoman at the Theatre Royal until at least November 10, 1682 (PRO, Lord Chamberlain 5/191, p.102). In 1687 she was said to have become a Roman Catholic ("The Converts," *POAS*, Yale, IV, 157).

135. *Young Griffin.* James Griffin (1667–1715), M.P. for Brackly 1685–87, was the son of Edward Griffin, Treasurer of The Chamber to Charles II and James II. On December 3, 1688, King James created Edward Baron Griffin of Braybrooke, a title which his son never assumed. If the son was like the father, he was a very unpleasant person. In "A Supplement to the Late Heroic Poem," c. 1681 (Harleian MS. 6913, p. 227), Edward is called "Clown Griffin,"

> Griffin, with whom even Killigrew durst fight,
> Whose horses lose their fellow servants' right,
> Griffin, the falsest that e'er friend deceived,
> Yet by the best of friends too well believed.

147. *Newburgh.* Charles Livingston, Earl of Newburgh (c. 1662–94), was honored by a single short libel, "The Complete Fop," 1685 (Dyce MS. 43, II, 618). The *Jewess*, evidently his mistress, is not identified.

155. *Henningham.* Henry Heveningham, lieutenant of the Band of Pensioners.

156. *villain Frank.* Francis Villiers; see Appendix, Villiers (Grandison).

163. *Lady Bellamont.* Frances (born 1642, daughter of William, sixth Lord Willoughby of Parham, married (1) Sir John Harper of Swarkeston, Derby; (2) Charles-

Henry Kirkhoven, Earl Bellamont (Ireland); and (3) on July 3, 1684, Henry Hevening-ham. A countess who married a commoner retained her title.

166. *hectic.* Fever.

167. *Kildare.* John Fitzgerald, Earl of Kildare (1661–1707), married his second wife, on June 2, 1684, Elizabeth, a daughter of Richard Jones, Earl of Ranelagh. According to the gossips, she became mistress to Lawrence Hyde, Earl of Rochester.

169. *Rochester.* Hyde, Earl of Rochester (who suffered by comparison with the poet John Wilmot, second Earl of Rochester) was Lord Treasurer from 1685 to January 4, 1687, when he was "cast," i.e., dismissed by King James.

175. *Huntington.* Theophilus Hastings, seventh Earl of Huntington (1650–1701), was famed as the possessor of an overlarge penis. In "The Quarrel between Frank and Nan," 1681 (*POAS*, Yale, II, 235) he is described as

> . . . Huntington with his long tool,
> Not as the mark of man but fool.

Originally a Whig, in 1681 Huntington recanted and was accepted again at Court. *wheaking whey visage.* Whining pale face.

179. *villain Frank.* Francis Villiers was appointed one of the four Tellers of the Exchequer in February, 1685 (*CTB*, 1681–85, p. 1524).

182. *a mandamus.* A mandamus was an order issued in the King's name, usually under the Great Seal. *S.P.* The initials may stand for Lord Sunderland, who usually signed the King's orders with "Sunderland P.", i.e., President of the Council.

186. *jus divinum.* Divine right; a hit at King James II.

189. *Maudlins.* Magdalens. On April 13, 1687, King James ordered the fellows of Magdalen College, Oxford, to elect as their new president a young convert to Catholicism, Anthony Farmer, noted for his debauchery He had never been a fellow of the college, and as a Catholic he was disqualified by law. On April 15, refusing the King's command, the fellows elected a qualified man, John Hough. In June the Ecclesiastical Commission declared Hough's election invalid, but said no more about Farmer. This seems to be where matters stood when the present satire was written. In August James ordered the fellows to elect Samuel Parker. Bishop of Oxford and a crypto-Catholic. They refused, saying that they had made their election. In September James installed Parker, deprived the fellows of their appointments, and replaced them with Roman Catholics (David Ogg, *England in the Reigns of James II and William III*, 1955, pp. 183–85). *assistants.* The Exchequer clerks.

190. *Sir Courtly.* Sir Courtly Nice, the fool in John Crowne's *Sir Courtly Nice*, 1685.

197. *rem in re.* Coition. This is surely an exaggeration, yet on August 23, 1688, Etherege wrote of the ladies of Ratisbon, where he was stationed, "the Devill's in't, marriage is so much their buisness that they cannot satisfy a Lover who has desires more fervent than Franck Villars" (*Letters*, p. 232).

202. *Sister Nancy.* On April 13, 1687, Anne Villiers and Edward Rumbolt took out a license to marry; see Villiers (Grandison).

204. *Sir Nice.* Sir Courtly Nice.

206. *Mountfort.* William Mountfort, a popular actor, had created and continued to play the character of Sir Courtly Nice.

209. *Teague.* A common pejorative name for an Irishman.

211. *Lumley*. Henry Lumley, younger brother of Richard, Viscount Lumley; see Appendix.

214. *rammish Williams*. Lascivious, lustful Susannah Williams, a widow; see Appendix, Skipwith.

215. *a blemish*. See above, "wry-mouthed Lumley," in "A Satire," c. 1680 (Add. MS. 34, 362, p. 131).

219. *Montagu*. Charles Montagu (1661–1713), fourth son of George Montagu (a younger son of Henry, first Earl of Manchester). In July, 1687, Montagu joined with Matthew Prior in writing a famous parody, *The Hind and the Panther Transversed* (see *POAS*, Yale, IV, 116). In 1688 Montagu was successful "with the fair," marrying (c. February) Anne, Dowager Countess of Manchester (Luttrell, I, 432). In the next reign, Montagu, as a Lord of the Treasury, was largely responsible for the founding of the Bank of England and the National Debt. Arrogant, vain, and ambitious, Montagu was created Earl of Halifax on October 19, 1714.

227. *Constable*. William Constable (1654–1719), younger brother of Robert, third Viscount Dunbar.

235. *Little Rowley*. I have found no courtier named Rowley. Perhaps the poet meant to suggest that his victim was a libertine, a diminutive version of "Old Rowley," King Charles II, and, like that king in his younger days, was now living in exile on the continent. Of the many exiled Whigs in Holland ("Dutchland") at this time, only one fits most of the circumstances: Dr. Gilbert Burnet, a Whig clergyman (1643–1715), often accused of lechery. It is possible, too, that the poet may have had in mind's Dryden's *The Hind and the Panther*, published in May, 1687. In Part II, lines 2547 to 2630, "the noble Buzzard"—Burnet—is crowned king of the Doves—the intransigent Anglican clergy. Burnet is described as

> A portly prince and goodly to the sight,
> He seemed a son of Anach for his height,
> Like those whom stature did to crowns prefer;
> Black-browed and bluff, like Homer's Jupiter,
> Broad-backed and brawny, built for love's delight,
> A prophet formed to make a female proselyte.

Dr. Burnet (not an "Oxford scholar") had fled from England in May, 1685, and, after a year of travel, had arrived at The Hague, where he became an unofficial "lieger," or resident envoy, from the English Whigs to the Court of William of Orange. Certainly "politics employed all his time," and his written blasts against Catholicism so enraged King James that he had Burnet outlawed in Scotland for treason, and tried to get him sent back to England for execution. As for his wife, in March, 1687, Burnet married (as his second wife) one Mary Scott, a lady who was heiress to a considerable fortune (*Portland MS*, III, 398).

247. *Wem language*. Intemperate, like the wild speech of George Jeffreys (1645–89), lawyer and judge who was created Baron Jeffreys of Wem in 1685.

251. *Feversham*. Lewis de Duras, Marquis de Blanquefort and Earl of Feversham (1641–1709), a Frenchman who was naturalized in 1673. He was technically in command of the King's army at the Battle of Sedgemoor, the climax of Monmouth's rebellion. In 1687 he was Master of the Horse and Lord Chamberlain to Dowager Queen Catherine.

252. *the Treasurer.* Lawrence ("Lory") Hyde, Earl of Rochester, was noted for his arrogance and petulance. He was no longer Lord Treasuer; after his dismissal on January 4, 1687, the Treasury was put into commission.

259. *Mordaunt.* The poet seems to have had a special spite against Charles, Viscount Mordaunt, a rabid Whig. Stanzas 65 through 67 hint at an erotic adventure in St. James's Square (between Pall Mall and Piccadilly), in which the boastful hero met defeat. For a comparable adventure see "A Faithful Catalogue of Our Most Eminent Ninnies," 1687 (*POAS*, Yale, IV, 200).

271. *Hayes.* Sir James Hayes was a Privy Councillor and Lord Falkland's stepfather.

274. *Dapperwit.* A character in Wycherley's *Love in a Wood*, 1671, Dapperwit was "a brisk, conceited, half-witted fellow of the Town." The name is applied to Falkland.

279. *Northumberland.* George Fitzroy (1665–1716), third son of the Duchess of Cleveland by King Charles II, in 1686 married Catherine, widow of Sir Thomas Lucy, and, regretting his folly, kidnapped her to Flanders and placed her in a nunnery. See above, "The Two Tom Lucys," 1686.

291. *Grafton.* Henry Fitzroy, Duke of Grafton (1663–90), a rough, uneducated fellow, took to the sea and was appointed Vice-Admiral of England.

295. *Duncomb.* Duncan Abercromy (see Appendix), a captain in Grafton's Royal Regiment of Footguards, was Grafton's follower and and crony.

296. *Eland.* Henry Savile, Lord Eland, son of the Marquis of Halifax, married Esther de Gouvernet, a French heiress, on June 20, 1684. Eland died in early October, 1687.

298. *he.* I.e., Grafton, often called "tarpaulin."

303. *lawyer.* Marginal note in Harleian MS. 7317, "Sr John Mayne," identifiable as Sir John Maynard, aged 86. An eminent and learned lawyer, he headed a Commission for the Great Seal in 1689. He died in 1690.

314. *haggard.* An untamed hawk.

316. *Apsley.* Sir Peter Apsley, Cofferer to King James II, lost his first wife, Anne, on September 5, 1681. Finally, in September, 1687, he married Catherine Fortrey, a Maid of Honor to Queen Marie. The use of "can" instead of "could" in line 315 suggests that the satire was written before Apsley's marriage. *Clifford.* Probably Charles Boyle (1639–94), styled Viscount Dungarvan but commonly called Lord Clifford. He was forty-eight years old and long a widower.

319. *fair Montague.* Anne, aged twenty-two, eldest daughter of Robert Montague, third Earl of Manchester, became c. June, 1682, the third wife of James Howard, Earl of Suffolk (1620–89).

322. *Newport.* In December, 1681, Katherine, daughter of Francis, Lord Newport, married Henry Herbert, fourth Baron Herbert of Cherbury (1640–91). The author of "Satire," 1682 (Harleian MS. 6913, p. 237) had a different view:

> Let Herbert be a slave to Newport's brat,
> Charmed with the siren's base seducing chatt. (pudendum)

326. *young Luck.* This temptress has eluded me. In "The Session of the Ladies," 1688 (below) her name is marginally given as "Mrs. Luke," with the notation "Sir

John Maynard's Lady." In "A Letter to Julian," 1687 (Harleian MS. 7319, p. 522), Julian is asked,

> What dost thou hear of Mrs. Luck?
> Will she for love or money truck?
> Shall Willoughby, as people say,
> Get her by over-bidding Grey?

In "A Letter to Lady Osbourn," 1688 (*POAS*, Yale, V, 80), we learn that "that pigmy, Grey" (of Ruthin) had been pursuing Mrs. Luck, but

> . . . Nancy Luck refused [the] wicked chit,
> She liked his gold, but not his childish wit.

JULIAN'S FAREWELL TO THE COQUETS

[*September, 1687*]

"Julian's Farewell" (in which, of course, Julian, now out of prison, is only a *persona*) is unusual because it is an attack upon a family; in one version it is entitled "Julian's Farewell to the Family of Coquets." The three ladies pilloried are Anne (Long), Lady Mason, widow of Sir Richard Mason, Clerk Controller of the Royal Household (died March 12, 1685); her first daughter, Dorothy Mason, and her second daughter, Anne, Lady Brandon (Gerard), estranged ("cast") wife of Charles Gerard, Lord Brandon. Lady Brandon, separated from her husband since 1685, was eventually divorced by him (*a vinculo*) in 1698, on the well-proven grounds of her adultery with Richard Savage, fourth Earl Rivers, by whom she had two by-blows (see Appendix, Gerard, Brandon). According to the gossips, Lady Brandon had had many lovers, including Henry, Duke of Grafton. Possibly Lady Brandon's mother and sister were damned by association.

The copy text is Harleian MS. 7317, p. 122; see also Add. MS. 29, 497, p. 49. The date is derived from internal evidence; for example, late summer is indicated by the invocation to the players, whose patrons had left town for the summer.

> Give o'er, ye poor players, depend not on wit,
> The best play you have the cost will not quit;
> They are gone who each day filled your boxes and pit.
> Near Epsom are two civil ladies retired,
> Whom all the Town for good nature admired;   *5*
> With hopes, not with beauty, our oglers they fired.
>   Not a day any public place did they fail,
> And, as slight baits to inveigle gudgeons prevail,
> Each still had a fry of young fools at their tail.
> Confess not, O Rosamund's pond, the rare pranks   *10*
> Which at midnight they played on the sides of your banks,

199

Nor tell with what member the men gave them thanks.
   Cast Brandon, on whom the small pox are scarce dry,
Seems resolved by her conduct the greater to try;
They can ne'er want that who with Grafton will lie.   *15*
   His grace many months in her favor hath been,
But as he was carrying on the sweet scene,
A sea voyage and Radnor popped just between.
   No wonder if Radnor grew fast in her grace;
His foppery and falseness with hers may take place,   *20*
And for pock holes and paint he'll not bate her an ace.
   As about her the other day I did hover,
'Twas hard for the sharpest eye to discover
Who laid it on thickest, the mistress or lover.
   But she'll not lose hold of a blue ribbon so;   *25*
A woman, she says, as the fickle times go,
Should ne'er be without two strings to their bow.
   This made her to Worcester Park to invite
Tarpaulin to give her one dear parting night,
And pay ere his voyage his *foi* of delight.   *30*
   Two days he was missing, if rumor not lies,
And from Windsor posting away in disguise,
In a grove near the house he lay hid from all eyes.
   Long live you mute pimps of that well-wooded park,
For 'twas under your bawdy shades in the dark   *35*
The hungry nymph clung like glue to her spark.
   Wisely Doll Mason from London does steal,
A new miscarriage to make and conceal;
Her belly else soon would her secrets reveal.
   For Hubbard came up in an amorous fit,   *40*
Stayed here long enough a young fopling to get;
His damned pocky seed in her womb is just knit.
   The spark oft in song tells the state of his case;
His rhymes to his dullness give just such a grace
As fine close-stool to his sickly, sniveling face.   *45*
   A fop he is both of the pen and the feather,
And she a coquet of a skin of tanned leather;

His wit to her beauty may e'en go together.
 Poor bechamber Lawson, how hard is thy hap
To purchase another man's bastard and clap, 50
And where Phil Kirke had 'scaped, to fall souse in the trap.
 But shall I forget their sage lady mother,
Who to set herself out doth keep such a pother,
In hopes she may snap some raw younger brother?
 Determined she is the first offer to marry, 55
If any whose wants like hers cannot tarry
Will venture to dig in her dangerous quarry.
 As false as her heart are her frizzes and locks,
Of her teeth she could save but the black rotten stocks,
From the flux she endured in France for the pox. 60
 Old Admiral Holmes, in the gay days of yore,
Attacked her full oft both behind and before;
He engaged her so long till his mainmast she bore.
 Her favor in nodes still his gouty joints wear;
Half his life he since spends in an old velvet chair, 65
Abhoring and cursing the *fleurs de bergère*.
 Young men from this fireship keep yourselves free.
For all his great skill, our famed seaman you see
By coming too nigh forced to lie by the lee.
 Beware then how of your prowess ye swagger; 70
Though age and disease both join to be-hag her,
She has a mouth that will eat your long sword to a dagger.
 Unhappy is he who to this galley's a slave;
That wide barren womb forever will crave,
Insatiate 'tis grown as hell and the grave. 75
 Thus ladies I have my compliment paid,
As is fit, to the chief supports of my trade,
And by whom I hope my fortune will be made.
 For were you but once well settled in town,
And would you still live as this winter you've done, 80
Never more would Julian want a lampoon.
 Oh, let not your stay in the country be long;
For till you come back this dull urban throng

Will breed but small business for satire or song.

But your return will supply all my wants,   *85*

That day after which my thirsty soul pants,

And turn all my Bordeaux to champaign and Nantes.

4. *civil ladies.* The two civil (i.e., complaisant) ladies, Dorothy Mason and her sister, Anne, Lady Brandon, lived at Sutton, Surrey, near Epsom.

10. *Rosamund's pond.* A trysting place in St. James's Park. The two sisters were popular, and appeared often together in public. On May 12, 1688, a gossip wrote, "There was a ball lately at my Lord Sunderland's; the women were the Duchess of Grafton, my Lady Brandon, Mrs. Mason, and two of the Maids of Honor" (*Rutland MS,* II, 119).

13. *small pox.* On May 28, 1686, Henry Savile wrote to Lord Halifax, "My Lady Brandon has the smallpox, which may possibly alter some circumstances in a matter you know of" (*Savile Correspondence,* p. 289).

14. *the greater.* the "great pox," venereal disease.

15. *Grafton.* Henry Fitzroy, Duke of Grafton (1665–90).

18. *a sea voyage.* On July 5, 1687, Grafton sailed in command of a squadron of war ships to the Brill, whence he carried to Lisbon the new Queen of Portugal, Mary Elizabeth, daughter of William, Prince Palatine. From Lisbon Grafton sailed into the Mediterranean to discourage the Algerine pirates. *Radnor.* Charles Robartes (1660–1723), Earl of Radnor, a well-known rake.

25. *a blue ribbon.* Grafton wore the Order of the Garter.

28. *Worcester Park.* In 1670 King Charles II gave Nonsuch House in Worcester Park, near Epsom, Surrey, to Grafton's mother, the Duchess of Cleveland (*Victoria History of Surrey,* III, 268–69).

29. *Tarpaulin.* A contemptuous name for a sailor, i.e., the rough Duke of Grafton, who was bred for the sea.

37. *Doll Mason.* At twenty-two Dorothy was still unmarried, although she was reputed a great beauty and had a dowry of £16,000. In August, 1688, she married William Brownlow (1665–1701), who succeeded his brother, Sir John, as baronet on July 16, 1697 (*Ellis Correspondence,* II, 99; *London Post,* January 18, 1700).

40. *Hubbard.* Perhaps Sir Henry Hobart, 1658–98 (the name was usually pronounced "Hubbard"), son of Sir John Hobart, Bart., of Blickling, Norfolk.

45. *close stool.* A commode.

49. *Lawson.* Usually Lewson or Leveson. Richard Leveson of Staffordshire was sworn as a Groom of the Bedchamber ("bedchamber Lawson") in May, 1685 (*CSPD,* 1685, p. 144), and he was still listed as a Groom in Chamberlayne's *Angliae Notitia,* 1687. He became M.P. for Lichfield and an army officer.

51. *Phil Kirke.* "Beardless Phil" Kirke, Housekeeper of Whitehall Palace, died September 8, 1687. Possibly the Masons had been in treaty with Kirke to marry Doll. He had "'scaped" a horrible fate by dying, and now Leveson was the chosen groom. It is, of course, highly unlikely that Doll Mason was pregnant.

52. *lady mother.* Anne Margaretta (Long), widow of Sir Richard Mason. The poet's coarse treatment of Lady Mason is not justified by any obtainable evidence.

61. *Holmes.* At this time Admiral Sir Robert Holmes (1622–92) was Governor of the Isle of Wight. A rough, quarrelsome sea dog, his greatest exploit was the capture of New York from the Dutch in 1664.

64. *nodes.* Swellings developed during the secondary stage of syphilis.

66. *fleurs de bergère.* According to Randle Cotgrave (*A Dictionarie of the French and English Tongues*, 1611), *fleurs* could mean "a woman's monthelie flux, or flowers." *Bergère* can be translated as shepherdess or nymph. In this case, Lady Mason is supposed to be the nymph who infected Holmes.

67. *fireship.* In naval usage a fireship was a small vessel filled with combustibles, set afire, and sent into the midst of an enemy fleet. As a cant term, a fireship was a whore of low degree. See Richard Ames, *The Female Fireship, a Satire against Whoring*, 1691.

87. *Nantes.* Brandy, originally from Nantes, France.

THE SESSION OF LADIES

[*April, 1688*]

Obviously written in imitation of "The Lovers' Session," the following "session" satire depicts a gathering of lecherous ladies: half a dozen duchesses, a covey of countesses, and a miscellaneous huddle of harlots. All are competing for the favor of "Adonis," who represents Cardell Goodman, a famous actor and Gentleman of the Horse to the Duchess of Cleveland. Appropriately the scene is a playhouse, with the contestants crowding the pit and Cupid and Adonis enthroned on the stage. The outcome, when Venus interferes and gives Adonis to the Duchess of Cleveland, would have been no surprise to the Court of James II; everyone knew that Goodman was the duchess's "stallion." The poet carefully avoids any political allusion.

The date is probably April, 1688, not long after the Duke of Grafton's return from his nautical mission in the Mediterranean. It must have been before May 28, 1688, when the Duchess of Monmouth owned her secret marriage to Lord Cornwallis.

The copy text is Harleian MS. 7319, p. 557. It is there dated 1688, as it is also in Harleian MS. 7317, p. 148, and in Bodleian MS. Firth c. 25, p. 292. It is undated in Dyce MS. 43, II, 816, and "A Choyce Collection," p. 280.

A session of ladies was held on the stage,
And Cupid himself was judge of the court,
Adonis the beauty for whom they engage,
And did from each corner in legions resort.

2.

Though such an Adonis before was not known,   5
He exceeded the other in beauty and grace;

With age and diseases though impotent grown,
He resembled the other exactly in face.

3.

To this new Adonis, in park and at plays,
Whose eyes had the power of life and of death,   *10*
Each beautiful lady an altar did raise,
But all their perfumes could not sweeten his breath.

4.

Here none were debarred at the purchase to strike;
A boundless commission the court did unfold,
Where all might put in their pretenses alike,   *15*
The young and the handsome, the ugly and old.

5.

And therefore the ladies of every degree,
From the miss of the Court to the bawd of the stews,
To win our Adonis a mercury fee,
His pockets each night stuffed with *billets a doux.*   *20*

6.

The gallery vizor, the mask of the pit,
The great ones who take in the boxes their place,
At the tavern appointed would afterward sit,
And prostrate their honor to purchase his grace.

7.

There were monkeys in top-knots and owls in settee,   *25*
High jilts in sultana and bulkers in crepe,

205

Who flocked from each quarter Adonis to see,
Admiring his beauty, his person and shape.

8.

There was pockey lewd Hinton and Howard's pert Mall,
With Grafton's chaste widow of Worcester Park, *30*
Fantastical Brandon and her sister Doll,
Who had many a bout with his grace in the dark.

9.

There was chestnut-maned Boutell, whom all the Town fucks,
Lord Lumley's cast player, the famed Mrs. Cox,
And chaste Mrs. Barry, i'th'midst of a flux, *35*
To make him a present of chancre and pox.

10.

The old and the ugly, the youthful and fair,
All flew at the sound of Adonis his name.
Poor Cuffley, alas, broke her neck in a chair,
Making overmuch haste to put in her claim. *40*

11.

The whores by profession and whores in religion,
All summoned, appeared at the deity's call;
The Court parakeet and the citizen widgeon;
There were whores of Whitechapel and whores of Whitehall.

12.

That harridan Cromwell and Silence, the bawd, *45*
Like mayor and recorder had brought an address;

Betty Mackerel, a favorite of the blind god,
In behalf of her function procured 'em access.

13.

One took him for Pompey, another for Caesar;
That he Alexander was another straight swore,   *50*
And thought he could do as great wonders to please her
As the great triumvirate mentioned before.

14.

Chaste Norfolk the first was that put in her claim,
A privilege due to her person and place.
The court had respect to her title and name,   *55*
And was at the point to comply with her grace,

15.

But Cupid, recalling the German to mind,
Said 'twas pity Adonis should e'er be her prize,
Whose lust the Town stallions, though never so kind,
And all the whole family could not suffice.   *60*

16.

Next Richmond the relic, once youthful and fair,
With matronly modesty put in her claim;
Adonis, she thought, would have fall'n to her share
Out of very regard to her honor and name.

17.

But Cupid replied, it should not be so;   *65*
Adonis must never expect to prevail

Where Howe and proud Mulgrave and Houghton the beau
Could not as yet lay the heat of her tail.

18.

Her sister Sophia the next crowded in,
At which Adonis damned, hectored, and swore   *70*
That he loved adultery, because 'twas a sin,
Yet he loathed in his heart so religious a whore.

19.

Another grave widow, in sables' deep veil,
Did send in by proxy her claim to the court;
She pleaded, since Monmouth his project did fail,   *75*
None could but Adonis make recompense for't.

20.

But she was soon answered that she had her choice
Of Stamford, Cornwallis, and brawny Dunbar;
Or take 'em all three, if one could not suffice,
For Adonis never should fall to her share.   *80*

21.

Next Grafton in vizor did put in her plea,
Saying none had such weighty pretenses as she;
Since lusty Tarpaulin was sent out to sea,
Her Grafton, her Mord[aun]t, Adonis should be.

22.

This plea would have took, but the court was informed   *85*
That his grace was with Duncan arrived in the Downs;

At the name of that hero, Adonis he stormed,
Being scarcely recovered of his dressing-room wounds.

23.

Her prettiness thus for this reason set by,
A foreign-built duchess stepped in her place;   *90*
Such a claim, such a beauty, what god could deny,
Much less anything of inferior race?

24.

But all these temptations of birth and high blood
Would never go down with Adonis's palate;
His prick to a courtesan never yet stood,   *95*
Who is fucked by her black and frigged by her valet.

25.

North[umber]land, ashamed of her ill gotten grace,
Yet proud of new conquests, came in with fresh charms;
But wisely Adonis removed from his place,
For fear of a philter to die in her arms.   *100*

26.

Pert Mulgrave, well flustered with brandy and sack,
To Cupid in passion her story applied;
Since her lord was grown feeble and weak in the back,
She might purchase Adonis to lie by her side.

27.

But Cupid replied in Adonis his praise,   *105*
Though he had an esteem for a lecherous punk,

The pox or the plague he could freely embrace,
But could not dispense with a whore would be drunk.

28.

Old Bellas[yse] next with the number did thrust,
But Cupid provoked rose up in a rage,   *110*
And since she was nothing but wrinkles and lust,
To allay her rank itch, bid her fuck with her page.

29.

With her, Lady Clifford sneaked out of the pit,
Ashamed to behold how the former had sped;
The god smiled to think she should have a sweet bit,   *115*
Who scarce had remaining a tooth in her head.

30.

Witty Dorchester next, like a queen took her place,
And bragged she a monarch subdued to her arms,
"If Jove in a shower does court my embrace,
Can Adonis deny to submit to my charms?"   *120*

31.

But Cupid, who always in mischief took pleasure,
Returned her this answer, and did not dissemble,
"If the full royal standard falls short in the measure,
What can you expect from Adonis's wimble?"

32.

The tall Lady Mary next mounted the stage,   *125*
The spawn of a stroller and sperm of a king,

210

Who has married a viscount, yet fucks with her page,
For which she's advised to abandon the ring.

33.

Her natural mother came in for a snack,
That ballocking squirter and shitten arsed whore,   *130*
But she an old Frenchman has got by the back,
And of that poor Adonis enough had before.

34.

Old Freschville, for drinking and hunting so fit,
With Lowther her crony, for swiving so famed,
By the court for the crime they do daily commit,   *135*
Were to catso and dildo forever condemned.

35.

Here Villiers, who passed for a Maid of the Queen,
Came ramping along to supply her great need;
But Cupid advised her behind the new scene
To leave off her lewdness or she never would speed.   *140*

36.

Next Frazer, the old and deformed enough,
And had for that cause juster claim to admit,
But she from the court did receive a reproof
For pretending to beauty, to conduct, or wit.

37.

Unfortunate South did approach in the rear,   *145*
She never yet ventured but met a mishap;

211

But the court did advise her to come no more there
Until she was perfectly cured of her clap.

38.

Roscommon with passion even ready to burn,
Adonis had much, much ado to appease her;   *150*
But he told her a poor whore was ne'er for his turn,
And bid, to recruit her, keep close to Sir Caesar.

39.

Kildare, of whose beauty the palace does ring,
Did make him a present, in hope he would sieze her;
But what would she do with a poor chitterling,   *155*
When a thousand stiff Irish pricks could not please her?

40.

Lady Orrery, once both a beauty and wit,
With the box and [the] dice had great hopes to prevail;
But she had a trick, when she was in her fit,
To throw off with her hand what she got with her tail.   *160*

41.

Last fair Mrs. Luck did bring up the rear,
But she was soon told of her folly before;
And since she had made so wise a choice there,
She never should choose for herself anymore.

42.

While thus from all nations and lands they resort,   *165*
Of every humor, complexion, and age,

Dame Venus herself arrived at the court,
And thus she bespoke the blind god in a rage:

43.

"Am I thy own mother, from Jove's mighty race?
And this fair Adonis, the amorous boy?   *170*
Such beauty is fit for a goddess's embrace,
A blessing for mortals too great too enjoy."

44.

This said, he laid by both his bow and his dart,
Which at his own mother he drew to the head;
And with one word she (resigning her heart)   *175*
To Cleveland put rakehelly Goodman to bed.

45.

This startled the court, to see her so pleased,
From a dish for a monarch and feeding so nice,
But all in a moment the court was appeased,
Since the goddess had made so equal a choice.   *180*

---

3. *Adonis*. Cardell Goodman (1653–c.1714), actor, highwayman, and Jacobite conspirator; for details of his life, see J. H. Wilson, *Mr. Goodman, the Player*, 1964. We may be sure that he was not as ugly, old, or diseased as he is represented by the satirist, who seems to be angry that a mere player should dare to become the lover of a duchess.

18. *miss*. Kept mistress, prostitute.

19. *a mercury fee*. This phrase, plus the following stanza, seems to mean that besotted women would "prostrate their honor" in taverns to get money to pay Adonis's medical bills.

21. *the gallery vizor*. Poor whores, wearing masks, sat in the theatre galleries, paying eighteen pence for a seat; more prosperous trollops sat in the pit, paying two shillings and sixpence.

25. *monkeys*. In his *The Female Fireship*, 1691, Richard Ames listed three kinds of whores: kept mistresses, playhouse punks, and "the cracks of the night." Apparently the "monkeys" were playhouse punks. *top-knots*. Elaborate head dresses. According to Mary Evelyn (*Mundus Muliebris*, 1690) this was called a "Fontange . . . so called from Mademoiselle de Fontange, one of the French king's mistresses, who first wore it." *Owls in settee*. Ames wrote of nightwalkers,

> Like owls all day they still remain within,
> And seldom are until the twilight seen.

A "settee" was a caplike head dress, "the double pinner," according to Mary Evelyn.

26. *sultane*. "A gown trimmed with buttons and loops" (Mary Evelyn). *bulkers*. Whores who performed at night on empty bulks, or stalls, before shops.

29. *Hinton*. Mall Hinton; see Appendix, *pert Mall*. Mall Howard; see Appendix.

30. *chaste widow*. Anne, Lady Brandon (Gerard), was a widow because she was separated from her husband. For her affair with "his grace," the Duke of Grafton, see above, "Julian's Farewell to the Coquets."

31. *Doll*. Lady Brandon's sister, Dorothy Mason.

33. *Boutell*. Elizabeth (Ridley) Boutell, actress and wife of Lieutenant Barnaby Boutell. She was with the King's Company c. 1670–78; the United Company 1688–90; and the Lincolns Inn Fields Company 1695–96.

34. *Lumley*. Richard, Lord Lumley (c.1650–1721). *Cox*. Elizabeth Cox, an actress with the King's Company 1671–82.

35. *Barry*. Elizabeth Barry (1658–1713), the greatest actress of the seventeenth century. She was on the stage from 1675 to 1708. Her reputation as an actress was equalled by her notoriety as a mercenary strumpet.

39. *Cuffley*. A well-known woman of the Town; see the verse epistles between "B---" and "Mr. E --" in Rochester's *Poems on Several Occasions*, ed. James Thorpe, 1950, pp. 77–87. Mrs. Cuffley was so notorious that in 1680 the editor of *The Courant Intelligence* (April 17) was obliged to apologize because he had reported that a witness in a trial was "Mrs. Cuffly of Scotland Yard," when in fact she was Mrs. Cufeler, widow of one Dr. Cufeler (*The True Protestant [Domestic] Intelligence*, April 25, 1680).

43. *parakeet*. A gaudy bird as opposed to the dull grey and brown of "the citizen widgeon," a duck.

45. *Cromwell and Silence*. Two well-known bawds. For Cromwell see "Jenny Cromwell's Complaint against Sodomy. 1692/3," in Harleian MS. 7315, f. 224. For Silence see Nahum Tate's "The Battle of the B[aw]ds in the Theatre Royal, December 3, 1680," an account of a hair-pulling match between Mesdames Silence and Stratford (*Poems Written on Several Occasions*, 1684, p. 153).

46. *recorder*. The Recorder of London was a counsellor experienced in the law, one who spoke in the name of the City, and read and presented addresses and petitions to the King.

47. *Betty Mackerel*. A famous trollop and orange girl. By this date she functioned also as a bawd.

49. *Pompey*. etc. Cardell Goodman was celebrated as Alexander in Lee's *The Rival Queens*. He certainly played *Julius Caesar* in a revival in 1684, and may have played the role earlier. It is unlikely that he ever played Pompey, unless in a revival of *Pompey the Great* (1664), by Sedley, Waller, Dorset, et al.

53. *Norfolk*. For the amorous exploits of Mary (Mordaunt), Duchess of Norfolk, see Appendix. In January, 1688, the duchess was legally separated from her husband, Henry Howard, seventh Duke of Norfolk.

57. *the German*. John Germaine, a Dutch adventurer, professional gambler, and the Duchess of Norfolk's lover.

61. *Richmond*. Frances Teresa, widowed Duchess of Richmond; see Appendix.

67. *Howe*, etc. John Grubham Howe; John Sheffield, Earl of Mulgrave; John Holles, Lord Houghton. The poet is merely repeating earlier charges; see above, "A Ballad to the Tune of Cheviot Chace."

69. *Sophia*. Sophia (Stuart), wife of Henry Bulkeley, Master of the Household, was a Lady of the Bedchamber to Queen Marie.

73. *grave widow*. Anne, daughter of Francis, second Earl of Buccleuch, and widow of James Scott, Duke of Monmouth.

78. *Stamford*. Thomas Grey, Earl of Stamford. His wife, buxom Elizabeth (Harvey), died on September 7, 1687. *Cornwallis*. Elizabeth, daughter of Sir Stephen Fox and first wife of Charles, third Baron Cornwallis, died February 28, 1681. As his second wife, Cornwallis married privately, on May 6, 1688, Anne, the widowed Duchess of Monmouth. The marriage was widely known by or before May 28 (*Clarendon State Papers*, II, 45). *Dunbar*. The first wife of Robert Constable, third Viscount Dunbar, was Mary (Belasyse). In July, 1687, she gave birth, and under pressure admitted that the infant's father was not Dunbar but her own confessor. She seems to have died soon afterward (*Rutland MS*, II, 115, July 21, 1687).

81. *Grafton*. Isabella (Bennet), Duchess of Grafton. The "lusty tarpaulin" was Henry, Duke of Grafton. Adonis would be the substitute for Grafton, and for Charles, Viscount Mordaunt, reputedly the duchess's lover.

86. *his grace*. The Duke of Grafton, with a small fleet, left England on July 5, 1687, to convoy Mary Elizabeth, Princess Palatine and bride of Peter the Second of Portugal, from Holland to Lisbon. After that he was ordered to make a show of force before Algiers. His fleet returned to England about March 19, 1688 (Luttrell, I, 434). *Duncan*. Duncan Abercromy; see Appendix.

88. *wounds*. According to John Dryden, the duel between Goodman and Duncan Abercromy took place, not in a dressing room, but in Covent Garden, "where they say Alexander the Great [Goodman] was wounded in the arm" (*Letters*, ed. C. E. Ward, p. 27, February 16, 1687).

90. *a foreign-built duchess*. Hortense, Duchess Mazarin, was still beautiful and should have been tempting to a mere actor, a member of an "inferior race."

96. *her black*. Mustapha, page to the Duchess Mazarin.

97. *Northumberland*. Katherine, Duchess of Northumberland, formerly widow of Captain Thomas Lucy. *ill-gotten* suggests that she used mean devices to snare George Fitzroy, Duke of Northumberland, in March, 1686.

100. *a philter*. Usually a love potion.

101. *pert Mulgrave*. On March 11, 1686, Ursula, the widowed Lady Conway, married John Sheffield, Earl of Mulgrave. The marriage was not happy, and apparently the countess took to drink. The author of "A Faithful Catalogue of Our Most Eminent Ninnies," c. 1687 (*POAS*, Yale, IV, 197), asserted that

> But now, poor wretch, she lies as she would bust,
> Sometimes with brandy and sometimes with lust.

108. *dispense with*. Accept.

109. *Bellasys*. Susan (Armine), widow of Sir Henry Bellasys and once mistress of James, Duke of York. She was created Baroness Bellasys of Osgodby in 1674. Died March 6, 1713.

113. *Lady Clifford*. Probably (because she is old) Elizabeth (Martin), widow of Thomas, Baron Clifford of Chudleigh, who had been Lord High Treasurer, 1672–73. Lady Clifford died on September 21, 1709.

117. *Dorchester*. Katherine Sedley, created Countess of Dorchester by her lover, King James II.

124. *wimble*. A gimlet or auger.

125. *Lady Mary*. On August 18, 1687, Lady Mary Tudor, daughter of King Charles II by the actress Moll Davis, married Edward, Viscount Radcliffe, later second Earl of Derwentwater.

129. *natural mother*. On December 4, 1686, Moll Davis took out a license to marry a French musician, James Paisible. She gave her age as "abt 25," and Paisible claimed to be "abt 30" (*Marriage Allegations, Vicar-General*, 1890). The epithets echo the tradition that Nell Gwyn gave Moll a purgative dose before she was to have a night with the King.

133. *Old Freschville*. Anne Charlotte (De Vic), widow of John, Baron Freschville, and a Lady of the Bedchamber to Princess Anne, died in 1717.

134. *Lowther*. Probably Katherine (Thynne), 1653–1713, wife of Sir John Lowther of Lowther, Westmorland, created Viscount Lonsdale in 1696.

136. *catso*. *Membrum virile. dildo.* An artificial priapus.

137. *Villiers*. Mary, a daughter of Sir Edward Villiers and a Maid of Honor to Queen Marie (and later to Queen Mary), married in April, 1691, William, Lord O'Brien.

141. *Frazer*. Mary (Carey) Frazier, widow of the royal physician, Sir Alexander Frazier, was a dresser to Queen Dowager Catherine. Lady Frazier died in January, 1696.

145. *South*. Elizabeth South, a Maid of Honor to the Queen.

149. *Roscommon*. Isabelle (Boynton), c. 1654–1721, widow of Wentworth Dillon, Earl of Roscommon, 1637–85, had been a Maid of Honor to Marie, Duchess of York and was now a Lady of the Bedchamber to the Queen. Her poverty is vouched for in "News from Whitehall," Harleian MS. 7317, p. 154,

> Though 'tis too well known she hath ne'er a penny,
> And that sneaking Sir Ceasar is all her revenue.

152. *Sir Caesar*. Sir Caesar Wood Cranmer, one of the Queen's equerries.

153. *Kildare*. Elizabeth (Jones), 1665–1758, wife of John, Earl of Kildare (Ireland), was often accused of promiscuity.

155. *chitterling*. A piece of entrail, stuffed with meat; i.e., a small sausage.

155. *Orrery*. Mary (Sackville), 1642–1710, widow of Roger Boyle, second Earl of Orrery, seems to have been a compulsive gamber; hence she threw off "with her hand" at the gaming tables what she earned abed.

166. *Mrs. Luck*. In Harleian MS. 7317, p. 148ff, this lady's name is given as "Mrs. Luke," with the marginal note, "Sir John Maynard's Lady," not his wife. For more about Anne (or Nancy) Luck, see above, "The Lovers' Session."

176. *Cleveland*. Barbara (Villiers), Duchess of Cleveland.

SATIRE ON BENT[IN]G

[*March, 1689*]

From June 10, 1688, when a son ("the Old Pretender") was born to King James and Queen Marie, through the fearful summer and autumn, the Dutch invasion on November 5, the flight of the King and Queen, the triumph of William of Orange, and the deliberations of the Convention Parliament, Englishmen had little interest in scandalous Court libels. When the dust had settled and the Court satirists went to work again, they found that scandal was in short supply. If the Court of gloomy King James offered little nourishment to sinners, that of William and Mary starved them. Surly King William had his private vices, but he kept them private, and Queen Mary was forbiddingly virtuous. The writer of "Satire on Bent[in]g" (c. March, 1689) could do little more than sneer at Bentinck and Overkirke, rake up some past scandals, and descend to attacking such naughty ladies as the old bawd Sue Willis, the actresses Moll Davis and Elizabeth Barry, and the aging Duchess of Cleveland. Like most Englishmen, the poet detested the Dutch, even though William and his army had saved them from the bigoted tyranny of King James II.

The copy text is "Satyr 1688/9," in Bodleian MS. Firth. c. 15, p. 311. A version in "A Choyce Collection," p. 299, lacks the last fifty-seven lines, on Barry.

> Long had my pen lain dull and useless by,
> My fancy dozed, as in a lethargy,
> The charms of satire could not raise it up,
> My spleen still palled, nor could one notion hope.
> The government (which ever was the theme   5
> Of witty malice) so correct did seem
> That I resolved to sit contented down,
> Scorn the transactions of the Court and Town,
> To some dear solitary place retire,
> Where groves and rivers should my muse inspire;   10

217

But such a lump of whores and fools fell in
My way that to compel my tickled spleen
I found was harder far than to devise
How to make bishops humble or South'ton wise.
   Bent[in]g, that topping favorite at Court   *15*
(The King, though, has some private reasons for't),
To whom all for preferment now resort,
As mercenary as Petre or [as] Brent,
As proud as Mulgrave, fitter to be sent
To Italy with Villiers and Kildare   *20*
Than nose his master with his buttocks here;
Who, like a coxcomb, made blunt Grafton wait
To show's Dutch breeding in his English state.
Could the tarpaulin get him once from Court,
He'd spoil his parts for e'er more making sport.   *25*
   Sue Willis has this darling's heart secured;
He too has hers; the damsel is ensured,
Two only by themselves to be endured.
This whore at first her life with Moseley led,
The bawd's least profit and her bully's bread,   *30*
Thence in a playhouse, where a goatish peer,
Feeling her cunt, liked it but never her.
So much though to this cunt he was allied
He sacrificed his all to feast her pride.
And when he had made over his estate,   *35*
She put him to board wages and to wait,
Fucking with all but him; which heavy fate
So violently on his spirits fell
He's gone before to keep her a place in hell.
May Bent[in]g Culpeper's ill usage find,   *40*
And all who to the prostitute are kind.
   Davis was looking out too for a hero,
Weary already of her piping lero.
O Peaceable! thy own sad farewell set,
And make words to it of thy want of wit.   *45*
A fiddler's name alone is vile, we know,

Must thou then be a pimp and cuckold too?
This lady must a Dutchman somewhere get,
For they've huge pricks, much money, and no wit.
She would have had Count Solmes, but he being told   50
How she beshit King Charles, cried, "Though I'm old,
I want no dung to fertilize my land."
Her nature was too strong for his to stand;
And if she wanted fuck in her old age,
She might set up with Boutell on the stage.   55
That whore, we hear, poor Armstrong's life betrayed
And passed upon Maccarty for a maid.

   Queer Overkirke, our Master of the Horse,
That came into his place, forsooth of course
Because he did i'th' Hague the title bear,   60
Is there no difference in the office here?
I think as much 'twixt England and his home
As distance 'twixt a helper and a groom.
Norfolk or Somerset, the best i'th'land,
Are only fit for such a great command;   65
A place i'th' royal bedchamber or so,
A troop of guards, had recompensed the beau.
That dressing, whining, peaking, creeping mien,
Which he affects because 'tis like the King,
He'd better leave it off and take more pains   70
To imitate his master in his brains.
He's farther from him yet than truth is from Jo. Haynes,
From Rivers honor, or from Oxford wealth,
From Cleveland virtue, or from Goodman health.

   How poor and despicable is she grown,   75
The most famed beauteous harlot of the Town,
Nelly and she long struggled for the crown;
One strove the other always to outlive,
And likewise both each other to out-swive.
Nelly is dead and left St. Albans more   80
Than Cleveland can her bastards or the poor,
A duchess though she die and Goodman's whore.

219

Who can to such a spendthrift grant relief
That gives her children's birthright to a thief?
The vaunting vagabond lives high, looks great,   *85*
Whilst she not plays, but begs gold at basset.
Pretending 'tis a purse for charity.
Indeed it is, since her it must supply.
In Goodman's grave may fate her carcass lay,
And every man avoid that foul highway.   *90*
   Another lass, whose virtues far exceed
The arts of Moseley's, Cresswell's, Strafford's breed,
Expert in all the arts of thriving sin
From Posture Mall to Machiaevellian Behn,
Who can the pride of the late queen affect,   *95*
And all the lewdness of the Hintons act;
Shameless, mercenary, always craving,
Dextrous in wheedling, scandalous in saving,
Whose cunt, as Paradise by priests, is sold,
You cannot want that Heaven if you have gold.   *100*
More languages at Babel were not known
Than into it have different seeds been thrown;
An issue in it too it has, that flows
Enough to stock her sex almost with those.
Had she been living in famed Pharaoh's reign,   *105*
He and even all his fierce and num'rous train
In her red sea might have been surely slain.
'Tis Barry, the illustrious of her kind,
Whose charity the poor could never find.
Rochester taught her first how to be lewd,   *110*
Fathered a cheddar child as his own brood;
And had he lived to Hesty's fifteen year,
He'd fucked his girl t'have been a grandfather,
But dying left it to his niece's care.
She likewise dies and leaves three thousand pound   *115*
To dower the girl provided she be sound.
T. Wharton is to have her maidenhead,
And if not sound, the dowry's forfeited.

If he to gain the sum should pox her now,
And swear before the judge he found her so,   *120*
The mother would (if she were him) all know.
Oh Barry, Barry, speedily repent,
Or else be doubly damned by my consent.
Bring forth thy mighty magazine of lust,
And in thy vile account be sure, be just.   *125*
As thou expectst to waste thy crimes away,
The trophies of thy countless fuckings lay
Sincerely at the shrine of Modena,
With a strict catalogue of every sin,
If paper can be found to put 'em in.   *130*
That wonder-working dame and none but she
Can intercede for such a bitch as thee.
Thy Jewish presents, howsoe'er they're prized,
Give 'em the duchess, 'tis well advised;
They'll [stink?] of trading with the circumcized.   *135*
Unlucky Whitmore's presents, all that pride,
The locket too that changed the day [he] died,
The citizens' rich silks and their fine linen,
The necessaries which thou ne'er wert seen in,
But shoes and stockings which thou ne'er went   *140*
     clean in.
Bring Goring's medals, all the wealth he gave
To purchase of a punk a shameful grave,
Which, though foreseen, himself he could not save.
Bring too the name of every occupation,
Each bidding fair, according to his station,   *145*
A list of every sect thou'st swived with, of each nation;
And if the duchess can thy pardon gain,
I'd not despair, though I'd my father slain.

---

14. *bishops humble.* An allusion to James's conflict with the seven bishops who
refused to read his Declaration of Indulgence during divine services. Tried for seditious
libel, the seven bishops were pronounced not guilty on June 30, 1688. *South'ton.*

Charles Fitzroy, Duke of Southampton (1662–1730), first son of the Duchess of Cleveland by King Charles II, was generally considered a simpleton.

15. *Bent[in]g.* Hans Willem Bentinck (1649–1709) had long been Prince William's devoted servant as Page of Honor and later Nobleman of the Chamber. On February 13, 1689, King William appointed him Groom of the Stole, First Gentleman of the Bedchamber, and Keeper of the Privy Purse. On April 9, 1689, William created him Earl of Portland. Thereafter the King heaped wealth upon Bentinck until Parliament protested. The "private reasons" were presumed to be homosexual.

18. *Petre.* Father Edward Petre, S.J., was a Privy Councillor and King James's most reckless adviser. *Brent.* Robert Brent, "the Popish attorney," was an extremist Catholic and a justice of the peace for Westminster. After James fled, Brent was arrested, bailed, and fled to France. A reward of £200 was offered for his capture (Luttrell, I, 388, 496, 506).

19. *Mulgrave.* ("King John"), Earl of Mulgrave.

20. *to Italy.* The poet is suggesting that Sir Edward Villiers, the Earl of Kildare, and Bentinck, all reputed homosexuals, should be sent to Italy, the reputed center of epicene vice.

22. *Grafton.* Henry Fitzroy, Duke of Grafton, a rough sailor, was out of favor because on January 29, 1689, he had voted for a regency. In March he lost his commission as Colonel of the First Footguards.

26. *Sue Willis.* A notorious bawd and whore; see Appendix. I have found no evidence that she was ever an actress. The "goatish peer" was Thomas, Lord Colepeper of Thoresby (1635–January 27, 1689).

42. *Davis.* In December, 1686, Moll Davis, actress and whilom mistress of King Charles II, married James Paisible, French musician (1636–1722). On May 12, 1687, Etherege commented on the match: "Mrs. Davis has given a proof of the great passion she always had for musick, and Monsieur Paisible has another (guess) Bass to thrum than that he playd so well uppon" (*Letters*, p. 118).

43. *Iero.* Properly "lira." A lira tedesca was a bowed instrument of the viol class.

50. *Solmes.* Heinrich, Comte de Solmes, an arrogant old Dutch general, was slain at the Battle of Landen, July 19, 1693.

51. *beshit.* The story of Nell Gwyn's giving her rival a dose of purgative jalap before Moll's engagement with the King has often been told and may be true. For a verse account of the affair see Samuel Butler's "The Court Burlesqued," 1678 (*Posthumous Works*, 1715, II, 19–23).

55. *Boutell.* Elizabeth Boutell, ingenue (King's United, and Lincoln's Inn Fields companies to 1696) returned to the stage after ten years' absence in May, 1688.

56. *Armstrong.* Sir Thomas Armstrong (1624–84), a follower of Monmouth, was outlawed for complicity in the Rye House Plot, captured in Holland, brought back to England, and executed without a trial on June 20, 1684. I have found no evidence that Mrs. Boutell was involved in his capture; however, her husband, Barnaby Boutell or Bowtell, was a lieutenant in the Holland Regiment of Foot. She might have been in Holland with him at the time of Armstrong's capture (Wilson, "Biographical Notes on Some Restoration Actresses," *Theatre Notebook*, XVIII, 2 (1963–4), 43).

57. *Maccarty.* Justin, third son of Donogh McCarty, first Earl of Clancarty, and colonel of a regiment of foot, was created Viscount Mountcashel on May 23, 1689 (Dalton, I, 207). He was said to be very nearsighted.

58. *Overkirke.* Henry van Nassau, Heer van Ouwerkerk, Master of the Horse to William III.

64. *Norfolk*. Henry Howard, seventh Duke of Norfolk and Lord Marshall (1655–1701). *Somerset*. Charles Seymour, "the proud" Duke of Somerset (1662–1748).

72. *Haynes*. Joseph Haynes, actor, farceur, and famous liar (d. April 4, 1701).

73. *Rivers*. Thomas Savage, third Earl Rivers (c. 1628–94), must not be confused with his more famous son and successor, Richard ("Tyburn Dick"), Lord Colchester (1654–1712). *Oxford*. Aubrey de Vere, twentieth Earl of Oxford (1622–1703), a compulsive gambler, wasted his wealth at the Groom Porter's lodge.

74. *Cleveland*. Notorious Barbara, Duchess of Cleveland; see Appendix. *Goodman*. Cardell Goodman (c. 1653–c.1714), actor and the Duchess of Cleveland's Gentleman of the Horse.

77. *Nelly*. Nell Gwyn died November 14, 1687.

80. *St. Albans*. Charles Beauclerc, Duke of St. Albans, son of King Charles II by Nell Gwyn.

84. *a thief*. In 1681 Goodman was arrested, charged with highway robbery. The case never came to trial, but on April 18, 1681, King Charles II gave him a pardon for "all felonies, robberies upon the highways or elsewhere" (Wilson, *Mr. Goodman the Player*, p. 73).

86. *begs gold*. This was a frequent charge against the duchess. For example, Mrs. Manly (*The New Atlantis*, 1720, I, 57) asserts that one night the duchess lost all her money at basset and begged Lord Marlborough, her former lover, to "lend her twenty pieces, which he absolutely refused."

92. *Moseley*, etc. "Mother" Moseley was a famous bawd. In the Epilogue to Duffett's farce, *The Empress of Morocco*, 1674, healths are proposed to five bawds: Madam Cresswell, Mrs. Gifford, "Sister" Temple, Betty Buly, and finally,

> But of all the brisk bawds, 'tis M[oseley] for me,
> 'Tis M[oseley], the best in her degree;
> She can serve from the lord to the squire and clown,
> From a guinea she'll fit you to half a crown.

Cresswell. "On Tuesday last the famous Madam Cresswell was in a trial at *nisi prius* at Westminster convicted after above 30 years practise of bawdry, some, of her 'Does' most unkindly testifying against her" (*Impartial Protestant Mercury*, no. 64, November 29–December 2, 1681). Madam Cresswell is the chief character in *The Whore's Rhetorick*, 1683 (rpt., London, 1960). *Stratford*. In *The Female Fireship*, 1691, Richard Ames listed a number of famous bawds as candidates for monuments of brass,

> Then would no Buly, Stratford, Temple, Whipple,
> Cresswell nor Cozens, who so loved the nipple,
> Nor other female fachesses unknown,
> Want that disgrace is due to vice alone.

In May, 1695, Sarah Stratford was "convicted of being a woman of ill fame, and for enticing Elizabeth Farrington into a common tavern in the parish of St. Clement Danes." She was fined twenty nobles, condemned to the pillory three times, one hour each time, and to spend three months in Newgate (*Middlesex County Records*, 1689–1709, p. 133).

94. *Posture Moll*. Apparently a woman who made her living doing Italian posture dances in a stall or booth at one of the London fairs. In the prologue to his comedy

The Banditti, 1686, Thomas D'Urfey represented a "rusty dry'd up Debauchee" complaining about bawdry on the stage,

> "Their plays are cramm'd with such a Bawdy Rout,
> Damme if I've the Face to sit 'em out."
> Yet this Nice Spark whose modest Tast we pall,
> Shall sit Two Hours admiring Posture-Mall.

Behn. Aphra Behn, playwright (1640–April 16, 1689). In "To Julian. 1688" (Harleian MS. 7317, f. 58) she is called a "lewd harlot" and a "poetic quean."

96. *the Hintons.* Whores like Mall Hinton; see Appendix.

103. *those.* A common euphemism for menses. At regular intervals Pepys would write such phrases as "my wife sick of those in bed," or "my wife, being ill of those, kept her bed all day" (*Diary*, February 7, May 12, 1664).

108. *Barry.* Elizabeth Barry (1658–1713), the greatest English actress in the years 1674 to 1709, had a scandalous reputation as a mercenary whore.

111. *a cheddar child.* A child with many fathers. In December, 1677, Mrs. Barry, then mistress to John Wilmot, Earl of Rochester, gave birth to a daughter, named Elizabeth Clerke. When Rochester died in 1680 he left the child an annuity of forty pounds, secured on the manor of Sutton Malet (V. de S. Pinto, *Enthusiast in Wit*, 1962, p. 228). Betty (not "Hesty") died in 1689 or 1690.

114. *his niece.* This is probably fiction. Rochester's niece Anne, daughter of his half-brother, Sir Henry Lee of Ditchley, was the poetess Anne Wharton. She married Thomas Wharton on September 16, 1673, and died in 1685.

117. *T. Wharton.* Thomas Wharton (1648–1715), eldest son of Philip, Lord Wharton, was a famous libertine; see Appendix. The poet suggests that Wharton, apparently Betty's guardian, will seduce her and "pox" her in order to get the forfeiture of her dowry.

121. *if she were him.* If Mrs. Barry were the judge, she would know who was responsible for her daughter's disease.

128. *Modena.* Laura, Duchess of Modena, mother of Queen Marie Beatrice, died in Rome in July, 1687. King James's priests attributed the Queen's pregnancy to a pilgrimage her mother had made to the shrine of Loretto, shortly before she died; hence "wonder-working dame."

133. *Jewish.* Obtained by haggling and sharp practise.

135. *stink.* Conjectural; there is a blank in the MS.

136. *Whitmore . . . [he].* The copy text has "Whitmore . . . she," clearly a mistake. Whitmore may have been Sir Thomas Whitmore of Bridgenorth, who died in 1682. When his widow, Frances (Brooke), who had remarried, died in 1690, Dryden wrote an "Epitaph on the Lady Whitmore."

140. *Goring.* Henry Goring was a captain in Lord O'Brien's Regiment of Foot (Dalton, I, 217). On June 13, 1685, Robert Southwell wrote, "Our brother, Charles Deering . . . on Wednesday night at the playhouse, had the misfortune to kill Captain Goring. . . . They were both very drunk, and upon a sudden quarrel that arose they both drew in one of the tiring rooms, where none were there present, and Mr. Goring received a wound in his throat and never spoke more" (*Egmont MS*, II, 153). This may be the episode referred to by Robert Gould in "The Playhouse. A Satyr," 1685; he mourned the death of a friend "behind the scenes," one who "fell the victim" of a "sudden death,"

The shame, the guilt, the horror and disgrace
Light on the punk, the murderer, and the place.

Subsequently it is clear that "the punk" is Elizabeth Barry.
147. *the duchess*. The Duchess of Modena.

SELECTED BRIEF BIOGRAPHIES

ABERCROMY, DUNCAN

Colonel Duncan Abercromy, a Scotsman, appears under versions of both names as surnames: Duncan, Duncombe, Duncome, Dungan, Abercromy Duncan, Dungan Abercromow, or Abercromby. He was an army career officer, a rake, and a furious duelist. Appointed lieutenant in Colonel Russell's Regiment of Footguards on April 13, 1681, he became a captain on April 1, 1687, served under the Duke of Grafton in the Royal Regiment of Footguards, and became a lieutenant-colonel in 1688. King William discharged him for Jacobite activities.

Military titles were used very loosely or not at all. For example, on November 8, 1682, "Capt. Godolphin, governor of Scilly, was killed in a duel by Col. Dungan in a yard in Drury Lane" (*CSPD*, 1682, p. 526). According to Luttrell (I, 236) the duel was between "Mr. Godolphin and one Lieutenant Duncomb." According to a third account, Godolphin was killed by "Mr. Duncome, who also received three wounds" (*Seventh Report*, p. 480A). On February 2, 1686, Abercromy seconded the Duke of Grafton in a duel which resulted in the death of John Talbot, the Earl of Shrewsbury's brother. A Scotsman wrote, "This morning Jake Talbot, the Earle of Shrosberry's brother, was kilde in a diuell by the Duke of Grafton. . . . Our countryman Abercromby was his second and Captain Fitzpatrick to the other. Neither of them has any hurt" (*Buccleuch MS*, II, 97). Another correspondent named Grafton's second "Dungan Abercromow" (*Downshire MS*, I, 116). On February 16, 1687, Dryden, in a letter to Etherege, reported a duel in Covent Garden between "Abercromy" and Cardell Goodman, the famous actor, in which Goodman was wounded.

On September 9, 1690, "Abercromy" was one of a group of Jacobites who "surrendered themselves," and in March, 1691, "Capt. Duncan Abercromy" was one of a party of Jacobites picked up in a tavern (*Le Fleming MS*, p. 289; Luttrell, II, 189.)

227

A troublesome fellow, Abercromy seems to have been a follower of the rough Duke of Grafton, sharing in his escapades and debaucheries. Yet he must have been a good soldier. An entry in *The Secret Service Accounts* (1851, p. 111) for September 29, 1685, reads "To Lieut. Duncan Abercrombey, bounty to him in consid'ac'on of the wounds he rec'd at Tangier, in the service of King Char 2d. £100 0 0."

Some time after 1688 Abercromy married Caroline, daughter of Sir George Carteret and widow of Sir Thomas Scott. On May 21, 1695, Luttrell wrote (II, 475), "Some gentlemen, coming out of a tavern in Convent Garden on Sunday morning, quarreled and fought, and Captain Abercromby Duncomb killed."

Dalton, I, 285, 316; II, 129; Dryden, *Letters*, p. 27; Evelyn, *Diary*, III, 358, note 5.

ARP , HARP, ORPE, OR ORBY

Thomas Orby was the son of Peter Orby, alias Arpe, of Burton Pedwardine, Lincs. Thomas was a gentleman usher to Queen Henrietta Maria during her long years in exile at Paris. At Brussels, on October 9, 1658, the exiled King Charles created him a baronet, and in 1671 Queen Henrietta Maria rewarded his fidelity with a twenty-one years lease of Crowland Abbey and Manor. Sir Thomas, called indifferently "Orpe" and "Orby" married Katherine, daughter of one ----- Guernier, of France; as Katherine Arp or Orpe, she became a dresser to Queen Henrietta Maria.

Sir Thomas fathered two sons and probably one daughter, Henreitta Orby, who was a dresser to Queen Catherine, 1669–77 (*CTB*, 1669–72; *CTB*, 1672–75; *CTB*, 1676–79). Sir Thomas died at his house in St. Paul's, Covent Garden, c. March 23, 1692.

The Arp, Harp, Orpe, or Orby occasionally mentioned in the Court satires was no doubt Charles, Sir Thomas's first son and heir (c. 1640–1716), an officer in the Guards and a very minor courtier. A duel between Mr. Fenwick and Mr. Churchill, reported on February 6, 1671, involved as seconds "Mr. Harpe and Mr. Newport, son to my Lord Newport" (*CSPD*, 1671, p. 71). On April 11, 1671, Charles Orby (Arp) and James, Lord Annesley, were granted pardons, apparently because they had been involved with the Dukes of Albemarle and Monmouth, Viscount Dunbar, Edward Griffin, Peter Savage, and John Fenwick in the murder of Peter Vernall, a watchman slain by the band of young savages in a riot in Whetstones Park, February 26, 1671 (*CSPD*, 1671, p.183). No doubt, too, Charles was the "Mr. Harpe" or "Mr. Orpe" who appeared as one of the gentleman dancers attending upon the Duke of Monmouth in Crowne's masque, *Calisto,* February, 1675.

In "An Ironical Satire," 1680 (*POAS*, Yale, II, 203), the poet lists among the half-wits who adorned the Court,

> . . . Arp, to whom Heav'n no distinction gave
> From John-an-apes, but that the brute can laugh.

In the *Gyldenstolpe MS* version of the poem (p. 284) "Arp" becomes "Harp." In "Satire," 1680 (*POAS*, Yale, II, 305), the poet protests against Court fools,

> Must I meet Heveningham where'er I go,
> Arp, Arran, villain Frank, nay Poulteney too?

In the Portland Miscellany version of Sir Carr Scroope's "In Defense of Satire," the "vain fop" who mortgaged all his land to get "that gawdy Play-thing, a Command" is identified in a key as "Mr. Arpe: Orpe" (V. de S. Pinto, *Rochester's Poems*, 1964, p. 226). In "Satyr Unmuzzell'd," 1680 (*POAS*, Yale, II, 209) we have Arp again,

> Who to the sin of pride does lay most claim:
> Need you say Tollemach, Arp, or Heveningham?

Eventually Charles Arp-Harp-Orpe-Orby became colonel of the Queen's Regiment of Foot, only to be removed by William of Orange in December, 1688. Arp married (1) Anne, widow of Thomas Winter, and (2) Anne, widow of Sir William Beeston. He died in May, 1716, and was succeeded in the baronetcy by his younger brother, Thomas (c. 1658–1725).

Complete Baronetage; *Angliae Notitia*, 1671; Boswell, *The Restoration Court Stage*; Dalton, I, 188, 253, 312; II, 89, 117, 206.

BULKELEY, HENRY AND SOPHIA

Sophia Stuart (c. 1648–1715), younger daughter of Walter Stuart, third son of Lord Blantyre, Scotland, and sister of Frances Teresa (later Duchess of Richmond), came to England from France in 1663 as one of Queen Henrietta Maria's dressers. Pepys first saw her on January 30, 1668, and considered her "very handsome." In December, 1671, she became one of Queen Catherine's Maids of Honor. In November, 1673, she married Henry Bulkeley (1638–98), fourth son of Thomas, Viscount Bulkeley of Baron Hill, near Beaumaris, Wales, and captain of a company of the King's Guards in Ireland (*Williamson Letters*, II, 71). Bulkeley became Master of the Household to Charles II and James II, a Groom of the Bedchamber, and M.P. from Beaumaris, 1679–81 and 1685–87.

A lesser member of the coterie of Court Wits, Bulkeley was a pugnacious fellow, frequently involved in brawls and duels. In 1668 he killed his man in a duel in Ireland, was convicted of manslaughter, sentenced to be burned in the hand, and promptly pardoned. In July, 1673, with his friend Lord Buckhurst, he was in a riotous brawl outside the Theatre Royal and was wounded in the neck (*Williamson Letters*, I, 87). In February, 1675, he was sent to the Tower for challenging James Butler, Earl of Ossory, who had been too free with Sophia. In December, 1677, he fought a bloodless duel with Lord Ossory— "the old quarrel about Mr. B. wiffe is the town talk" (*Rutland MS*, II, 42). In July, 1691, he fought another bloodless duel with Dr. Charles Frazier (*Seventh Report*, p. 100).

According to the gossips, Sophia was promiscuous, and a series of entries in the Secret Service accounts suggests an intimacy with King Charles II. In 1680 a Court intrigue against the Duke of York brought forth the gossip that "Godly [Sidney] Godolphin being enamored and intoxicated with Mrs. Buckly was trusted to manage the intrigue" (*Ormonde MS*, N.S., V, 561). On February 28, 1684, Sophia was granted the place and precedency of an earl's daughter for unspecified services (*CSPD*, 1684, February 28). In the reign of James II she became a Lady of the Bedchamber to Queen Marie Beatrice. At her leisure she presented her husband with two sons and four daughters.

An ardent Jacobite, Lady Sophia followed King James into exile. Bulkeley, who often went to France to see his wife, was certainly a Jacobite agent and was accused as a spy but never convicted. He died in 1698. In 1700 his daughter Anne was married to James, Duke of Berwick, a natural son of King James II. Lady Sophia was still living in December, 1718, and petitioning for leave to return to England (*Stuart Papers*, VII, 605).

DNB; *Tenth Report*, V, 67; *Bulstrode*, I, 212; Luttrell, December 30, 1690; C. H. Hartmann, *La Belle Stuart*, 1924; J. H. Wilson, *Court Wits of the Restoration*, 1948.

CLEVELAND, BARBARA, DUCHESS OF

Barbara Villiers, daughter of William, second Viscount Grandison, and Mary Bayning, daughter of Paul, Viscount Bayning, was baptized on November 27, 1642. A beautiful wanton, Barbara lost her virginity to Philip Stanhope, second Earl of Chesterfield, about 1656. On April 14, 1659, she married a wealthy law student, Roger Palmer. She became mistress to King Charles II in April or May, 1660, and ruled him for the next ten years. Barbara was created Countess of Castlemaine (I) in December, 1661. In December, 1663, she became a Roman Catholic. According to the French Ambassador, "The King has been asked by the relations of the lady to interfere and prevent her; but he answered that as for the souls of the ladies, he did not meddle with that" (Jusserand, *French Ambassador*, p. 95). In August, 1670, when her liaison with the King came to an end, Barbara was created Duchess of Cleveland.

In 1676 the duchess took up residence in France, returning to England at intervals. In 1682 she came back to stay and took the famous actor, Cardell Goodman, as her Gentleman of the Horse and lover. Barbara's husband, Roger, Earl of Castlemaine, died July 21, 1705, and on November 25 the duchess (now 63) married Robert ("Handsome") Fielding. When she learned that Fielding was already secretly married, the duchess had her marriage annulled on May 23, 1707. She died on October 9, 1708.

Generally acclaimed as the most beautiful woman in England, Barbara was tall, shapely, with blue eyes and auburn hair. She was said to be skilled in "all the tricks of Aretin that are to be practised to give pleasure" (Pepys, May 15, 1663). Among her numerous lovers besides Chesterfield, the King, and Goodman were (according to the gossips) Sir Charles Berkeley, Henry Jermyn, James Hamilton, Charles Hart (an actor), Jacob Hall (a ropedancer), William Wycherley (a playwright), John Churchill (to whom she gave £5,000), Henry Savile, Ralph Montague, and John, Earl of Mulgrave. She was avaricious, extravagant, foolish, and an inveterate gambler. In spite of immense sums given her by King Charles she died poor.

Barbara's children (the first five acknowledged by King Charles II) were the following:

1. *Anne*, born February 25, 1661, and married on August 11, 1674, to Thomas Lennard. Lord Dacre (1654–1715), who was promptly created Earl of Sussex. As handsome and wanton as her mother, Anne fled to France with King James II and died there on May 16, 1722. She was "debauched" in 1678 by Ralph Montague, then Ambassador to France (*Rochester-Savile Letters*), p. 64.

2. *Charles Fitzroy*, baptized June 18, 1662, and created Duke of Southampton on September 10, 1675, was a student at Christ Church College, Oxford, from 1675 to 1678. He married (1) Mary, daughter of Sir Henry Wood, in 1671 (the ceremony was repeated in 1677); Mary died of smallpox on November 15, 1680, aged seventeen. He married (2) in November, 1694, Anne daughter of Sir William Pulteney of Misterton, Lincs. (Luttrell, III, 397). Southampton, a simple-minded, if not feeble-minded, man, inherited as Duke of Cleveland in 1709 and died September 9, 1730. His widow remarried and lived until 1746.

3. *Henry Fitzroy*, born September 20, 1663, was created Duke of Grafton on September 11, 1675. On August 1, 1672, he married Isabella, the five-year-old daughter of Henry Bennet, Earl of Arlington. (The wedding ceremony was repeated on November 7, 1679, and the marriage was consummated in April, 1681). Grafton, a rough, ill-educated sailor and soldier, was killed at the Battle of Cork, October 9, 1690. In October, 1697, his widow married Sir John Hanmer, a young Buckinghamshire baronet. Her reputation for promiscuity was well established, both before and after Grafton's death. Hearne wrote (*Collections*, July 19, 1714), "She is still living, and was once a beautiful woman. Several people were supposed to have had the use of her body after the death of the Duke of Grafton . . . before Hanmer married her." The duchess died on February 7, 1723.

4. *Charlotte Fitzroy*, born September 5, 1664, married on May 16, 1674, Henry Lee, Earl of Lichfield (consummated in February,

1677). An amiable and prolific spouse, she brought her husband thirteen sons and five daughters. Lichfield died on July 14, 1716; his countess died on February 17, 1718.

5. *George Fitzroy*, born December 28, 1665, was created Earl (October 1. 1674) and Duke (April 6, 1683) of Northumberland (q.v.). He married (1) c. March 12, 1686, Catherine Lucy, the penniless widow of Sir Thomas Lucy, and (2) on March 10, 1715, Mary, daughter of Thomas Dutton. Northumberland died in 1716.

6. *Barbara Palmer*, born August 23, 1670, was probably the daughter of John Churchill (future Duke of Marlborough). On May 31, 1691, Lady Barbara gave birth to an illegitimate son, sired by James Douglas, Earl of Arran. Barbara retired to a nunnery in France, where she died in 1737.

DNB; *Complete Peerage*; Abel Boyer, *History of the Life and Reign of Queen Anne*, 1722; G. S. Steinman, *A Memoir of Barbara, Duchess of Cleveland*, 1871; Philip W. Sergeant, *My Lady Castlemaine*, 1911; J. H. Wilson, *Mr. Goodman, the Player*, 1964.

DEVONSHIRE, WILLIAM, DUKE OF

William Cavendish (1641–1707), styled Lord Cavendish, inherited as fourth Earl of Devonshire in November, 1684, and was created Duke of Devonshire on May 12, 1694. On October 28, 1662, he married Mary (1646–1710), second daughter of James Butler, Duke of Ormonde.

Cavendish was a spendthrift and a reckless gambler; once he lost one thousand pounds in two nights at the Duchess Mazarin's gaming tables (Cartwright, *Sacharissa*, p. 284). Quick to anger, he was often involved in duels. In June, 1669, on the stage of a Paris theatre, he quarreled with several French officers, who attacked him *en masse*. Only the intervention of a servant, who threw Cavendish bodily into the pit, saved his life (*Sixth Report*, p. 366A).

Notorious for his extramarital affairs, Cavendish had several illegitimate children by one Mrs. Heneage. His liaison with the lady was well known. One night in November, 1676, at a Court ball, Cavendish insolently took his stand in front of some women spectators. An Irish officer, "one Mr. Powre," remarked audibly that "if it had been Mrs. Henage, his lordship would have stood more civilly and given them place to see." Cavendish called Powre a rascal, and was promptly challenged. The duel ended without immediate fatalities, but Cavendish's second, Lord Mohun, "was run into the guts." Mohun died several months later (*Rutland MS*, II, 32; *Le Fleming MS*, p. 14í).

According to Baronne D'Aulnoy (*Memoirs*, p. 243), Cavendish had an affair also with Olive, daughter of George Porter (q.v.). The gossips accused him of liaisons with Mrs. Barbara Berkeley, Lady Betty Felton, and Lady Elizabeth Isham. In his old age the duke took as his mistress a pretty young actress, Anne Campion; when Anne died at nineteen (May 19, 1706), he erected a monument with an epitaph describing her virtues.

In his younger days, Cavendish was a Member of Parliament from Derbyshire. An outspoken, but not violent, Whig, he was strongly opposed to the Catholic Duke of York; however, he preferred William of Orange over the Duke of Monmouth as a substitute successor to the throne, and in October, 1681, he made his peace with King Charles II. In the reign of James II, the earl was in trouble because of altercations with Colonel Thomas Colepeper, and in 1686 he struck Colepeper in Whitehall. He was fined £30,000 (never paid), and imprisoned until he gave a bond for the fine. Understandably, the Earl of Devonshire was one of the seven peers who, on June 30, 1688, signed an "Invitation" to William of Orange (Macaulay, III, 222).

Devonshire took an active part in "the Glorious Revolution" of 1688 and became an important office holder in the reigns of William and Mary, and Queen Anne. He was a Fellow of the Royal Society, a connoisseur of music, architecture, painting, and literature, and a trifling poet. John Macky said of him, "He hath been the first and handsomest gentleman of his time; loves the ladies and plays; keeps a noble house and equipage; is tall, well made, and of a princely behavior. Of nice honor in everything but the paying his tradesmen" (*Memoirs*, p. 18). A typical Restoration gentleman.

DNB; *Complete Peerage*; Frances Bickley, *The Cavendish Family*, 1911; D'Aulnoy, *Memoirs*; Evelyn, *Diary*, July 9, 1685; *The Hazard of a Death-Bed Repentance*, 1708.

DUNBAR

Robert Constable (1651–1712) inherited as third Viscount Dunbar (S.) in 1668. In his youth he was a drunken bully. In 1670 Lady Newton wrote, "Poor Henry Savill and the Lord Dunbar both foule drunk, quarreled and cuff'd, then drew, Henry could not stand, but fell, then Dunbar run him through but 'tis hoped not through the body, though he hath a terrible wound" (*The House of Lyme*, 1917, p.245).

On February 26, 1671, Dunbar with a riotous band of wild blades attacking a bawdy house in Whetstones Park, fought with the watch and killed a beadle, one Peter Vernall. All were guilty, but Dunbar gave the mortal wound, stabbing Vernall with a rapier and giving him "a wound on the right side of the head" (*Middlesex County Records*, IV, 24). Because the Dukes of Albemarle and Monmouth were in the riot, the King pardoned all the rioters (*CSPD*, 1671, p. 183).

In or before 1672, Dunbar married Mary, daughter of John, first Baron Belasyse of Worlsby. Fifteen years later, she was the scandal of the town. "The thinge that makes most noise about towne is my Lady Dunbar being brought to bed, and oweneing the child to bee got by Father Confessor, upon her lord's persuadinge her she would die, and telling her shee would certainly be damned unless she told who got the infant, his lordship being very certaine 'twas none of his. This is a very great mortification to my Lord Bellasis in particular, who is her father, and to the whole [Catholic] party in general" (*Rutland MS*, II, 115, July 21, 1687). Probably Lady Dunbar died in childbed. About August 1, 1697, Dunbar married Dorothy (Brudenell), widow of Charles Fane, third Earl of Westmorland.

Opinions about Dunbar differed. Mulgrave wrote in his *Essay upon Satire*, 1679,

> Who would not be as silly as Dunbar,
> As dull as Monmouth, rather than Sir Carr?

But Etherege wrote on May 22, 1687, "Pray . . . send me some news of all my friends, particularly of my Lord Dunbar and of Ned Lee, whose prosperity I have always wished" (*Letters*, p. 118). Completely undistinguished, Dunbar died on January 2, 1712. His widow died January 26, 1740, aged ninety-three.

Complete Peerage.

FALKLAND, ANTHONY, VISCOUNT

Anthony Carey (1656–94) was son and heir to Anthony (1634-63), fourth Viscount Falkland in the peerage of Scotland. His grandfather, Lucius, was a noted Cavalier poet. Young Anthony succeeded as fifth viscount in April, 1663. He attended Winchester School (1668), traveled in France (1671), and briefly attended Christ Church College, Cambridge. He married a great fortune, Rebecca Chapman of Knebworth, Hants. (1662–1709) and set about amassing more wealth.

Falkland was a rather useless Treasurer of the Navy from April, 1681, to September, 1689; a Lord Commissioner of the Admiralty, December 20, 1690, and First Lord, April 15, 1693. A member of the House of Commons and an accomplished debater, he was appointed to the Privy Council in March, 1691. He was a financial speculator, engaged in some shady deals, and on January 17, 1694, he was committed to the Tower charged with peculation, but quickly freed. He died of smallpox on March 24, 1694.

Falkland was a little man, described in contemporary satires as a "monkey," "A frivolous chit," a bad mimic, and a would-be wit. Charitable John Evelyn (May 30, 1694) described him as "a pretty, brisk, understanding young gentleman; had formerly been faulty, but now much reclaimed; had also the good luck to marry a very great fortune, besides being entitled to a vast sum, his share of the Spanish wreck, taken up at the expense of divers adventurers"—Christopher, second Duke of Albemarle, Sir James Hayes, Sir John Narborough, Lord Falkland, Francis Nicolson, and Isaac Foxcraft.

Although Falkland was frequently mentioned as a writer of lampoons and prologues, only two pieces can be confidently identified as his: the prologue to Otway's *The Soldier's Fortune*, 1680, and the prologue to Congreve's *The Old Bachelor*, 1693. "To Mr. Julian"— "Julian, in verse, to ease thy wants, I write"—1679, is assigned to Lord Falkland in Dyce MS. 43, p.180; Harleian MS. 7319, p. 41; and Folger MS. m.b.12, f. 34.

Complete Peerage; Arthur Bryant, *Samuel Pepys: The Years of Peril*, 1935; E. F. Ward, *Christopher Monck, Duke of Albemarle*, 1915.

FANSHAW, MARY AND WILLIAM

In the course of Charles II's long exile on the continent, he shared his bed with a number of light ladies; notable among them were Lucy Walter, Elizabeth Killegrew, Eleanor (Needham), Lady Byron, and Catherine Pegge. On April 9, 1649, Lucy Walter (1630–58) gave birth to a son, later to be known as James Crofts, Duke of Monmouth, the King's favorite. After separating from the King, Lucy, on May 6, 1651, gave birth to a daughter, Mary, whose father was (conjecturally) Nicholas, Viscount Taafe. Although King Charles never acknowleged Mary, he gave her a pension of £600 a year. Mary and her family made much of the fact that she was Monmouth's half-sister, and therefore touched with royalty.

About 1670 Mary married William Sarsfield (elder brother of Patrick Sarsfield, q.v.). Sarsfield died in 1675, and a year later Mary married William Fanshaw, a Master of Requests and eldest son of John Fanshaw of Parsloe, Essex.

Apparently Mary (ironically called "princess") once touched for the King's Evil and cured one Jonathan Trott, son of a fruit-woman. In his *Historical Observes* (1840, p. 29) Sir John Lauder noted "at the end of February, 1681," "A pamphlet against Monmouth which suggested that he prove his legitimacy by approaching a lion in the Tower . . . and why might not he try this experiment as well as his sister, Madam Fanshaw [who] had cured on[e] of the King's evill by touching and using the words which his Majesty does."

William Fanshaw was a meagre person, of small attainments and unpleasant habits. On November 1, 1677, Henry Savile wrote to Lord Rochester that Nell Gwyn had advised Fanshaw "to buy him new Shooes that hee might not dirty her roomes, and a new periwigg that she might not smell him stink two storeys high when he knocks at the outward door" (*Rochester-Savile Letters*, p. 48).

A minor member of the coterie of Court wits, Fanshaw visited Lord Rochester in his last illness and was one of the witnesses to his will. In 1681 he was put out of his place "for talking little less than treason upon all occasions that he can" (*Ormonde MS*, N.S., V, 48). Thereafter the Fanshaws and their five children lived in poverty, depending on the charity of friends and on Mary's pension, which was reduced by James II and often in arrears.

Mary died before her husband, whose will (proved July 13, 1708) directed that he be buried in Barking Church "by the side of his dearly beloved wife Mary, sister of the Duke of Monmouth." For arguments that Mary's mother, Lucy Walter, was married to King Charles II, see Lord George Scott, *Lucy Walter, Wife or Mistress*, 1947.

A True Account of a Wonderful Cure of the King's Evil perform'd by Mrs. F[anshaw], sister to his Grace the Duke of Monmouth, 1681; Fea, *Some Beauties,* pp. 142–44; Johannes Prinz, *Rochester,* 1927, pp. 232, 300; A. I. Dasent, *The Private Life of Charles II,* 1927; Wilson, *Court Wits.*

FELTON, LADY BETTY

Lady Elizabeth Howard, born in 1656, was the only daughter of James, third Earl of Suffolk, by his second wife, Barbara, widow of Richard Wenman and a daughter of Sir Edward Villiers. Nineteen years later, Madam D'Aulnoy described her thus: "Madam Betty had a beauty and youth that were almost dazzling, and won her the love of all who saw her, and being of a very gay disposition she seldom frightened her lovers away by her looks" (*Memoirs,* p. 130). In July, 1675, against her parents' wishes, she stole a marriage with handsome Thomas Felton, Esq., a Groom of the King's Bedchamber. Henry Savile wrote, "Mr. Felton has at last got my Lady Betty, and has her in lodgings in the Mall. Her parents are very disconsolate in the point, and my Lord Suffolk swears all manner of oaths never to be reconciled" (*Savile Correspondence,* p. 39). Eventually Suffolk was reconciled to the marriage and gave his daughter a large allowance.

Once married, gay Lady Betty gloried in her conquests. In 1679 Lady Sunderland commented on "the fine airs of the great beauty, my Lady Betty Felton, who turns the heads of all the men, and quarrels with all the women, and lies in bed and cries when things are not altogether to her taste" (Cartwright, *Sacharissa,* p. 240). The *enfant terrible* could not endure rivals. In March, 1681, Lady Russell wrote that "Lady Betty Felton threatens to mortify [Lady Arundell] above all sufferance; for she vows she will not suffer Lord Shrewsbury to adore there any longer . . . and for my Lord Thanet, she says, the world shall see how much more powerful her charms are than those of a great monarch" (*Letters,* p.77). True to her vow, Lady Betty made a scene in public, and on October 2, 1681, Lady Russell added (p. 81), "The ladies' quarrel [Lady Betty and Lady Arundel] is the only news talked of: Lady Betty lies abed and cries. Lord

238

Newport came yesterday morning and says he never saw the King more enraged; he sent to Lord Suffolk to chain up his mad daughter, and forbid her the Court, so at present neither Lord nor Lady Suffolk sees her, and little Felton is leaving her."

Passion has its penalties: Lady Betty died "of an apoplexy" on December 13, 1681. The gossips charged that she had committed adultery with Frank Newport, William, Lord Cavendish, and James, Duke of Monmouth, but she may have been more coquette than *cocotte*. Lady Betty's husband, who succeeded his older brother as fourth baronet in February, 1697, was Comptroller of the Household under Queen Anne. He died March 2, 1709, a harmless little man and an excellent jockey.

FRAZIER, CAREY

Sir Alexander Frazier (c.1610–81), a Scots physician and an ardent royalist, was chief physician to Charles II in his years of exile. Shortly after the Restoration he was knighted, and his wife Mary (Carey) was appointed a dresser to Queen Catherine. According to Pepys (September 19, 1664), Frazier was "so great" with the Court ladies "in helping them to slip their calfes when there is occasion, and with the great men in curing of their claps, that he can do what he pleases with the King." Dr. Frazier had a house in Scotland Yard, close to Whitehall. He fathered two children, a son, Charles, who also became a physician, and a daughter, Carey, one of the Queen's Maids of Honor from 1674 to 1680.

Carey was famous for her beauty and her finery. On November 2, 1676, Lady Chaworth wrote, "Mighty bravery in clothes preparing for the Queen's birthday, especially Mrs. Phraser, whose gown is ermine upon velvet imbroidered with gold and lined with cloth of gold. 'Twill come to £300 and frights Sir Carr Scroope, who is much in love with her, from marrying her, saying his estate will scarce maintaine her in clothes." On January 30, 1677, Lady Chaworth reported a quarrel between Sir Carr and Katherine Sedley (the Duke of York's mistress) as the result of libels each had written against the other. Scroope (said the gossip) accused Katherine of being "as mad as her mother and as vicious as her father," Sir Charles Sedley.

239

Katherine retorted with a lampoon "of him being lapt in searcloth, Mrs. Phraser being with child, but her father able to cure both" (*Rutland MS*, II, 31, 37).

Sir Carr's verses are lost, but the following squib, discovered by David M. Vieth (*Manuscripts*, VI, 160–65) may be Katherine Sedley's retort. It presents a supposed conversation between Carey Frazier and George Douglas, Earl of Dumbarton.

> As Frazier one night at her post in the drawing room
> stood,
> Dumbarton came by, and she cried, "My lord, would
> you—would—"
> "What is your will, madam, for I am in haste and can't
> tarry."
> "The thing is soon done, for I swear it is nothing but
> marry."
> He laughted and cried out, "Do you think that the devil
> is in me,
> To marry with one that in time will be mine for a
> guinea?
> Nay, look not so coy, nor toss your dangling locks,
> But marry Car Scroope, and your father may cure his pox."

It seems that Carey was both ambitious and promiscuous. The charge that she was once mistress to John, Earl of Mulgrave, a Knight of the Garter, was first expressed in another short squib, "Upon Madam Fra." (Add. MS. 34,362, f. 118).

> There was a lass in Scotland yard,
> A haughty lass of high degree;
> She common was to all the Guard,
> And all upon her father's fee.
>
> There was a knight made love to her,
> He wore a star and garter blue;
> He got the better of Sir Carr,
> Although his love was not so true.

In December, 1677, when the King's reigning mistress, the Duchess of Portsmouth, was ailing, the rumor ran that "Mrs. Frazier, the doctor's daughter, and Mrs. Elliott, and one or two more strive for the preferment" (*Seventh Report*, p. 469). The duchess recovered, but in 1679, according to the author of "Colin" (see above), "stately Carey Frazier" was still striving for regal preferment.

In or about 1679, Carey fell into the hands and bed of Charles, Viscount Mordaunt (q.v.), with the usual biological consequence. On May 20, 1680, a gossip reported that "Mrs. Frazer is marched off from Court; how honorably time will try" (*Seventh Report*, p. 496). Two days later another gossip continued the tale, "It is said that the marriage between my Lord Mordaunt and Mrs. Frazer will now be speedily consummated, the lady being discovered with child, and my lord seeming to own something of a contract" (*Ormonde MS.*, N.S., V, 325). But it was not until December, 1681, that Mordaunt "brought out as well as owned his lady" (*Rutland MS*, II, 62, December 12, 1681).

Carey proved to be a devoted wife and gave her eccentric husband two sons, both of whom died of smallpox in 1710. Carey died in March, 1709.

GERARD, CHARLES AND ANNE, LORD AND LADY BRANDON

Charles Gerard (1659–1701), styled Lord Brandon or Lord Brandon Gerard from 1679 to 1694, was the elder son of Charles, first Viscount Brandon and first Earl of Macclesfield, by Jane, daughter of Pierre de Civelle. Brandon Gerard was a young spark of dissolute habits. On May 18, 1676, a gossip wrote, "Last night the Lord Charles Cornwallis and Mr. Gerard, the Lord Gerard's son, being in drink, abused the sentinels in St. James's Park, and after, Mr. Gerard meeting Captain With's footboy, upon what provocation is not known, struck him so that the boy fell down dead" (*Hatton Correspondence*, I, 127). The boy's neck was broken. Lord Cornwallis was tried for murder and acquitted. Gerard fled to France and soon won a pardon. In December, 1677, Gerard seconded Henry Bulkeley in his duel with Lord Ossory, disarmed his own opponent, and forced Ossory to yield (*Hatton Correspondence*, II, 119).

On June 18, 1683, Lord Brandon Gerard, aged twenty-four, married Anne, aged fifteen, second daughter of Sir Richard Mason of Sutton, Surrey, Comptroller of the Household, by Anne Margaretta, daughter of James Long of Draycott, Wilts. The young people were completely mismatched, even in their politics; Anne came from a Tory family;

Gerard was a violent Whig. After a year and a half of constant quarrels, Brandon took his wife to his father's house and left her there, vowing never to live with her again. Two weeks later his father, Lord Macclesfield—according to Pepys (December 9, 1667) "a very' proud and wicked man"—turned her out of Gerard House in Soho and left her to shift for herself.

On November 26, 1685, Lord Brandon, accused of complicity in Monmouth's Rebellion, was convicted of high treason and sentenced to death. His wife pleaded for him with King James. In January, 1687, he was released from prison, and in November his attainder was reversed. He succeeded as second Earl of Macclesfield on January 7, 1694.

His unhappy, deserted wife was no beauty, and what looks she had were damaged by smallpox in 1686, yet she seems to have had several lovers, among them Henry, Duke of Grafton. Early in 1693 Richard Savage ("Tyburn Dick"), Lord Colchester and future Earl Rivers, "a tall handsome man of a very fair complexion" (Macky, p. 160), became her lover. He fathered two children: a daughter, called Anne Savage (1695) who died in infancy, and a son, baptized Richard Smith (1697), who may have been the eighteenth century poet, Richard Savage. Lady Brandon's affair with Colchester was well known, and in "Satyr. 1692/3" (Holkham MS., p.124), Jack, Howe bemoaned

> Poor Brandon's fate; she loves a battered bully,
> An ill performer, yet by descent no cully.

In the summer of 1697, Brandon (now Lord Macclesfield) sued for a divorce *a mensa et thoro* in the Court of the Arches. His wife contested the suit bitterly. Impatient of ecclesiastical delay, on January 15, 1698, Macclesfield offered a bill of divorce *a vinculo* (with permission to remarry) in the House of Lords. The countess continued to fight. The Bishop of St. Davids wrote, "She hath brought proofs of his ill usuage, his leaving her, her seeking for reconciliation, her trouble upon the letter he left when he went first from her, her sending to his father and him at Lancaster for provision, her application when he was condemned, her letter delivered by J. Tillotson when he was pardoned, for reconciliation. She sues for liberty to recriminate, which I fear will be denied" (*Hastings MS*, II, 306).

But the countess's adultery, however justified, was fully proved, even though she claimed that she had tricked Macclesfield into spending a night with her, thinking her a stranger, and that little Richard was the result! On March 3, 1698, the House of Lords granted Macclesfield a divorce with permission to remarry, bastardized Richard Smith, and returned the ex-countess's dowry.

In 1700 Anne married Colonel Henry Brett and became a faithful, loving wife, so exemplary that (it is said) Colley Cibber used her as the model for his Lady Easy in *The Careless Husband*, 1704. She died in 1753.

In July, 1688, Anne's older sister, Dorothy (1665–1700), a beauty with a large dowry, married William Brownlow of Humby, Lincs., who succeeded as baronet July 11, 1697. Macclesfield died on November 5, 1701, and was succeeded by his brother, Fitton Gerard (c.1665–1702).

DNB; *Complete Peerage*; *Reasons for the Earl of Macclesfield's Bill in Parliament*, 1697; James Boswell, *Life of Johnson*, 2 vols., 1904, I, 119, Note 2; Frederick Clifford, *A History of Private Bill Legislation*, 1885, p. 400; Clarence Tracy, *The Artificial Bastard, a Biography of Richard Savage*, 1953.

GERARD, SIR GILBERT COSINS AND LADY MARY

Gilbert Cosins Gerard (c. 1662–1720) was the son of Sir Gilbert Gerard, Bart., of Fiskerton, Lincs., and his second wife, Mary, daughter of John Cosins, Bishop of Durham; he was also a great nephew of Charles Gerard, first Earl of Macclesfield. He inherited as second baronet c. September 20, 1687.

On May 2, 1681, young Gerard married Mary, daughter of Charles Berkeley, Earl of Falmouth, and his notorious wife, Mary (Bagot). Born c. 1665, Mary Gerard was an emancipated young woman who quickly ran wild. For example, on November 27, 1683, a gossip wrote, "The other night Lady Mary Garett and her woman and some other of her companions was at a tavern, whear they had musick; and after some time they went away and would not pay the musick; and so there was a quarrell amongst them, and some of the fiddlers were killed, and those that did it was taken, and one of them was the Ladys woman in mens cloaths, who was a French woman; and she is much concerned and tells many storys of her lady, who there is a warrant from my Lord Chief Justice to take; but I fancy she will not be easyly found, for, if she should, it is believed she will be punished" (*Hatton Correspondence*, II, 39–40). According to more sober accounts, several ladies dressed in male attire for "the frolic"; there were gentlemen in the party, and two musicians were killed. Apparently no one was punished. Mary's conduct then and thereafter brought her the distinction of a libel, "Advice to the Ladies," (Dyce MS. 43, II, 479–80),

> She that designs to make a virtuous wife
> Must not like lewd Mall Gerr-d lead her life;
> Not (like her) in vice place her chief delight,
> Sleep all the day and revel all the night;
> Not (like her) run on every tavern score
> To treat those bawds that taught her first to whore;
> Not (like her) 'mongst a crowd of strumpets roll,
> Nauseous alike both in body and in soul;
> Not (like her) should another frost arrive,
> In every booth with every blockhead swive;
> Not (like her) a salacious jilt become,
> And from the stews each night come reeling home;
> Not (like her) scour the stews, with brandy drunk,
> And fight for stallion, as he fights for punk;
> Not (like her) think't a scandal to be good,
> And make a jest of spilling human blood.
> No—
> She who'd acquire that name, her course must steer
> Just opposite to what is painted here;
> And that will waft her safe to the port of fame,
> While t'other splits on rocks of pox and shame.

Perhaps Mary Gerard was protected by the Earl of Dorset, her step-father and, after her mother's death in 1679, her trustee. But Gerard divorced his errant wife in 1684; she died in April, 1693.

Apparently Gerard, called by one satirist "whiffling Topus" ("To Julian," 1687, Harleian MS. 7317, p.109), was a confirmed rakehell and "keeper" and "by leading such a vicious life / He justifies the lewdness of his wife." In February, 1687, he conspired to marry one of his whores to Sir Samuel Morland (q.v.), but continued his own relations with her. No one seems to have had a good word for him. On April 6, 1712, Gerard took a second wife, one Mary Wheeler, spinster. He died in 1720.

Complete Baronetage; *Verney Memoirs*, II, 339; *Seventh Report*, p. 375 B; Harris, *Dorset*, p. 79.

GREY, FORD, LORD

Ford Grey (1655–1701), third Lord Grey of Werke, was the eldest son of Ralph, Lord Grey, and Katherine, daughter of Sir Edward Ford. A tall, slender, handsome young man, he married, c. 1674, Mary Berkeley, fourth daughter of George, Earl of Berkeley. Grey was clever, adventurous, a devout libertine, and a convinced Whig, an intimate of the Earl of Shaftesbury and the Duke of Monmouth.

Grey succeeded to his title in June, 1675. In 1679 and 1680 there were persistent rumors of an intrigue between Mary, Lady Grey, and the Duke of Monmouth. In January, 1680, Grey took his wife off to Northumberland, and Lady Sunderland wrote, "My Lord Grey was long in believing the Duke of Monmouth an unfaithful friend to him. He gave [Lady Grey] but one night's time to take leave, pack up, and be gone" (Cartwright, *Sacharissa*, p. 233). One result of the scandal was a scurrilous pamphlet entitled *A Relation of the Apparition which appeared to Lady Grey*, January, 1681. Nevertheless, there is no conclusive evidence that Lady Grey was ever Monmouth's mistress.

There is, however, abundant evidence that Lady Grey's younger sister, Henrietta ("Harriet") was Grey's mistress. Although the Berkeleys did not discover the incestuous intrigue until the end of June, 1682, the Town knew all about it. As one gossip wrote on June 9, 1682, Lord Grey, "as the report goes, saith that he married [Henrietta's] eldest sister and expected a maidenhead, but not finding it, hee resolved to have one in the family, if any be left" (*Kenyon MS*, p. '43).

Berated and confined by her family, Henrietta—"a young lady of a fair complexion, fair haired, full breasted, and indifferent tall"— ran away from home in August, 1682. Although Luttrell (I, 215) reported on August 24 that "one Mr. Forester hath lately stole the

Lord Berkeley's daughter, and married her," Grey was arrested, charged with "conspiring the final ruin of Lady Henrietta Berkeley . . . to commit whoredom, fornication, and aultery," committed to the King's Bench Prison, and tried on November 23. Henrietta appeared in court to testify in his defense. A witness of the trial commented, "It is the foulest story that ever eyes saw or ears heard; in short, the lady was pretty round about the wast, and the proofs given in court made it too plain (if she is with child) who is the father" (*Kenyon MS*, p.154). But Henrietta introduced one William Turner as her husband, and eventually Grey was freed. Thereafter he and his wife lived separate lives.

On June 25, 1683, Grey was arrested for complicity in the Rye House Plot. With his usual ingenuity he managed to escape to France with Henrietta and her complaisant "husband." A child was born to Henrietta during the sojourn abroad.

On June 11, 1685, Grey returned to England with the Duke of Monmouth's invading force, as commander of the cavalry. As a soldier he was useless, as a coward contemptible. After Sedgemoor he was captured, forced to plead for his life, and eventually freed after writing a full confession, testifying at the trials of Lords Delamere and Brandon Gerard, and giving up his fee-simple estates and most of the income from his entailed properties. In King William's reign, his attainder was reversed and most of his estates and income returned. On May 11, 1695, William created him Earl of Tankerville and appointed him to the Privy Council. He became a successful politician and an acknowleged orator. He died on June 30, 1701. Henrietta Berkeley died in obscurity August 13, 1706. Lady Grey took a second husband, Richard Rooth of Epsom, in 1712, and died May 19, 1719.

DNB; *Complete Peerage*; *A New Vision of the Lady Gr--s Concerning her Sister the Lady Henrietta Berkeley*, 1682; Aphra Behn [?], *The Love Letters of a Nobleman to his Sister*, 1683; Cecil Price, *Cold Caleb*, 1956.

GWYN, NELL

The origins of Ellen Gwyn are obscure. She was born (supposedly in an alley near Covent Garden, London) on February 2, 1650, the second daughter of Helena Gwyn (said to have been an apple woman) and an unknown father. Nell's older sister, Rose, once declared that their "father was a gentleman that did faithful service for his late Majesty [Charles I] and lost all that ever wee had for him" (PRO, State Papers 29/86/62).

According to her own account, Nell was employed in a bawdy-house "to fill strong waters to the guests" (Pepys, October 26, 1667). At about thirteen, through the agency of her sister, she became an orange girl in the Theater Royal. A year later she was a probationary member of the King's Company, and probably mistress of Charles Hart, the Company's leading man. Quick-witted and clever, she learned to read and even to write after a fashion, although to the end of her life she signed documents with a scrawled "E. G." At fifteen she was already noted as a dancer and as "pretty, witty Nell" at the King's House. At seventeen she was a star, especially in comedy, and briefly mistress of Charles Sackville, Lord Buckhurst. (It is said that she called King Charles II her "Charles the Third".)

In 1668 and 1669, Nell was an occasional mistress of King Charles. In May, 1670, she gave birth to a son, named, of course, Charles. In December, despairing of recognition by the King, she returned to the stage. Two months later she left theatrical life for good; the King gave her a house in Pall Mall and an allowance. Her second son by the King, James, was born on Christmas Day, 1671. Late in 1676 her son Charles "Beauclerc" was created Earl of Burford, and James became Lord Beauclerc.

During the Popish Plot years (1678–81) Nell was popular with the mob as a Protestant and a friend of the Whig Party. When a mob mistook Nell's coach for that of the King's Catholic mistress, the Duchess of Portsmouth, Nell stuck her head out the window and said sweetly, "Pray, good people, be civil. I am the Protestant whore." On July 28, 1679, old Mrs. Gwyn, living in Chelsea at Nell's expense, drank too much brandy, fell into a brook and drowned. In June, 1680, Lord James Beauclerc died in France. In January, 1684, Charles, Earl of Burford, was created Duke of St. Albans.

Nell was always a spendthrift, but she was also generous and charitable. On her journey to the meeting of Parliament at Oxford in March, 1681, she was "very liberal to the Ringers and Poor all the Road and especially at Beconsfield and Wickham where she distributed much money." At Oxford she was "very liberal here upon all occasions, and out of her charitable inclinations, has released Three Prisoners for Debt out of the Castle, and two out of Bocardo" (Smith's *Protestant Intellgence*, no. 20, April 4–April 7, 1681).

When King Charles died on February 6, 1685, Nell was deeply in debt to tradesmen. Eventually King James II, urged by his dying brother to "Let not poor Nelly starve," came to her rescue, paid her debts, and gave her a pension of £1,500 a year. She died "of an apoplexy" on November 14, 1687.

Although Nell was commonly attacked by contemporary satirists, the author of the following untitled song (MS. Don. b. 8. p.504) treated her with sympathy. Nell is represented as speaking to King Charles,

> Long days of absence, dear, I could endure,
> If thy divided heart were mine secure;
> But each minute I find myself without thee,
> Methinks I find my rival's arms about thee.
> She perhaps her interest may improve
> By all the studied acts of fraud and love;
> Whilst I, a poor, kind, harmless creature,
> A plain true passion show and trust good nature.
> In her white hand let thy gold sceptre shine,
> And what I must not name be put in mine.
> Crowned and in purple robes to her I'll fling thee,
> But naked every night let Nell unking thee.

DNB; Peter Cunningham, *The Story of Nell Gwyn*, 1852; Arthur I. Dasent, *Nell Gwynne*, 1928; J. H. Wilson, *Nell Gwyn, Royal Mistress*, 1952.

HERBERT, ELIZABETH, LADY

Elizabeth Brydges (1651–1718) was the second daughter of George, sixth Baron Chandos, by his first wife, Susan (Montague). In August, 1673, Elizabeth married (as his second wife), Edward, third Lord Herbert of Cherbury. She was "a great beauty of £10,000 portion" (*Williamson Letters*, I, 192). Lord Herbert died on December 9, 1678, aged 64.

Thereafter Lady Herbert and her widowed older sister, Mrs. Margaret Brownlow, seem to have lived together and to have been guilty of loose conduct; at least they became favorite subjects for satirists. In March, 1683, Captain Patrick Sarsfield (q.v.) abducted Lady Herbert, but could not persuade her to marry him. It is possible that she had been his mistress for a time. In September, 1686, Lady Herbert married (as his second wife) William O'Brien, second Earl of Inchiquin (I), who died in Jamaica in January, 1692, aged 52.

In August, 1694, Lady Inchiquin (now 43) took a third husband, Charles Howard, fourth Baron Howard of Escrick, a handsome young man many years her junior. In December he sold her jewels, took all her money and deserted her, leaving her with only £200 a year. On January 1, 1695, James Vernon wrote, "The Lord Howard of Escrick, who not long since married the Lady Inchiquin, has left her already for the sake of another woman, whom he was in league with before, and it is said they are both gone together for Holland. I find all his lady's concern now is to prove, if she can, that he was first married to that woman, for since she is like to lose her husband, she is desirous to preserve her jointure"—of £1,000 a year (*Lexington Papers*, pp. 37–38).

Lady Inchiquin brought suit against Howard at the Court of the King's Bench and proved that he had previously married his mistress, Mrs. Pike. In a suit at the Guildhall, in July, 1697, Lady Inchiquin tried to have her marriage anulled, but a jury decided against her. In December she petitioned the House of Lords, saying that she wanted to sue her husband in the ecclesiastical Court of the Arches, but that Howard stood upon his privilege as a peer and refused to answer. The Lords ordered him to submit to the Court, but before he did so he came back with a counter offer: to pay half her jointure annually and to give her £500 to pay the expenses of her suits. She refused. Finally her suit reached the High Court of Delegates, which, on February 4, 1701, declared her marriage null and void, "there being full proof of 5 witnesses of a prior marriage with Mrs. Pike of Stafford in the year 1689" (Luttrell, V, 141).

In 1712 Lady Inchiquin married a Mr. George, a French Protestant. She died February 3, 1718, aged 57. She had had a full life but, fortunately, no children.

Complete Peerage; *Calendar of Orrery Papers*, p. 320; *Hastings MS*, II, 243; Luttrell, III, 227; *House of Lords MS*, III, 10; G. S. Alleman,

Matrimonial Law and the Materials of Restoration Comedy, 1924, pp. 132–33.

HEWITT, SIR GEORGE

Sir George ("Beau") Hewitt (1652–89) was a famous fop, noted for his fine clothes and well-arranged cravats. The only surviving son of Sir Thomas Hewitt, Bart., of Pishiobury, Herts., he succeeded to the baronetcy on August 4, 1662. He had six sisters, all of whom married.

On June 25, 1673, Sir George, "the young gallant", bought a commis-
ꞏsion as cornet in the Queen's Troop of Guards. On July 2 he was caned by Mr. Ravenscroft for an insult in the theatre "halfe a year since." Hewitt challenged Ravenscroft, but the King ordered the Earl Marshall to sieze both men and prevented the duel (*Williamson Letters*, I, 67, 87, 94). Hewitt did not lack courage, although references to him as "purblind" suggest that he may have been nearsighted. On the other hand, the word also meant "slow of understanding," or "dim-witted."

In April, 1676, Hewitt fought a set duel with maniacal Philip Herbert, Earl of Pembroke; Hewitt was "wounded in the thumb and arm, but little hurt" (*Seventh Report*, p. 467B). On February 28, 1680, he fought a duel with Charles, Earl of Plymouth; Lords Cavendish and Mordaunt were their seconds. "My Lord Plymouth was disarmed, and my Lord Mordaunt hurt in the shoulder. The quarrel was upon some idle messages that passed in the park by an orange wench that, they say, reported lies to one another to make herself sport" (*Hatton Correspondence*, II, 222). In "An Ironical Satire," 1680 (*POAS*, Yale, II, 202), a satirist reported a different result and made light of the affair, sneering at

> Plymouth, who lately showed upon the plain,
> And did by Hewitt's fall immortal honor gain.
> So Mouse and Frog came gravely to the field,
> Both feared to fight, and yet both scorned to yield.

No doubt Sir George was a fop, although there seems to be no truth in the tradition that he was the model for Etherege's Sir Fopling

Flutter in *The Man of Mode*, 1676. Contemporary libelers described him as a "tittle-tattle fool" and "a moving thing without one grain of wit" and called him "fop Hewitt" and "Sir Amorous La Fool." Nevertheless, as a soldier he was considered competent enough to command the Queen Dowager's Regiment of Horse in the campaign against King James in Ireland. As a man of business he must have been at least adequate. When King Charles bought Lord Scarsdale's house in Pall Mall for Nell Gwyn (April 1, 1671), Hewitt acted as the King's agent. He was also one of Nell's trustees when she acquired Burford House in Windsor on September 24, 1680. According to Lord Clarendon, when Prince George of Denmark wanted to get rid of his Groom of the Stole, Lord Scarsdale ("a pitiful wretch"), he thought of replacing him with Hewitt, who was not a peer, but could be ennobled "when things were settled" (*Clarendon State Papers*, II, 150, January 17, 1689). Sure enough, in April, 1689, King William created Hewitt Baron of Jamestown and Viscount Hewitt of Gowran (I). However, on his return from the campaign in Ireland, Hewitt died at Chester, December 2, 1689. He never married. The chances are that he was never as much a fop and fool as he was painted.

Complete Peerage; Arthur Sherbo, "Sir Fopling Flutter and Beau Hewitt," *Modern Languages Notes*, LXIV, 1949; *CSPD*, 1673, p. 393, June 25; Luttrell I, 520; Wilson, *Nell Gwyn*, pp. 118. 233.

HINTON, MARY

"Moll" Hinton was a notorious strumpet who, to judge by contemporary comments, flourished from about 1680 to 1692. In "The Playhouse. A Satyr. 1685," Robert Gould described the audience at a theatre:

> In the side box Moll Hinton you may see,
> Or Howard Moll, much wickeder than she;
> That is their throne, for there they best survey
> All the young fops that flutter to the play.

Moll was the daughter of Sir John Hinton (1603–82), a physician in ordinary to the King. He was knighted by King Charles early in 1666. According to one report he was honored for "giving his positive opinion that the Queen is with child again" (*Sixth Report*, p. 338A). However, in a begging "Letter of Memorial" to the King in 1679, Hinton himself said that he was knighted for procuring an advance of money to enable the Duke of Albemarle to pay the army (Henry Ellis, *Original Letters*, 3rd Series, 1846, IV, 296).

According to his own account, Hinton had worked and fought for both Charles I and Charles II. However, he was never a popular physician and never prospered. Said Samuel Pepys (December 18, 1665), "Lord, to see how Dr. Hinton come in with a gallant or two from Court, and do so call 'Cozen' Mr. Hinton, the goldsmith, but . . . I know him to be a beggar and a knave."

Moll Hinton was well known in Court circles. In an undated letter, Charles, Earl of Dorset, thanked her ironically for giving him the pox, "a greater favor than any of your sex have bestowed on me this five year" (Harris, *Dorset*, p. 91). On January 26, 1682, we learn that the Russian Ambassador to England "is so taken with Moll Hinton that he intends to carry her over with him" to Russia (*Rutland MS*, II, 64). About that time a satirist took the item as his spring board for "On Three Late Marriages" (see above), insisting that Moll was about to get "an honorable spouse."

Since she is still referred to as "Moll" or "Mall" Hinton after 1682, we must presume that the marriage never took place. Moll was called "pocky lewd Hinton" in "The Session of Ladies." 1688 (see above), and in "The False Favorite's Downfall," 1692 (*POAS*, Yale, V, 332) Arabella Churchill is said to be "as pocky as Hinton, as lewd as Peg Hughes." Moll's reputation for lechery lasted into the next century. Eustace Budgell (*The Spectator*, no. 77, May 29, 1711) presented his *persona*, Will Honeycombe, in a coffee-house, giving "an account of the person and character of Moll Hinton" to an admiring crowd. Unfortunately Budgell did not record Honeycombe's imaginary account.

HOWARD, MARY

Often linked with Moll Hinton (q.v.) as a notorious whore, "Dirty Mall" Howard was also famous as a bawd. Her dates are unknown, and her origins obscure, but apparently she was one of the numerous

Howards who claimed gentility. In "Evidence Mall" (Harleian MS. 7319, p.313) she was said to be "kin to an evidence lord"—William, Lord Howard of Escrick. In "Cheviot Chace" (see above), a stanza ending with the line, "No man will need Mall Howard" is followed by a stanza beginning "Escrick's daughter's much the best/ That family can show."

Related by marriage to Mary Howard, Countess of Arundel, Mall seems to have become that lady's companion or superior lady-in-waiting some time after August, 1678, when the countess's former companion, Frances Skinner, married Sir William Buck (*Complete Baronetage*, III, 142; *Cold Caleb*, p. 30). Mall quickly became famous for her double function. See "A Pert Imitation of all the Flatteries of Fate," c. 1680 (Harleian MS. 6913, p. 91),

> All the world can't afford
> Such a bitch as Mall Howard,
> She procures for my lady and fucks with my lord.
> If this she deny
> 'Tis time she should die,
> For she's able to bawd for a whole Council board.

See also "A Court Satyr. 1682" (Harleian MS. 7317, p. 91. The "Countess" is Lady Arundel),

> Alas for poor St. James's Park
> Since Moll Howard left the Town;
> Baber himself, that very spark,
> Is turned a very clown.
> The withered lime trees cast no shade,
> The jolly Dillons droop,
> And Jack Howe's parts are so decayed
> You'd take him for Sir Scroope.
>
> Since none but Roger Martin's there,
> And stately Stamford stalks,
> Now both the witty and the fair
> Retire to Gray's Inn walks.
> Ah, Countess, since unkind you be
> To rob us of our dear,
> May Shrewsbury lose the other eye,
> And Arundel see clear.

In 1683 it was rumored that Mall was to marry an Irish lord. Evidently the author of "A Letter to the E. of Kildare dissuading him from marrying Mall Howard" (Harleian MS. 7319, p. 326) was successful. Mall never married.

There is no way of knowing how long Mall continued as Lady Arundel's companion. The author of "News from Tunbridge. 1684" (Dyce MS. 43, II, 470) saw at Tunbridge

> none but knaves; the D of N[orfolk]'s bride,
> With dirty Mall attending by her side;
> Mall, who is proof against all human nature,
> Mall, who was never foiled by any creature,
> Insatiate, yet foul in every feature.

Mall's name was often linked with that of Harry Wharton, third son of Philip, Lord Wharton. In "Satire on the Court Ladies," 1680 (see above), he is called "Mall Howard's witty Harry." On February 4, 1687, Thomas Maule wrote to Etherege at Ratisbon, "I cannot forbear telling you that Harry Wharton is no more the constant . . . for he has forsaken Mrs. Mary [Howard?] and makes violent love to Mrs. Drumar" (Etherege, *Letters*, p. 275). The author of "A Letter to Julian," 1687 (Harleian MS. 7319, p. 522) asks,

> Has Mall Howard made her peace with Harry,
> Will they still fornicate, or marry?

In 1688 Mall appears as "Howard's pert Mall" in "The Session of Ladies" (see above), and in 1690 she is "silent Moll Howard" in "Tunbridge Dance" (*POAS*, Yale, V, 379). The rest is silence.

HOWE, JOHN GRUBHAM

Jack Howe's father, John Grubham Howe of Lingar, Notts., married Annabella, third natural daughter of Emanuel Scrope, Earl of Sunderland (1585–1630), by Martha Janes, a servant. Annabella and her two sisters, Mary (who married [1] Henry Carey, and [2] Charles Pawlet, Marquis of Winchester) and Elizabeth (who married Thomas Savage, Earl Rivers) were legitimized and given the rank of an earl's daughters on June 1, 1663. Annabella survived her husband, dying on March 21, 1704.

The Howes had five daughters ("Lady Annabella's girls"), of whom Bridget married John, Lord Ossulton; Elizabeth married Sir John Guise of Rendecomb, and Diana married Sir Francis Molineux of Tiverfall. The Howes had also four sons, Scroope, John, Charles, and Emanuel; of these only the first two were in any degree distinguished.

Scroope Howe (1648–1712) was a staunch Whig in Parliament and became a Groom of the Bedchamber to King William. He was knighted on March 16, 1663 and on May 6, 1701, he became Viscount Howe (I). Under Queen Anne he was Comptroller of the Excise. In April, 1672, he abducted and married Anne Manners, daughter of the eighth Earl of Rutland. His second wife (1698) was Juliana, daughter of William, Lord Allington. Lord Howe died January 15, 1713.

John ("Libeling Jack") Howe (1657–1722), was at first merely "a young amorous spark of the Court." In August, 1679, he tried to make love to Frances, the widowed Duchess of Richmond. When she scorned him, he plotted revenge and reported abroad "several testimonies of her kindness, as well by letters as otherwise." The duchess complained to King Charles who appointed four lords to look into the matter. Howe could produce only one letter, which the King declared was neither the duchess's "hand nor style" (Sidney, *Diary*, I, 100). Nevertheless, for years the Court satirists listed Howe among the duchess's putative lovers.

In November, 1679, Howe, with George Porter, Jr., and Henry Wharton, all drunk and disorderly, "came and broke down Mrs. Willis's balls [on her gateposts] and called her all to naught, upon which she sent for the constable, but he was so civil as not to secure them" (*Seventh Report*, p. 477B). Howe's talents were better employed in writing libels than in beating up bawdyhouses.

Originally a violent, noisy Whig, Howe was a member of the Convention Parliament of 1689, and represented Cirencester in several later Parliaments. He served as Vice-Chamberlain to Queen Mary from 1689 to March, 1692, when he was dismissed (*Portledge*, p. 133). According to Macaulay (VII, 170), "If rumor could be trusted, he had fancied that Mary was in love with him, and had availed himself of an opportunity which offered itself while he was in attendance on her as Vice Chamberlain to make some advances, which had justly moved her indignation." In early November of the same year he cut and wounded his own servant in the verge of Whitehall— a heinous crime. He was forced to plead guilty and sue for a pardon, but the double blow was too much for his pride. From then on he was a violent Tory and "showed the most rancorous hatred of his royal mistress, of her husband, and of all who were favored by either." When Tory Queen Anne came to the throne, Howe became a member of the Privy Council and Paymaster of the Guards (1702– 14). Howe was an eloquent speaker, with a gift for telling epithets, but wrong-headed, fractious, and malicious.

Howe married Mary, daughter of Humphry Baskerville, Herts., and widow of Sir Edward Morgan of Monmouthshire. Macky said that he was "endued with good natural parts, attended with an un-accountable boldness, daring to say what he pleases, and will be heard out; so that he passes with some for the shrew of the House. . . . He is a tall, thin, pale-faced man, with a very wild look; brave in his person, bold in expressing himself, a violent enemy, a sure friend, and seems always to be in a hurry" (*Memoirs*, p. 118).

Although Howe was famed "For smutty jests and downright lies" in verse (see above, "An Answer to the Satire on the Court Ladies"), only a few poems can be positively identified as his: two agreeable songs in Dryden's *Miscellany Poems*, 1716, "A Song by Mr. John Howe" (II, 214) and "A Song. By Mr. J. H." (II, 344). "An Epistle to Somerton, Secretary to the Muses, 1691" is signed "Your Servant, Jack Howe", and "Satyr 1692/3" is signed "Jack Howe" (Holkham MS, pp. 96, 129). Apparently he was also author, or coauthor, of the second-day Prologue to Rochester's alteration of *Valentinian*, 1684.

DNB; *Complete Peerage*; Burke, *Extinct Peerages*, 1938; *Buccleuch MS*, I, 317; *Lady Giffard's Letters*, 1911, p. 14.

JULIAN, ROBERT

In 1667 "Captain" Robert Julian was clerk or secretary to Admiral Sir Edward Spragge. He seems to have served in that capacity, or as Judge Advocate of the Mediterranean Fleet, until Spragge was killed in action in 1673. (In 1685 Julian claimed that he had "served the late King nine years at sea.")

About 1670, Julian entered upon the trade which earned him the ironic title "Secretary to the Muses." Perhaps aided by a clerk or two, he copied and sold libels and lampoons written by the wits of the Town and Court, who either gave or sold him the rights to their satires. Evidently he did a thriving trade. Numerous references to him in contemporary satires, and a number of lampoons addressed to him, or pretending to speak for him, testify to his reputation as a purveyor of scandal. It is unlikely that he wrote any of the verses attributed to him. He seems to have been a big, heavy man, much addicted to brandy.

On May 31, 1684, he pleaded not guilty to the charge of writing and publishing a libel on King Charles II entitled "Old Rowley the King, to the tune of Old Simon the King." On November 12 he was convicted of publishing this and other "scandalous libels," and sentenced to pay one hundred marks fine, to stand in the pillory at Westminster, Charing Cross, and Bow Street, and to give bonds for his future good behavior. Unable to pay the fine, he languished in the King's Bench Prison until June, 1685, when he was released, "he being an ancient man and almost blind and very poor."

After he was free, Julian returned to his old vocation. Several lampoons were addressed to him in 1686 and 1687, and on February 16, 1688, Sir George Etherege wrote from Ratisbon, "I was thinking of inviting Mr. Julian to a correspondence that I might at least know how scandal goes" (*Letters*, p. 328).

The date of Julian's death is unknown, but it must have been early in the 1690s. An undated epitaph (*POAS*, 1698, Pt.III, 226) ironically sang his praises and concluded:

> But, ah, his loss 'tis now too late to mourn!
> He's gone, and Fate admits of no return!
> But whither is he gone? To Heaven, no doubt,
> Where if there's any drink, he'll find it out.

Brice Harris, "Captain Robert Julian, Secretary to the Muses," *ELH*, X, 4 (December, 1943), 294–309; Judith Slater, "The Early Career of Captain Robert Julian, Secretary to the Muses," *N&Q*, N.S., XIII, 7 (July, 1666), 260–62; Tom Brown, *Amusements Serious and Comical*, ed. A. L. Hayward, 1927, pp. 248–55.

KIRKE, PERCY, PHILIP, DIANA, AND MARY

Although it is possible that famous Percy Kirke was the son of George Kirke, Groom of the Bedchamber to King Charles I, by his first wife, Anne Killigrew, who died in 1641, it is more likely that his mother was George's second wife, Mary (daughter of Aurelian Townshend), who married him on February 26, 1646. Mary was a beautiful wanton, whose reputation did not improve with years. However, she gave her husband two sons, Percy and Philip, and two daughters, Diana and Mary. At the Restoration George Kirke became Housekeeper of Whitehall Palace. He died on April 6, 1675.

Percy Kirke (c. 1647–91) was commissioned as an ensign July 7, 1666. He moved regularly up the military ladder, and in 1682 he became Governor of Tangier and Colonel of Fairborne's Regiment at Tangier. Kirke was a first-rate soldier, a brutal fighter, a duelist, and a wencher. Brought back from Tangier in 1684, his regiment, known as "Kirke's Lambs" distinguished itself bloodily after Monmouth's rebellion in 1685. Kirke was general of the English force which raised the siege of Londonderry in July, 1689. He died at Brussels on October 31, 1691.

Kirke married Lady Mary Howard, daughter of George Howard, who became fourth Earl of Suffolk in 1689. Lady Mary had her gallants as Kirke had his whores.

Philip Kirke, Percy's younger brother, also chose a military life. He was a captain in the King's Holland Regiment in 1678, a captain in the First Footguards in 1683, and lieutenant-colonel of the Queen's Regiment of Foot in 1684. In June, 1675, he became Under-Housekeeper of Whitehall (*CSPD*, 1675–76, p. 192), and on October 8, 1679, he became Housekeeper (PRO, L.C. 7/1). He held the post until his death, c. September 8, 1687, when his brother Percy succeeded him. Philip seems not to have married, but he was a true Kirke with the ladies.

About April, 1673, Diana Kirke married Aubrey de Vere, twentieth Earl of Oxford. She produced a daughter, also Diana, who on April 17, 1694, married Nell Gwyn's son, Charles, Duke of St. Albans, and died on January 15, 1742.

George Kirke's second daughter, Mary ("Mall") Kirke, was a Maid of Honor to Marie Beatrice, Duchess of York, c. 1673–75. She seems to have been mistress (1) to the Duke of York, (2) to the Duke of Monmouth, and (3) to the Earl of Mulgrave. Apparently she tried to juggle all three at once. On October 1, 1674, a gossip reported that "The Duke of Monmouth, being jealous of Lord Mulgrave's courting his newest mistress, Mall Kirke, watched his coming thence late four or five nights ago, and made the Guards keep him amongst them all night" (*Rutland MS*, II, 27). On June 27, 1675, we learn that Mall had long known that she was pregnant, had turned Roman Catholic, and had planned to retire to a nunnery on the continent for her confinement. But she waited too long "and spoiled all." Her infant was born that morning with no midwife in attendance, just "the young Mother of the Maids and her own servant." The child died a few hours after birth (*Bulstrode*, I, 303). Mall was turned out of St. James's Palace and found refuge with her mother in Whitehall. On July 4 Percy Kirke challenged Lord Mulgrave "for having debauched and abused his sister." Mulgrave denied everything, and Mall denied any carnal relations with him, but the Restoration Hotspur would not be appeased; he fought with Mulgrave and wounded him seriously. On August 30 Mall fled to France and a nunnery "to do penance for the rest of her life for her past follies" (*Bulstrode*, I, 305, 313; *Savile Correspondence*, p. 39).

Even in a nunnery, Mall was pursued by lovers. In the spring of 1676, Honoré Courtin, newly appointed Ambassador to England, visited her and pumped her about English Court affairs. He wrote to the French Minister, Louvois, "She is a pretty bit of stuff, as pretty as I've seen for a long time, and if I had as much money and opportunity as you, she would not escape me" (Delpech, *Portsmouth*, p. 101). On August 15, 1676, there was "a warm report" that Mall had married Lord Mordaunt at Paris. "Mrs. Kirke hopes it is false, for she does not look upon him as a good match" (*Rochester-Savile Letters*, p. 42). Finally Mall became mistress to Sir Thomas Vernon, of Hodnet, Salop (1637–84), a man at least twice her age, who finally married her at Paris in May, 1677 (*Savile Correspondence*, p. 57). Mall gave Sir Thomas, a Teller of the Exchequer, three children; according to the Court gossips, she was still promiscuous. She "ended her life in miserable circumstances at Greenwich in 1711" (G. S. Steinman, *N&Q*, November 12, 1853, p. 461).

DNB; *Complete Peerage*; *Letters and the Second Diary of Samuel Pepys*, ed. R. G. Howarth, 1933; Dalton, *Army Lists*; *CTB*, 1679, p. 563; 1685–89, p. 1558; Luttrell, I, 413.

LAWSON, ELIZABETH [?]

By his wife Catherine, third daughter of Sir William Howard, Sir John Lawson of Brough Hall, Yorks., had five sons and three daughters. In 1680 Sir John's sister-in-law, Mary, Duchess of Richmond (who had married "Northern Tom" Howard, fourth son of Sir William Howard) tried to interest King Charles in one of her nieces by marriage, probably Elizabeth, the youngest. Her aim was to oust her enemy, the Duchess of Portsmouth, and "to bring the Duke of Buckingham [her brother] into favor" (*Portland MS*, III, 368).

In "Flatfoot the Gudgeon Taker," 1680 (*POAS*, Yale, II, 190) we are told that Mistress Lawson was "managed" by "Two rev'rend aunts, renown'd in British story/ For lust and drunkenness with Nell and Lory." ("Aunt" still carried the connotation of bawd). One "aunt" was the Duchess of Richmond; the other, "my Lady Mary", is sometimes erroneously identified as Lady Mary (Mordaunt), wife of Henry Howard, then Earl of Arundel. At this time, of course, Arundel's wife was properly identified as "Lady Arundel," and is so called by contemporary satirists. Probably "Lady Mary" was Lady Mary Fenwick, granddaughter of Sir William Howard, wife of Sir John Fenwick, and Mistress Lawson's first cousin. Lady Mary Fenwick was a great intriguer with a scandalous reputation.

Mistress Lawson was too timid to attract a jaded old roué; she never became the King's mistress. In "The Ladies' March," 1681 (see above), we learn that

> Lawson, she who's disappointed,
> Grieves to lose the Lord's anointed,
> Follows next in the reverend clutches
> Of her old aunt and bawd, the duchess.

In 1682, Mistress Lawson was still about the Court, apparently drinking heavily (see above, "Satire. 1682"). In 1684–85 she was in Paris, and there was a false report that she had married Lord Grey of Ruthven. In fact, she was living in the nunnery to which the Duke of Norfolk (Arundel) took his wife and left her for a year. In 1696 an Elizabeth Lawson (presumably Sir John Lawson's daughter) was in London and intimate with the Duchess of Norfolk and Lady Mary Fenwick at the time of Fenwick's trial for high treason. Apparently she never married.

Complete Peerage; *Rutland MS*, II, 85; *State Trials*, XII, col. 926; *House of Lords MS*, 1695–97, pp. 283–89; Luttrell, IV, 166.

LOFTUS, ADAM

Adam Loftus (1647–91), a Roman Catholic, second son of Sir Arthur Loftus of Rathfarnham, co. Dublin, was Ranger of Phoenix Park and of the King's parks in Ireland and a Master of the Court of Requests. He was hot tempered, a compulsive gambler, and a heavy drinker. On December 27, 1677, a gossip wrote, "Lord Pembroke hath hurt Mr. Loftus att a quarrell at dice, but a slight wound, many being present at the tavern where they played" (*Rutland MS*, I, 44). In June, 1684, the Earl of Ranelagh lost a suit for £30,000 in Dublin. "Mr. Loftus, who has appeared all along in this business for his lordship, threatened the judges that my Lord Ranelagh would have them turned out, and in a drunken fit did very much abuse the Chief Baron at his own house, but it seems upon Mr. Loftus asking pardon, my Lord Chief Justice promised not to complain, or else it should not have gone so with him; Mr. Loftus is like to lose by this £4,000 or £5,000 so that he may be allowed a little anger" (*Ormonde MS*, N.S. VII, 248).

On January 29, 1686, King James II, who loved to elevate Roman Catholics, created Loftus Baron of Rathfarnham and Viscount Lisburne. Nevertheless, Lord Lisburne took the Whig side in the Glorious Revolution and in 1689 he commanded an English regiment in Ireland. He aroused no enthusiasm in his superiors. On December 30, 1689, Marshall Schomberg wrote to King William, "My Lord Lisburne's conduct is not good. He passes his life at play and the bottle; a little wine fuddles him" (Sir John Dalrymple, *Memoirs*, 1773, App., Pt. II, 59). At the siege of Limerick, September 15, 1691, Lisburne was slain by a cannon ball.

Loftus married (1) on March 7, 1673, Lucy, aged twenty-two, second daughter of George Brydges, Lord Chandos (1620–55), by his second wife, Jane Savage. Although Lucy was a coheiress to her father's estates, Chandos left most of them to his second wife, who married (2) Sir William Sidley, and (3) George Pitt of Stratfieldsaye, Hants. Jane died June 6, 1676, and it is likely that Loftus sued Pitt for his wife's inheritance. Lucy Loftus gave birth to a daughter, also Lucy, who married, as his second wife, Thomas Wharton (q.v.).

After his first wife died in April, 1681, Loftus married (2) in May, 1682. Dorothy, daughter of Patrick Allen, Esq. From Paris on May

31, the Earl of Donegal wrote, "I hear Addy Loftus's wedding was very public. It was a great match for her [Dorothy]. I hear the furniture of the wedding room cost £1,000" (*Calendar of Orrery Papers*, p. 260). Dorothy (Lady Lisburne) died in July, 1689.

Complete Peerage; *London Marriage Licenses*; Mark Noble, *Biographical History of England*, 1806, I, 341; *Ormonde MS*, N.S., VI, 226; Francis Nichols, *The Irish Compendium*, 1756.

LUMLEY, RICHARD AND HENRY

Richard (c. 1650–1721) and Henry (c. 1659–1722) Lumley were the first and second sons of John Lumley, Esq., by his wife Mary Compton, and grandsons of Richard, Viscount Lumley, of Waterford, in the peerage of Ireland. The brothers were educated as Roman Catholics, but became Protestants c. 1685–86. Richard became Viscount Lumley of Waterford on the death of his grandfather in 1662. On May 31, 1681, Richard was created Baron Lumley of Lumley Castle, Durham; on April 9, 1689, Viscount Lumley of Lumley Castle; and on April 15, 1690, Earl of Scarborough. He was Master of the Horse to Queen Catherine 1680–82. He was one of the seven peers who signed an invitation to William of Orange on June 31, 1688, and he became a Gentleman of the Bedchamber to King William and a member of the Privy Council. Later he held numerous government and Court posts. As Deputy-Lieutenant of Sussex, Lord Lumley was responsible for capturing the Duke of Monmouth after the Battle of Sedgemoor.

On March 17, 1685, Richard Lumley married Frances (aged nineteen), daughter of Sir Henry Jones of Aston, Oxon., "a fine young woman and heiress of £1,000 per annum" (*Rutland MS*, II, 85). By her he had seven sons and four daughters. Frequently mentioned in satires as "Lumley" or "Lord Lumley," he was accused of affairs with Mary, Countess of Scarsdale, Mrs. Elizabeth Fox, and an actress, "the fam'd Mrs. Cox." Macky described him as "a gentleman of very good sense, a great lover of the constitution of his country, and an improver of trade . . . a handsome man of a brown complexion" (*Memoirs*, p. 74). Swift called him "a knave and a coward" (Burnet, *Own Time*, III, 264n.)

Henry Lumley, in his younger days known as a wit and a beau ("Lumley Beau"), took to the army in 1685, became a lieutenant-general in 1703, and achieved distinction in Marlborough's campaigns. He was Governor of the Isle of Jersey when he died on October 18, 1722. He married (1) Elizabeth Trimbleby and (2) Anne, daughter of Sir William Wiseman. He was said to have suffered much from the pox, as one result of which his mouth was drawn awry; hence "wry-mouthed Lumley" or "wry-mouthed tyzard." In contemporary satires he is usually associated with Susannah, Lady Williams and Mary, Countess of Arundel. Macky described Lieutenant-general Lumley as "a good officer, brave, but hot and passionate to a great degree . . . he is tall, fair, and [in 1703] 45 years old" (*Memoirs*, p.163).

Complete Peerage; Collins, *Peerage*.

MACKEREL, BETTY

An orange girl in the Theatre Royal, Betty Mackerel, a tall, handsome young wanton, had her moment of glory when she played the role of tiny Ariel in Duffett's *The Mock-Tempest*, November, 1674. In the last act she sang a parody of Ariel's song,

> Where good ale is, there suck I,
> In a cobbler's stall I lie
> While the watch are passing by;
> Then about the streets I fly
> After cullies merrily.
> And I merrily, merrily take up my clo'se
> Under the Watch and the Constable's nose.

Betty's wit was decidedly coarse. According to Sir Francis Fane (MS Commonplace Book, c. 1675), "Bet Mackell ye orange wench taught a sterlin to speake baudy & gave ye bird to ye King, on[e] day ye Bishop of Canterbury came into ye bed chamber & ye bird hopt on his shoulder & sade 'Wilt thou have a whore, thou lecherous dog?' "

Evidently she pleased the courtiers who thronged the playhouse. In 1685 Robert Gould wrote ("The Playhouse," Add. MS. 30,492),

> Here others, who no doubt believe they're witty,
> Are hot at repartee with Orange Betty,
> Who, though not blest with half a grain of sense

To leaven her whole lump of impudence,
Aided with that, she always is too hard
For the vain things and beats them from their guard.

According to "Satire to Julian," 1682 (see above), Betty had once been mistress to "Handsome" Robert Fielding, and then had fallen into bed with Sir Thomas Armstrong (Monmouth's follower). Incredibly, the author of "Sir Thomas Armstrong's Last Farewell to the World. 1684" (*POAS*, Yale, III, 563) asserted that she had been Armstrong's mistress "this fourteen long years."

Betty's size and harlotry were so famous that in John Phillips' *The History of Don Quixote*, 1687, p. 412, she was mentioned as "the Gyantess Betty-Mackerela, who . . . was one of the most diligent women of her time." In September, 1686, Sir George Etherege described the Countess de Windisgratz as "very like, and full as handsome as Mrs. Betty Mackerell" (*Letters*, p. 60). She must have been living in 1688, because she appears as "a favorite of the blind god" in "The Session of Ladies" (see above).

Montague Summers, *Shakespeare Adaptations*, 1922; Fane's Commonplace Book, Shakespeare Memorial Library, Stratford.

MAZARIN, HORTENSE, DUCHESS

Hortense, third daughter of Lorenzo Mancini and favorite niece of Cardinal Mazarin, Prime Minister of France, was born in Rome in 1646. Brought up at the French Court, at the age of fourteen she was married to a nobleman twice her age, Armand Charles de la Porte, Marquis de Meilleraye, who was created Duc Mazarin after the marriage. Mazarin was a religious bigot, a jealous tyrant, and so prurient minded that he defaced statues and paintings, and prohibited the women on his estates from milking cows—to preserve them from wicked thoughts. Hortense endured him for seven years and bore him a son and three daughters.

After long and fruitless litigation for a separation, Hortense took flight in June, 1668, and found refuge in Italy. For the next eight years she was free to indulge her romantic fancies in escapades and her libido in love affairs, some of which (the gossips said) resulted in biological consequences.

Late in 1675 Hortense traveled to England, dressed *en cavalier* and followed by half a dozen servants, including a Turkish page boy, Mustapha, who made her coffee. She reached London in January, 1676, and was heartily welcomed. The Duke of York bought Lord Windsor's house in St. James's Park and loaned it to her, rent free (*Rutland MS*, II, 28). King Charles gave her an allowance of £3,000 a year (Luttrell, IV, 528).

At thirty the duchess, a dark, pneumatic beauty, had the bloom and freshness of youth, and King Charles quickly joined the long train of her lovers. A woman of wit and learning, she soon had a brilliant salon, patronized by pimps, prostitutes, gamblers, politicians, and philosophers. Although she was often accused of unbounded lust, she discreetly concealed the names of her lovers. Only one, Luigi I, Prince of Monaco, gave King Charles the pangs of jealousy.

After the death of King Charles II, the duchess fell upon hard times. She gambled wildly and lost a great deal of money. She took to drinking heavily and went deeply into debt, but she was still beautiful and still surrounded by admirers. She died June 11, 1699, in a rented house in Paradise Row, Chelsea.

Memoires d'Hortense et de Marie Mancini, 1929; St. Evremonde, *Oeuvres*, V, 316–20; Delpech, *Portsmouth*, pp. 90–99; Fea, *Some Beauties*, pp. 1–26; C. H. Hartman, *The Vagabond Duchess*, 1926.

MIDDLETON, JANE

By his second wife, Jane, widow of John Worfield of All Hallows, Barking, Sir John Needham of Denbyshire had six daughters. The oldest, Jane, was born in January, 1646; the third, Eleanor, was born in July, 1650. For some years Eleanor was mistress to James, Duke of Monmouth, to whom she bore four children, all surnamed Crofts. After Monmouth's death in 1685, Eleanor married John South, a Commissioner of the Revenue in Ireland.

On June 18, 1660, Jane Needham married Charles Middleton Esq. (1635–91) of Morton Hall, Denbigh., sixth son of Sir Thomas Middleton of Chirk Castle. Jane's daughter Jane ("Jenny") was baptized December 21, 1661. Mrs. Middleton, a great beauty and a skilled painter, was very popular at the Court of Charles II, pursued by

Grammont, Viscount Ranelagh, Ralph Montague, Lawrence Hyde, Edmund Waller, and the Duke of York. Of these only Montague and York seem to have had some measure of success. In 1665 Mrs. Middleton was spoken of as a rival to Lady Castlemaine for the King's bed, and in "Colin. 1679" (see above), she was listed among the candidates for the Duchess of Portsmouth's place as chief mistress.

On October 3, Pepys, who greatly admired Mrs. Middleton, was told that she was noted "for carrying about her body a continued sour smell that is very offensive"; hence, perhaps, the frequent libelous allusions to "the fair one's funky hose." In her old age Mrs. Middleton was a close associate of the Duchess of Mazarin and her circle. She died in 1692.

As for her daughter, on June 4, 1678, Savile wrote to Lord Rochester, "My Lady Harvey [Ralph Montague's sister] who always loves one civill plot more, is working body and soul to bring Mrs. Jenny Middleton into play" as a new mistress for the King (*Rochester-Savile Letters*, p. 56). The rumor was confirmed by Ambassador Barillon, who wrote on July 25, 1678, that Mesdames Harvey and Middleton were trying to get the King "to honor Mrs. Middleton's daughter with his attentions" (Forneron, *Louise de Keroualle*, 1887, p. 202). Evidently their schemes failed. Jenny Middleton married a Mr. May, perhaps Richard May, a naval officer. Jenny died in 1740.

DNB; G. S. Steinman, *A Memoir of Mrs. Myddleton*, 1864; Fea, *Some Beauties*; Delpech, *Portsmouth*.

MORDAUNT, CHARLES, VISCOUNT

Charles Mordaunt (c.1658–1735) was the son of John, Viscount Mordaunt of Avalon, and Elizabeth Cary, daughter of Thomas, first Earl of Monmouth. Charles was semieducated at Westminster School and Christ Church, Cambridge; he succeeded as second Viscount on June 5, 1675. Taking to the sea "Romantic Mordaunt" spent two years as a volunteer in wars against the Algerines, 1675–77. In June, 1680, he accompanied Lords Mulgrave and Plymouth on an expedition for the relief of Tangier, which was not relieved. In 1681 Mordaunt was captain of *The Loyal Mordaunt*, a war ship built at his own expense. In later years Mordaunt held various commissions in the army, rising to the rank of general.

Mordaunt was an eccentric courtier, a would-be wit, and a poetaster. He is frequently named as a rhymer and writer of libels. Like all gentlemen of the time, he was always ready for a duel. On February 28, 1680, he and Lord Cavendish were seconds to the two principals, Lord Plymouth and Sir George Hewitt. Mordaunt was "hurt in the shoulder" (*Hatton Correspondence*, I, 222). On August 1, 1681, he fought "with sword and pistol" against James Douglas, Lord Arran. Both suffered sword wounds, "Lord Arran through the thigh, the other through the arm and into the body" (*Ormonde* MS, N.S., VI, 117).

A staunch Whig, Mordaunt became a Gentleman of the Bedchamber to King William in 1689. On April 9, 1689, he was created Earl of Monmouth and soon became First Commissioner of the Treasury. In 1690 he was one of the peers appointed as advisers to Queen Mary while King William was abroad. Queen Mary wrote to her husband that "Lord Monmouth is mad, and his wife [Carey] who is madder, governs him" (Marjorie Bowen, *The Third Mary Stuart*, 1929, p. 171). On the death of his uncle Henry, June 19, 1697, Monmouth became Earl of Peterborough. In 1705 he was in command of the allied forces in Spain, and on August 3, 1713, he became a Knight of the Garter.

Mordaunt married (1) Carey Fraizer, a Maid of Honor to Queen Catherine and daughter of the King's physician, Sir Alexander Frazier. She seems to have been his mistress first, and the marriage was secret. In December, 1681, Mordaunt "brought out as well as owned his lady" (*Rutland MS*, II, 62). By his first wife he had two sons. Mordaunt married (2), after keeping her for several years, a celebrated singer, Anastasia Robinson. Mordaunt (Peterborough) died October 25, 1735.

Bishop Burnet described Mordaunt as "a man of much heat, many notions, and full of discourse; he was brave and generous, but had not true judgement [and less virtue], his thoughts were crude and indigested, and his secrets were soon known. [He was both vain, passionate, and inconstant]" (*Own Time*, III, 262). Macky described him as possessed of "natural giddiness" and a "fiery, inconstant temper . . . He affects popularity, and loves to preach in Coffee Houses and public places; is an open enemy to Revealed Religion; brave in his person, hath a good estate; does not seem Expensive, yet always in debt, and very poor. A well shaped thin man, with a very brisk look" (*Memoirs*, pp. 65–66).

In contemporary satires there are references to the fact that Mordaunt lisped. For example, see above, "An Answer to the Satire on the Court Ladies," 1680,

> There's lisping Mordaunt and Beau Henningham,
> Much to be famed for two sharp writing men,

and in "Scandal Satyred," c. 1682 (Harleian MS. 6913, p. 209),

> Let Mordaunt please dull Monmouth and his rout,
> Lisp by the hour while they all crowd about.

Complete Peerage; Frank S. Russell, *The Earl of Peterborough and Monmouth*, 1887; Colin Ballard, *The Great Earl of Peterborough*, 1929; *DNB*.

MORLAND, SIR SAMUEL

Sir Samuel Morland, Bart. (1625–96) had been a clerk to Secretary Thurloe under Cromwell. In 1660 he was knighted at Breda for betraying Commonwealth secrets to the Royalists; later he was created a baronet. King Charles gave him a pension of £500 a year, which he sold for ready money.

Sir Samuel was famed as a mathematician and inventor. He invented the plunger pump, an ear trumpet, a perpetual calendar, a calculating machine, a naval gun carriage, the drum capstan, a device for opening letters without breaking the seals, and dozens of other gadgets. He wrote books on cryptography and compound interest. He served as an expert on ciphers for the Foreign Office, as the King's Master of Mechanics, and as a Gentleman of the Privy Chamber. He was a feckless man, and money slipped like water through his fingers.

Sir Samuel was married four times. His first wife was Susanne, daughter of Daniel de Milleville, Baron of Boissy in Normandy. He married his second wife, Carola, daughter of Sir Roger Harsnett, on October 26, 1670; she died October 10, 1674. On November 16, 1676, he married a third wife, Anne, "handsome [Robert] Fielding's sister," without a penny of portion. "She is handsomer for a woman than he [Fielding] is for a man" (*Seventh Report*, p. 467B). Anne died on February 20, 1680, aged nineteen.

At last the connoisseur of beauty decided to marry for money. On February 1, 1687, Morland married one Mary Aylif, who had been represented to him as a fortune with £4,000 in cash and £500 a year in land. Quickly he learned that he had been abused; Mary turned out to be a coachman's daughter, penniless, sadly diseased, and a whore who some months earlier had given birth to a bastard. Later Morland learned that for sixth months before the marriage Mary had been kept by Sir Gilbert Cosins Gerard. Morland sued for a divorce in the ecclesiastical courts, and after a long battle won his case on July 16, 1688. Gerard, who had continued his relations with Mary after her marriage and had been named as co-respondent in the divorce suit, appealed fruitlessly against the verdict.

On October 25, 1696, Evelyn visited Morland at Hammersmith and found him "entirely blind" and fanatically religious. Morland died in abject poverty December 30, 1696.

DNB; Pepys, *Diary*; *Letters and Second Diary of Samuel Pepys*, ed. R. G. Howarth, 1933; Evelyn, *Diary*.

MULGRAVE, JOHN, EARL OF

John Sheffield (1648–1721), son of Edmund and Elizabeth (Cranfield), succeeded as third Earl of Mulgrave at the age of ten. In 1666 he was a volunteer with Prince Rupert in the Fleet. On June 13, 1667, he was commissioned captain of a troop of horse. In February, 1673, he became a Gentleman of the Bedchamber to King Charles II. In the summer of 1673 he commanded a war ship, *The Royal Katherine*. In December he was commissioned colonel of the "Old Holland" regiment of foot. On April 23, 1674, probably by the influence of his then mistress, the Duchess of Cleveland, he was elected a Knight of the Garter.

A haughty, arrogant young man, Mulgrave made many enemies, and in his early years he was involved in a number of quarrels. In 1669 King Charles stopped a duel between Mulgrave and the Earl of Rochester. In July, 1670, the King, "having timely notice," prevented a duel between Mulgrave and Mr. Digby, second son to the Earl of Bristol (*Bulstrode*, I, 146). On October 30, 1671, a writer reported that "Lord Mulgrave has been wounded in a duel with Mr. Felton" (*Le Fleming MS*, p. 189). In June, 1675, Captain Percy Kirke accused Mulgrave of fathering his sister's stillborn child, fought with him and "worsted and wounded him" (Marvell, *Letters*, ed. H. M. Margoliouth, 1927, II, 318).

In 1677 Mulgrave served briefly in the French army under Marshall Turenne. In 1679 he became Lord Lieutenant of the East Riding of Yorkshire and Governor of Hull. In 1680 he commanded an expedition for the relief of Tangier. In October, 1682, he was forbidden the Court because he had tried to make love to Princess Anne. "Some believe his proceeding so far as to spoil her marrying to anyone else, and therefore the Town have given him the nickname of King John" (*Seventh Report*, p. 480A). He was also called, contemptuously, "Numps."

By 1684 Mulgrave was in favor again. A Tory by conviction but politically a time-server, he became a Privy Councillor, and on May 10, 1694, King William created him Marquis of Normanby. In March, 1703, Queen Anne created him Duke of Buckinghamshire.

On March 11, 1686, Mulgrave married a wealthy young widow, Ursula, Lady Conway. In Ratisbon, Sir George Etherege commented, "Numps is now in the stocks in earnest" (*Letters*, p. 28). Ursula died on August 13, 1697. Mulgrave's second wife (March 12, 1699) was Katherine, widow of the Earl of Gainsborough. His third wife (February 7, 1704) was Katherine (Darnley), natural daughter of James II by Katherine Sedley and divorced wife of the Earl of Anglesey. Mulgrave had many children, legitimate and illegitimate.

Mulgrave was a patron of poets, particularly of John Dryden. As a minor poet he was guilty of a number of weak lyrics and lampoons. He is best known for two long poems, *An Essay upon Satyr*, 1679 (at first attributed to Dryden) and *An Essay on Poetry*, 1682. His literary productions are embalmed in *The Works of John Sheffield*, etc., 2 vols., 1723. Macky described Mulgrave as "very proud, insolent, and covetous, and takes all advantages. In paying his debts unwilling; and is neither esteemed nor beloved. . . . He is of a middle Stature, of a Brown Complexion, with a sour, Lofty Look" (*Memoirs*, p. 20). Mulgrave died February 24, 1721.

DNB; *Complete Peerage*; V.de S. Pinto, *Rochester*, 1962; *Conduct of the Earl of Nottingham*, 1941, ed. W. A. Aiken; Wilson, *Court Wits*.

SELECTED BRIEF BIOGRAPHIES

Norfolk, seventh Duke and Duchess of

On August 7, 1677, Henry Howard (1655–1701), first son of Henry, Earl of Norwich (who inherited in December, 1677, as sixth Duke of Norfolk), married Mary Mordaunt (1659–1705), sole surviving daughter and heiress of Henry, Earl of Peterborough. Because the Howards were Roman Catholics and the Mordaunts were Protestants, "the wedding was perfectly private." Afterward the young couple seemed to be "very fond" (*Hodgkin MS*, p.65). Until the death of the sixth Duke of Norfolk on January 11, 1684, Henry and his wife were known as Lord and Lady Arundel. On his father's death, Lord Arundel became seventh Duke of Norfolk—premier duke of England—and Lord Marshall.

A few months after the marriage, Lord Arundel, a man of dissolute life, fond of fair hot wenches in flame-colored taffeta, returned to his old habits, and Lady Arundel, a pert, witty, if not beautiful young woman, and a Lady of the Queen's Bedchamber, found a number of admirers, among them Charles Talbot, Earl of Shrewsbury. Her relations with Shrewsbury brought her the open enmity of a rival, Lady Betty Felton (q.v.) and the slings and arrows of outraged Court poets.

In 1679, to keep his seat in the House of Lords, Lord Arundel turned Protestant and was rewarded with a number of appointments, including, on November 30, 1682, the office of Constable of Windsor Castle. At Windsor Castle, in the autumn of 1685, Arundel (now Norfolk) discovered an intrigue between his wife and John Germaine, a handsome Dutch adventurer and gambler (1654–1714), said to be a bastard brother of William, Prince of Orange. (Tradition has it that Germaine saved himself from the angry husband by jumping through a window into the Thames—a truly remarkable feat!) The duke took his wife to France and shut her up in a nunnery. After six month's incarceration (during which she turned Roman Catholic), the duchess promised to behave and was allowed to return to England. Thenceforth the duke and the duchess lived separate lives, and the duchess managed to live incognito with her lover, Germaine.

In January, 1692, the duke brought to the House of Lords a bill of divorce *a vinculo*, with permission to remarry. The Lords rejected it because he had not previously sued in the ecclesiastical courts for a divorce *a mensa et thoro*. In November, 1692, the duke sued Germaine for "committing adultery with the Duchess." The jury found for the duke "but gave only a hundred marks damage." Since Germaine was known to be wealthy, the small award (about £67) enraged the Lord Chief Justice, who told the jury that "he was sorry the world should know how low virtue and chastity were valued in England" (*Portland MS*, III, 508). The duke proceeded to bring a second divorce bill to the House of Lords, but the Lords rejected it for the same reason as before. Apparently the duchess was living almost openly with Germaine, who, in 1698, was created a baronet by King William.

In February, 1700, Norfolk's third bill of divorce *a vinculo* was presented, finally approved, and signed by the King on April 11. Unfortunately for Norfolk, who wanted to marry again and get an heir for his estates, his debaucheries caught up with him on April 4, 1701. In September, 1701, the ex-duchess, now merely Lady Mary Mordaunt, married her faithful lover and lived happily with him until her death on November 16, 1705.

State Trials, XII, cols. 833–948; M. A. Tierney, *History and Antiquities of the Castle and Town of Arundel*, 1834; H. K. S. Causton, *The Howard Papers*, 1862; *The Proceedings upon the Bill of Divorce, Between his Grace the Duke of Norfolk and the Lady Mary Mordaunt*, 1700.

NORTHUMBERLAND, GEORGE, DUKE OF

George Fitzroy (1665–1716), third natural son of King Charles II by the Duchess of Cleveland, was a tall, dark, handsome young man. He was created Earl of Northumberland on October 1, 1674, and Duke of Northumberland on April 6, 1683. On or about March 12, 1686, he married in haste beautiful but penniless Catherine Lucy, widow of Captain Thomas Lucy of Charlecote, Warwickshire. She was said to be "daughter to a poulterer near Fleet Bridge" (*Portland MS*, III, 395), but her father was a gentleman, Robert Wheatley, Esq., of Bracknell, Berks. Nevertheless she was no match for a half-royal duke. King James II, who had been trying to arrange a marriage for his nephew with a daughter of the Duke of Newcastle, was furious, and the Court was delightfully scandalized.

Evidently the young duke quickly came to his senses and was distressed by his action. His older brother, Henry, Duke of Grafton, seeing no legal remedy, suggested getting rid of the lady by the simplest means. On March 22, 1686, Northumberland took his bride for an airing in his coach, met Grafton at Chelsea, and the three boarded a barge for Gravesend, where they took ship for France. The two dukes returned on April 3, leaving the new duchess locked up in a nunnery.

Law and public opinion forced them to bring her back. On May 19, a yacht was sent for the duchess. She returned to England in June and took her proper place at Court. In Northumberland's otherwise harmless life, this episode alone kept the Court satirists happy for two or three years. Yet the marriage, although childless, seems to have been happy enough, in spite of many slanders against the duke and duchess.

Northumberland became a competent soldier and rarely meddled in politics. His first wife died on May 25, 1714, and on March 10, 1715, Northumberland married Mary, daughter of Henry Dutton, Esq. Macky described Northumberland as "a Man of Honor, nice in paying his Debts, and living well with his Neighbors in the country; does not much care for the Conversation of Men of Quality, or Business. Is a tall black man like his father the King" (*Memoirs*, p. 39).

Complete Peerage; *Downshire MS*, I, 135, 138, 140, 141, 146, 169; *Rutland MS*, II, 107, 110; *Ellis Correspondence*, I, 68.

OGLE, ELIZABETH, LADY

In November, 1679, at the age of twelve, Elizabeth Percy, daughter and heiress of Joscelyn, eleventh Earl of Northumberland, married Henry Cavendish, Lord Ogle, son of Henry, second Duke of Newcastle. Elizabeth was a pretty little redhead; Ogle was a puny, sickly youth, who conveniently died a year later, on November 1, 1680. The young widow, a great fortune, was beseiged by suitors, among them the Duke of Somerset; George Fitzroy, Earl of Northumberland by a new creation; the Earl of Kingston; Count Charles Koningsmarck, a German soldier of fortune; Sir Edward Villiers; and Thomas Thynne of Longleat—"Tom of Ten Thousand" pounds a year.

Lady Ogle's father was dead, and her mother had remarried. Influenced by her grandmother, the Dowager Countess of Northumberland, and by Colonel and Mrs. Brett, at whose house in Richmond she saw Mr. Thynne almost daily, Lady Ogle finally agreed to marry Thynne. The marriage was performed in haste, but, at the bride's request to be allowed to complete her year of mourning, not consummated. Regretting the match, she fled to Holland on November 7, 1681, aided by Henry Sidney. Her friends tried to get the marriage anulled on the ground that Thynne had been previously contracted to one of the Duchess of York's Maids of Honor, Mrs. Trevor, who had given birth to a bastard in 1678, assigning its paternity to Thynne. Squire Thynne denied everything.

On February 12, 1682, Thynne was assassinated in his coach in Pall Mall by three of Count Koningsmarck's mercenary soldiers, Vratz, Boroski, and Sterne. Koningsmarck was tried and acquitted; his three followers were tried, convicted, and hanged. Lady Ogle's character did not escape calumny, and she was said "to have had great intimacy with the Count in Holland, before he came over hither" (*Ormonde MS*, N.S. VI, 315). The author of "Satire in its Own Colors. 1682" (Harleian MS. 7319, p.187) was brutally specific,

> Ogle were a fine bitch
> If she were not so rich,
> For Coningsmark and lusty Harry,
> Ere she was fifteen
> Her bald tail-piece had seen,
> And taught her a trick to miscarry.

Lady Ogle returned to England March 15, 1682, and on May 30 she married "the Proud Duke," Charles Seymour, fifth Duke of Somerset (1662–1748). The rumors that Lady Ogle had somehow connived at Thynne's murder persisted for years. In 1711 Dean Swift incorporated them in his "The W--ds-r Prophecy," in which he called the red-haired duchess "Carrots,"

> And dear Englond, if ought I understond,
> Beware of Carrots from Northumberlond.
> Carrots sown Thyn a deep root may get,
> If so be they are in Somerset;

Their Conyns mark thou, for I have been told
They assassine when young and poison when old.

The duchess was then Mistress of the Robes to Queen Anne, and she made sure that Swift never became a bishop (Carl Van Doren, *Swift*, 1930, p. 114).

The Duchess of Somerset gave her husband thirteen children, of whom only one son and three daughters lived to maturity. The duchess died in 1722, aged fifty-three.

Complete Peerage; Allen Fea, *Some Beauties*; *Hatton Correspondence*, II, 9; "Ogle's History," *The Roxburghe Ballads*, V, 97.

PORTER, GEORGE, SENIOR AND JUNIOR

George Porter (1622–1683), eldest son of Endymion Porter by Olivia Botlier, had three sons and five daughters by his wife Diana, daughter of George Goring, first Earl of Norwich. Porter was a Gentleman of the Privy Chamber to Queen Henrietta Maria and later a Groom of the Bedchamber to King Charles II, but he took very lightly his duties as a courtier and as Surveyor of the Customs of the Port of London. He was hot-tempered, but much in demand as a jolly companion.

About 1673 Porter left his wife, took an actress, Jane Long, as his permanent mistress, and retired to Berkshire, making occasional visits to London. According to Baronne D'Aulnoy (*Memoirs*, p. 243) one such visit was made to break up a liaison between his daughter Olive and William, Lord Cavendish. Fearing Porter's temper, Lord Cavendish's father bought off the lady with "a handsome pension." On another occasion (November 17, 1677) Henry Savile reported that Porter was in London, and that "the rogue is grown so ravenous that he surfeits of everything he sees but Mrs. Long and his son Nobbs, which he can never have enough on" (*Rochester-Savile Letters*, p. 52). "Nobbs" was no doubt George Porter, Junior, who since 1663 had been a Gentleman Usher of the Privy Chamber to Queen Catherine. George Porter, Senior, died December 11, 1683.

"Nobbs" was wild and troublesome. One night in November, 1679, he, with Harry Wharton and Jack Howe, broke down the balls on the gate posts of Mrs. Willis's bawdy house, "and called her all to naught" (*Seventh Report*, p. 477B). In February, 1680, young Porter, with Sir Scroope Howe, Henry Wharton and others, invaded one of the playhouses, calling Lord Sunderland and the Duchess of Portsmouth names, acclaiming the Duke of Monmouth, and "throwing candles and links" (Cartwright, *Sacharissa*, p. 224). Porter and another rioter were challenged by Colonel Oglethorpe, "but the challenge was refused" (Newdigate Newsletter, February 17, 1680).

Although the Court satirists accused young Porter ("buggered Porter") of unnatural practices, he married Mary, daughter of John Mawson, and fathered several children. He died c. 1687.

DNB; *Calendar of Treasury Books*, 1685–89, pp. 1073, 1432; "Satyr," c. 1679, Add. MS. 34,362, f. 116v; Dorothea Townshend, *Life and Letters of Endymion Porter*, 1897; Gervase Huxley, *Endymion Porter*, 1959.

PORTSMOUTH, LOUISE, DUCHESS OF

Louise de Penancoët de Keroualle was born in September, 1649, first daughter of a poor but proud Breton nobleman, Guillaume de Penancoët, Comte de Keroualle. In 1668 she became a Maid of Honor to Henrietta, Duchess of Orleans, sister to King Charles II. Malicious chroniclers accused her of affairs with the old Duke of Beaufort, Chief Admiral of France, and with young Comte de Sault, son of the Duke de Lesdigiueres.

In May, 1670, King Charles saw Louise in his sister's train at Dover and promptly fell in love with her. When Henrietta set out for France, the King asked her to send him Louise. Two weeks later Henrietta died suddenly. King Charles offered Louise a post as Maid of Honor to Queen Catherine, and in October, 1670, the pretty little Breton arrived in London.

For a full year Louise was truly a Maid of Honor, in spite of constant temptation and the persuasions of the French Ambassador. At last, in October, 1671, she became the King's mistress after a mock marriage at Lord Arlington's country estate, Euston. According to Sir Francis Fane, the morning after the mock marriage Louise asked the King to make Arlington Lord Treasurer. The King replied,

"Madam, you should have asked me that yesterday" (MS Commonplace Book, Stratford Library).

Louise de Keroualle ("Madam Carwell" to the mob) quickly became the reigning royal mistress. On July 25, 1673, she was created Baroness Petersfield, Countess of Farnham, and Duchess of Portsmouth, with apartments in Whitehall and an income of some £10,000 a year. She succeeded in marrying her younger sister, Henrietta, to the rich but maniacal Philip Herbert, Earl of Pembroke, and on July 15, 1675, she succeeded in getting her son Charles (born July 29, 1672) acknowleged by the King and created Duke of Richmond.

However, Louise's lot was not easy. She was generally hated as a Roman Catholic, a French woman, and a French agent, commissioned to keep King Charles true to the interests of France. The Court satirists found her a vulnerable target, and her rivals, Nell Gwyn, and the Duchesses of Cleveland and Mazarin, united against her. She was often ill, once (in 1674) of venereal disease given her by promiscuous King Charles.

In 1679, at the height of the Popish Plot terror, Louise was so frightened that she seriously considered fleeing to France. Deciding to weather the storm, she made peace with the Whig faction, hoping that her son might be named as the King's successor. In March, 1682, she made a visit to France and was royally received. Back in England in July, she reigned alone over the King's heart and mind. She had only one moment of danger: in 1683 she foolishly listened to the ardent wooing of a handsome young libertine, Philippe de Vendôme, Grand Prior of France, and King Charles was forced to banish the besotted nobleman. In January, 1684, King Louis XIV created Louise Duchess of Aubigny.

After the death of King Charles on February 6, 1685, the duchess returned to France, where for a while she lived royally on the wealth she had saved from the gifts of two kings. Little by little her income dwindled, and in her later years she was deeply in debt. She died on November 14, 1734, at the great age of eighty-five.

Complete Peerage; *The Life of . . . Francelia, Late D---ss of P------h,* 1734; H. Forneron, *Louise Keroualle, Duchess of Portsmouth,* 1887; Fea, *Some Beauties*; Delpech, *Portsmouth.*

PULTENEY (POULTNEY), JOHN

Sir William Pulteney of Miskerton, Leics. (d. August, 1691), represented Westminster in several Parliaments and in 1690 was a Commissioner of the Privy Seal. His wife was a noted gamester. January 1, 1685, "Basset still keeps in credit at her grace of Portsmouth, the Duke of Norfolk, the Lady Poultney, and Mrs. Morine" (*Rutland MS*, II, 85). The Pulteneys had two sons and a daughter.

William Pulteney, the eldest, was commissioned a captain in the Royal Regiment of Dragoons on June 11, 1679. Twice married, his first wife was Mary, daughter of one Floyd, Esq.; his second was Arabella, third daughter of George, Earl of Berkeley. An inoffensive man, William died in 1715.

In contemporary satires, John, the second son, was often attacked for cowardice. In "To Mr. Julian," c. 1679 (*POAS*, 1705, p. 421) a satirist linked Pulteneny with Sir Carr Scroope,

> But for thy profit, Julian, have a care
> Of prying Poultney and of bully Carr,
> In them there's danger, for the one does write
> With the same prowess the other used to fight.

Apparently the charge was based on the fact that John was with the Dutch army routed at the siege of St. Omers, April, 1676. "An Ironical Satire," 1680 (*POAS*, Yale, II, 203), lists a number of "mighty knights,"

> Among all these 'twere not amiss to name
> Poultney to whom St. Omers' siege gave fame.

It seems that Pulteney was considered merely one of the Court hangers-on, a rather worthless young fop. The author of "Satyr," c. 1679 (Add. MS. 34,362, f. 116v), called him "Pimp-Prig Poultney," and accused him of being one of the Duchess of Cleveland's numerous stallions, concluding,

> He's famed for cowardice as his mother's for cheating,
> But she has some excuse: it is for eating.
> Were she as 'fraid of cards as he's of swords and guns,
> The spark might starve, for all his pantaloons.

Some time before 1682, John married (in France) Lucy Colvile of Northamptonshire. The marriage seems to have caused a duel between Pulteney and a rival, one Mr. Howard. Pulteney killed Howard; thereafter no one accused him of cowardice.

John became a useful public servant, first as secretary to Lord Shrewsbury, Secretary of State, in 1689, and after in various other secretarial positions. He became a Commissioner of Trade in 1707, and a Commissioner of Customs in 1714. Like his fellows, a poetaster, he is listed as the author of "Hermione to Orestes" in Dryden's *Ovid's Epistles*, 1680. He died in 1726.

On November 10, 1674, Anne Pulteney, Sir William's daughter, married, as his second wife, Charles Fitzroy, Duke of Southampton.

Dalton I, 255; *Le Fleming MS*, p. 136; *Seventh Report*, 497B; Luttrell I, 205, 579; III, 154, 397; *Rutland MS*, II, 85, 157.

RANELAGH, RICHARD, EARL OF

At the age of twelve Richard Jones (1641–1712) became a pupil of the great Puritan poet, John Milton, from whom he learned neither poetics nor virtue. After some time spent at Oxford and in foreign travel, Jones inherited as third Viscount Ranelagh, January 7, 1670, and on December 11, 1677, he was created Earl of Ranelagh in the peerage of Ireland.

Ranelagh was successively a member of the Irish Parliament from Roscommon (1661–66), Governor of Roscommon Castle (1661), Chancellor of the Irish Exchequer (1668–74), a Gentleman of the Bedchamber (1679), M.P. for Plymouth (1685–1702), and Paymaster of the Army (1685–1702). While Chancellor of the Irish Exchequer, he headed a company which "farmed" the Irish revenues, and by trickery, double dealing, and double taxation he richly lined his own pockets. Finally called to account, he was short by some £76,000, which the easy-going King forgave him. As Paymaster he continued his sharp practices until 1702, when he was convicted of misappropriating £72,000, dismissed, and expelled from the House of Commons.

Ranelagh married (1), Elizabeth, daughter of Lord Willoughby of Parham, by whom he had three daughters: Katherine, who became the King's mistress in 1679 and died unmarried; Elizabeth, who married on June 12, 1684 (as his second wife) John Fitzgerald, Earl of Kildare; and Frances, who married on April 23, 1698 (as his second wife), Thomas, Lord Coningsby of Clanbrassil. The first Lady Ranelagh died August 3, 1695, and on January 9, 1696, Ranelagh married Margaret, Dowager Baroness Stawell.

Ranelagh's private life was notoriously wicked. On December 28, 1677, Lord Conway wrote of Edward Seymour, Speaker of the House of Commons, "Mr. Speaker's lady is a most virtuous person, but her husband is worse for women than my Lord Ranelagh. If she [Conway's niece] were in either of those families, the world would judge I might better have ventured her in a bawdy house" (Marjorie Nicolson, *The Conway Letters*, 1930, p. 440). In 1679, when Ranelagh went to Ireland to defend his revenue accounts, he had his current mistress, one "Cocky," brought over to him, to the distress of his family. On January 20, 1680, a friend wrote drily, "Lord Ranelagh and his miss make much discourse in Ireland" (*CSPD*, 1679–80, pp. 272, 375, 417).

Ranelagh was a witty, clever, unscrupulous rascal; he spent all his peculations in luxurious living and died poor. According to Thomas Carte, Ranelagh "was a man of good parts, great wit, and very little religion; had a head turned for projects, and was formed for intrigue, artful, insinuating, and designing, craving and greedy for money, yet at the same time profuse and lavish" (*Ormonde*, IV, 501).

DNB; *Complete Peerage*; Lady Burghclere, *James, First Duke of Ormonde*, 1912; Carte, *Ormonde*; W. R. Parker, *Milton*, 1968, I, 476.

RICHMOND, DUCHESSES OF

From 1667 to 1685 there were two Duchesses of Richmond at the Court of Charles II. The older duchess, Mary (1622–85), daughter of George Villiers, first Duke of Buckingham, was married on January 8, 1634, at the age of twelve, to seventeen-year-old Charles, Lord Herbert. The next year Herbert died in Italy of smallpox. On August 3, 1637, Mary was married to James Stuart, first Duke of Richmond, who died in 1655, leaving Mary with a son, Esmé, who died in 1660, and a daughter, Mary, who married Richard Butler, Earl of Arran, and died without issue in 1668. In November, 1664, the duchess took a third husband, Colonel Thomas Howard, fourth son of Sir William Howard and brother of Charles, first Earl of Carlisle. A contemporary noted on November 26, "Northern Tom Howard is married to ye Duchess of Richmond, and they say [they] are the fondest couple that can be" (*Hatton Correspondence*, I, 42). Of course the duchess retained her title. Howard died in 1678, the duchess in 1685. According to Robert Harley, "The old Duchess of Richmond died a Roman Catholic" (*Portland MS*, III, 391).

The younger duchess, sometimes called "the Court Lady Richmond," was Frances Teresa (1647–1702), eldest daughter of the Honorable Walter Stuart, third son of Lord Blantyre of Scotland. A Roman Catholic, she was educated at the Court of France and brought to England in 1662 to be one of Queen Catherine's Maids of Honor. She was a great beauty and Rotier's model for Britannia on the new coins. Hotly pursued by King Charles, she resisted all his advances and seems to have retained her virginity. On March 30, 1667, she married privately Charles Stuart, third Duke of Richmond (a cousin of Esmé, the second duke), 1640–72. King Charles, who had marked the beauty for his seraglio, was hurt and angry. The Duke of Richmond was sent as Ambassador to Denmark, where he died on December 12, 1672.

In March, 1668, smallpox marred the duchess's beauty and left her with one eye blemished. In July the King appointed her a Lady of the Queen's Bedchamber, a post she seems to have held until 1689. In spite of Jack Howe's boasts and the allegations of incredulous libelers, she lived in the odor of chastity. She never remarried; she died October 15, 1702.

Complete Peerage; Fea, *Some Beauties*; Winifred, Lady Burghclere, *George Villiers, Second Duke of Buckingham*, 1903; Cyril Hughes Hartmann, *La Belle Stuart*, 1924.

SARSFIELD, PATRICK

Patrick Sarsfield, a bellicose soldier noted for his escapades, was the second son of Patrick Sarsfield of Lucan, c. Dublin. His older brother, William, was the first husband of Mary, daughter of Lucy Walter and half-sister to the Duke of Monmouth (see *Fanshaw*).

Patrick was educated at a French military academy, served a term in the French army, returned to England, and in 1678 was captain in a regiment of footguards. He was a very tall young man, impulsive, headstrong, and proud. On September 9, 1681, Luttrell wrote, "There [has] been a tall Irishman to be seen in Bartholomew Fair, and the Lord Grey [of Werke] being to see him, was pleas'd to say he would make a swinging evidence; on which one capt. Sarsfield, an Irishman, sent his lordship a challenge, taking it as an affront on his countrymen." Grey reported the challenge, and Sarsfield "was taken into custody, but hath since made his escape out of the messenger's hands" (I, 126, 127).

On December 6, 1681, Luttrell reported a duel "between the lord Newburgh and the lord Kinsale, as principals (two striplings under age), and Mr. Kirke and capt. Sarsfield as seconds: the principals had no hurt, but capt. Sarsfield was run through the body near the shoulder, very dangerously" (I, 150). Sarsfield had no luck in duels. On April 13, 1682, it was reported that "Last night Mr. Bridges & Capt. Sarsfield quarreled & the last was run through 'tis feared mortally" (Newdigate Newsletter). But Sarsfield bore a charmed life.

He had barely recovered from his wound when, in May, 1682, he joined Captain Francis Clifford and some other wild blades in abducting Mrs. Anne Siderfin, a wealthy young widow, with whose fortune Clifford was in love. They siezed the lady on Hounslow Heath, galloped off with her to the nearest landing, placed her in "an open shallop . . . and carried her to Calais." She refused to marry Clifford and managed to get in touch with the French authorites. Clifford and his cronies escaped to England. In due time Mrs. Siderfin returned and prosecuted the kidnappers. In February, 1683, Clifford was fined £1,000 and his accomplices £500 each. "She is to sue them again for her own damages" (*Seventh Report*, pp. 328A, 353A, 362A).

Undaunted, on March 24, 1683, Sarsfield tried his hand at abduction again. According to Francis Gwyn, "Last Saturday Capt. Sarsfield, the tall Irishman, ran away with Lady [Elizabeth] Herbert, widow to Lord Herbert of Cherbury, who was Loftus's wife's [half] sister. [He] carried her that night to [Sir John] Parsons' house at Enfield Chace, where, on her refusing marriage and promising not to prosecute him, he brought her back on Sunday. She has taken out a warrant from the Lord Chief Justice on him, but, notwithstanding, the Town says it will be a marriage and that all this is an artifice. Wagers are laid on it, and it appears there was a great familiarity between them" (*CSPD*, 1683, p. 136).

Apparently Sarsfield was besotted. When he learned that Lady Herbert had taken out a warrant against him, he "went to her lodging and either dissembling love or frenzy took forth a pen knife and opening his breast slashed his skin, and then stabbed himself therewith, at which the blood gushed out extremely before her presence and he was carried away, but is not yet dead. But 'tis thought he will scarce recover, he refusing to have his wounds dressed" (Lady Newdegate-Newdigate, *Cavalier and Puritan*, 1901, p. 183).

Sarsfield's wounds were only superficial, and he recovered quickly. Earlier he had left with Sir John Parsons Lady Herbert's written promise not to prosecute him. Now he asked for its return, and Parsons, sure that he would give it to Lady Herbert, refused. The two friends quarreled, and on April 29 they fought a duel behind Montague House. Both were run through the lungs; incredibly both survived.

Sarsfield, a brave soldier, distinguished himself at the time of Monmouth's Rebellion. In 1689 he followed King James II to France, and became successively colonel and brigadier when the deposed monarch invaded Ireland. After the decisive Battle of the Boyne, he is reported to have said to some English officers, "Change kings with us, and we will willingly try our luck with you again" (Macaulay, VI, 217). When hostilities ended, Sarsfield returned to France and took service in the French Army. In January, 1691, King James created him Earl of Lucan. He was killed at the head of a French division at the Battle of Landen in Flanders, July 29, 1693.

On or about January 9, 1690, Sarsfield married Honora, second daughter of William de Burgh, Earl of Clanrickard, who survived him.

DNB; Price, *Cold Caleb*; Macaulay, *History*.

SCARSDALE, ROBERT, EARL OF

Robert Leke, third Earl of Scarsdale (1654–1708), styled Lord Deincourt until January 27, 1681, seems to have been completely worthless. Yet he was captain of the Band of Gentleman Pensioners, 1677–83, a captain in Lord Gerard's Regiment of Horse, 1677–78, Governor of Hull, 1682, Lord Lieutenant of Derbyshire until 1688, and Groom of the Stole to Prince George of Denmark until 1688. On or about February 11, 1672, he abducted and married a very pretty girl, Mary, daughter of Sir John Lewis of York. Mary achieved notoriety as "the famous Scarsdale," and was accused of numerous affairs, notably one with Lord Lumley. She died February 17, 1684.

The Court satirists described Scarsdale as a "cully," a "cuckold," and "Scarsdale the stinking," and accused him of having a "pestilential breath." Yet he seems to have been very successful with women. More than a year after his wife's death, on May 30, 1685, we learn that "The great discourse of the Town besides Parliament affairs is of Lord Thomond's daughter, one of our great beauties, [who] last Sunday fell raving mad and so continues for love of Lord Scarsdale, who refuses to marry her, this is said to be the occasion" (*Portland MS*, III, 384). A year or two later, a libeler commented (*POAS*, Yale, IV, 200),

> Scarsdale, though loathed, still the fair sex adores,
> And has a regiment of horse and whores.

Yet according to Prince George, Scarsdale was "so pitiful a wretch" that he would have no more to do with him (*Clarendon State Papers*, II, 150).

In his old age, Scarsdale became infatuated with Anne Bracegirdle, "the Virgin Actress," famous for her supposed chastity. Whether or no she accepted him as a lover is a moot question, but in his will Scarsdale left her £1,000. He died at his house in Duke Street January 4, 1708.

According to Macky, Scarsdale "was always a man of pleasure more than business. No man loves the company of ladies more than he, or says less, when he is in it, yet is successful in his intrigues; a great sportsman, and hath neither genius nor taste for anything else; is of a middle stature, of a sanguine complexion, very fat" (*Memoirs*, p. 81).

Complete Peerage; John C. Hodges, *William Congreve*, 1941, pp. 88–89.

SHEPHERD (SHEPARD, SHEPPARD), FLEETWOOD

Sir Fleetwood Shepherd was born January 6, 1634, the second son of William Shepherd of Great Rowlright by Mary, daughter of Sir Fleetwood Dormer. In 1653 he received his B.A. at Christ Church, Oxford (M.A. in June, 1657), and in 1655 was at Gray's Inn in London. About 1673 he was a companion and steward of Charles Sackvile, Lord Buckhurst (later Earl of Dorset). About 1676 he was also tutor to Nell Gwyn's son, Lord Beauclerc.

According to Anthony Wood, Shepherd was "a debauchee and atheist, a grand companion of Buckhurst, Sedley, Buckingham, Rochester" and other wits, who "enlivened the suppers of Charles II in the private apartments of his favorite ladies" (*Athenae Oxonienses*, IV, 627). In 1690 Shepherd became a Gentleman Usher to King William, and on April 25, 1694, he was knighted and appointed Gentleman Usher of the Black Rod. He took advantage of his connection with Lord Dorset (now Lord Chamberlain) to engage in the selling of places, to the scandal of the Court.

On August 29, 1698, James Vernon wrote, "Sir Fleetwood Sheppard died this morning at Copt Hall, having been for some time bed-ridden. He left no will, and they say there was no occasion for it. If he has made even with the world, it is all that is to be expected" (*Letters, Reign of William III*, II, 159). Shepherd never married.

A man of jests and fancies, Shepherd wrote, among other squibs, "The Countess of Dorset's Petition to the late Queen Mary for Chocolate," *POAS*, 1698, Part III, 233; "Upon an Old Affected Court Lady," and "The Calendar Reformed," Buckingham's *Works*, 1704, I, 82, 217; "A Prophecy," "An Epitaph on the D. of G[rafton]," and "The Petition of Tom Brown," in *POAS*, 1705, 266, 272, and 373.

SHREWSBURY, COUNTESS OF AND DUKE OF

On January 10, 1659, Francis Talbot, eleventh Earl of Shrewsbury (aged 36), married, as his second wife, Anna-Maria Brudenell (aged 17), daughter of Robert Brudenell, who became second Earl of Cardigan. After the Restoration Lord Shrewsbury was appointed Housekeeper of Hampton Court Palace. He took his beautiful young wife to Court, where she was fair game for such libertines as Henry Jermyn

285

and "Northern Tom" Howard, who fought a duel over her. Jermyn's second, Giles Rawlins, was killed. In 1666 she became mistress to George Villiers, second Duke of Buckingham.

On January 16, 1668, in a six-man encounter on "the field of honor," Lieutenant William Jenkins lost his life and Bucks gave Lord Shrewsbury a wound which resulted in his death two months later. Thereafter Buckingham and Anna-Maria lived openly together, and in February, 1671, Anna-Maria bore the duke a son who died within a few days and was buried in Westminster Abbey as Earl of Coventry, a title in the duke's family. This was too much even for the Court of libertines. On January 31, 1674, the House of Lords ordered Buckingham and his mistress to cease cohabiting, and made them give bonds of £10,000 apiece to ensure obedience.

Lady Shrewsbury fled to France. She returned to England two years later, and in 1677 married George Rodney Bridges, Esq., for whom she bought a post as Groom to the King's Bedchamber. In July, 1678, she bore Bridges a son, also George. The countess died on April 20, 1702; Bridges died September 9, 1713.

Charles Talbot, twelfth Earl of Shrewsbury (1660–1718), Anna-Maria's first son by her first husband, was brought up in the Catholic faith in France and came to England in April, 1678. A handsome young man in spite of the loss of an eye (c. 1680), he was successful as a lover (although reputedly bisexual), and seems to have been a bone of contention between Lady Betty Felton (q.v.) and Mary, Countess of Arundel. In 1681 he became a Protestant and entered politics, holding many important posts under William and Mary and Queen Anne. On April 30, 1694, he was created Duke of Shrewsbury, On September 9, 1705, he married an Italian widow, Adelaide, daughter of the Marquis Paleotti of Bologna. Shrewsbury died February 1, 1718.

John Talbot (1665–86), Anna-Maria's second son, a libertine with a scandalous reputation, was killed by Henry, Duke of Grafton, in a duel on February 2, 1686. By a macabre coincidence, he had recently danced in a shroud at a ball given by the Earl of Devonshire.

John Macky described the Duke of Shrewsbury as "A great man, attended with a sweetness of behavior and easiness of conversation which charms all who come near him. . . . And although but one eye, yet he has a very charming countenance, and is the most generally beloved by the ladies of any gentleman in his time" (*Memoirs*, p. 15).

Complete Peerage; J. H. Wilson, *A Rake and His Times*, 1954; *Rutland MS*, II, 50; *Portland MS*, III, 394, Cartwright, *Sacharissa*, p. 225.

SKIPWITH, SIR THOMAS

Thomas Skipwith ("little Tom") of Metheringham (c.1652–1710) succeeded to the baronetcy on the death of his father, Sir Thomas, June 2, 1694. A would-be wit, his only qualification for distinction was an income of £2,000 a year. About 1685 he married Margaret, daughter of George Brydges, sixth Viscount Chandos, and widow of William Brownlow of Snarford, Lincs. His wife died January 1, 1731, aged 94; she was some fifteen years older than her husband.

Skipwith was a little man, weak, vain, and boastful. He became important in theatre annals in 1693 when he invested heavily in the United Company of players at the Theatre Royal. For ten years he and Christopher Rich controlled the company, and Skipwith improved neither his reputation nor his finances. When, in 1695, a group of the best actors, headed by Thomas Betterton, sought a license to open a new theatre at Lincolns Inn Fields, the patentees, apparently led by Skipwith, petitioned vainly against the rebels. No doubt the following verses (MS. Rawl. Poet. 159, f. 135) refer to the struggle. The MS is folded to letter size and marked on the back "Mrs. Bracegirdle's Petition to Sr Robert Howard. 1695."

To the Right Honble Sr Robt Howard

The humble Petition of Ann Bracegirdle.
Rinaldo-like, leave your Armida's charms,
And in our just defense resume your arms;
The dreadful Skipwith would again enslave us;
You who created, sir, can only save us.
Draw then your conquering sword in the defense
Of wit, youth, beauty, and my innocence,
And your petitioner shall ever pray.

In 1707 Skipwith gave his unproductive shares to Colonel Henry Brett, husband of the former Lady Brandon Gerard (q.v.). Two years later, when the two companies were reunited and prospering, Skipwith sued for the return of his shares, and Brett quietly returned them.

Skipwith's sister, Susannah, married April 30, 1673, Sir John Williams, Bart., of Minster Court, Kent. She was widowed in 1680. From 1681 on she seems to have lived at No. 13, St. James's Square, and to have acted as a purchasing agent for ladies of the Court and as a part-time doxy. She died September 26, 1689.

Complete Baronetage; An Apology for the Life of Mr. Colley Cibber, ed. R. W. Lowe, 2 vols., 1889; A. I. Dasent, *The History of St. James's Square*, 1895; Wilson, *Nell Gwyn.*

STAMFORD, ELIZABETH, COUNTESS OF

Sometime before April 13, 1675, Elizabeth (1657–87), oldest daughter of Sir Daniel Harvey by his wife Elizabeth (Montague), married Thomas Gray (1653–1720), who inherited from his grandfather as second Earl of Stamford on August 21, 1673. (From 1657 to 1675 Gray was styled Lord Gray of Groby). Soon after the wedding, Lady Russell wrote, "My Lord Stamford left his wife this morning at four o'clock and is gone to his uncle Gray" (*Letters*, p. 25). In spite of frequent separations, the countess had three children by her husband, all of whom died in infancy. Lady Stamford was apparently unstable; according to one account, she deliberately set fire to the Stamford mansion at Broadgate, and "the countess, with her infant daughter Diana narrowly escaped with their lives" (John Nichols, *History and Antiquities of Leicestershire*, 1795, III, 661–84). The countess was a famous beauty, tall, well-formed, and wanton. On September 5, 1682, when a rumor of the earl's death was current, Francis Gwyn wrote to Richard, Lord Arran, "The Earl of Stamford is lately dead; I need not acquaint your lordship how buxom [i.e., pliant] a widow he hath left behind him" (*Ormonde MS*, N.S., VI, 437).

The Earl of Stamford survived, was suspected of complicity in the Rye House Plot, and was in the Tower from July, 1685, to February, 1686. Lady Stamford died on September 7, 1687, and on March

12, 1691, Stamford married Mary, granddaughter of Sergeant Sir John Maynard.

DNB; *Complete Peerage.*

VILLIERS (GRANDISON)

George Villiers, fourth Viscount Grandison (I), the third of three brothers who inherited in succession, married (1) Lady Mary Leigh. His first wife died on July 7, 1671, and in November, 1674, he married (2) widowed Mary Starling ("about 40"), who died in June, 1700 (*London Marriage Licenses*). Lord Grandison (uncle to the Duchess of Cleveland) was Captain of the Band of Gentleman Pensioners from 1662 to 1689, when he was removed by King William. Grandison, who fathered four sons and two daughters, died December 16, 1699, aged about 75.

1. *Edward Villiers*, the first son, married in March, 1677, an heiress, Katherine, daughter of John Fitzgerald, and in accordance with the marriage settlement changed his name to Fitzgerald. However, at the Court of Charles II he was still known as Villiers. Edward died in 1693; his wife survived until December 26, 1725. Edward's son John became fifth Viscount Grandison.

2. *Francis Villiers* ("villain Frank") became Standard Bearer to the Band of Gentleman Pensioners in April, 1672, Lieutenant of the Band in 1679, and a Teller of the Exchequer in February, 1685. Ridiculed as an epicure and a fop, he never married. Dying February 4, 1694, he bequeathed his estate to his brother George and his sister Elizabeth.

3 & 4. *Charles* and *George Villiers* appear in a grant of the Clerkship of the Pipe to their older brother, Edward, for the lives of his two younger brothers in reversion, April 28, 1676. On September 20, 1679, a warrant was issued to swear in Charles Villiers as Clerk of the Cheque to the Yeomen of the Guard. On the death of their father, Charles and George became executors of his estate. Charles appears in various editions of *Angliae Notitia* as "third son of the Lord Viscount Grandison." Luttrell noted on February 14, 1693 that "Charles Villiers of the Guards is made colonel of Sir John Morgan's Regiment" (III, 35).

5. *Anne* ("*Nancy*") *Villiers* is frequently referred to in contemporary satires as Frank Villiers's sister. See above, "Advice in a Heroic Epistle to Mr. Fr. Villiers," 1683. On April 13, 1687, a license was issued to Edward Rumbold of Fulham, Middlesex, gent, aged 22, and Anne Villiers, of St. Margaret's, Westminster, aged 19, "daughter of the Rt. Hon. George Lord Viscount Grandison, who consents" (*Marriage Licenses Faculty Office*, p. 185)

6. *Elizabeth Villiers* appears only as Francis's legatee.

Complete Peerage; Luttrell, IV, 595; *CSPD*, 1672, p. 509; 1676–77, p. 91; 1679–80, p. 325; *CTB*, 1681–85, p. 1524; 1700–1701, p. 341; *Westminster Abbey Registers*, p. 233.

VILLIERS (JERSEY)

In the seventeenth century Villiers were as plentiful as blackberries, and their relationships as tangled as the vines. Colonel (later Sir) Edward Villiers, Knight Marshall, George Villiers, second Duke of Buckingham, and George Villiers, fourth Viscount Grandison, had a common grandfather, Sir George Villiers of Brooksby, Leicestershire. Colonel Villiers married Lady Frances Howard, daughter of Theophilus Howard, second Earl of Suffolk. In 1669 Lady Frances was governness to the Duke of York's children. She died at St. James's Palace on November 30, 1677; her husband in 1689. The Villiers had two sons and six daughters.

1. *Edward*, the first son (1656–1711), was knighted in 1676 and in 1677 went to Holland with William and Mary as the princess's Master of the Horse. In 1685, a gossip remarked, "Sir Edward Velors is Master of the Horse to the Princess, and he hath three sisters in Holland, and Bentyng and these Velores do govern all things" (*Seventh Report*, p. 535A). In December, 1681, Sir Edward married Barbara (aged 18), daughter of William Chiffinch, the infamous Closet Keeper to King Charles II. After "the Glorious Revolution" Sir Edward continued as Master of the Horse to Queen Mary and succeeded his father as Knight Marshall. He was created Viscount Villiers of Dartford, March 20, 1691, and Earl of Jersey, October 13, 1697. He was a Secretary of State in 1699 and Lord Chamberlain in 1700. In his younger days Edward was called scornfully "Scabby Ned."

2. *Henry*, the second son (1658–1707), was twice married and completely undistinguished.

3. *Elizabeth*, a Maid of Honor to Princess Mary, became mistress to William of Orange soon after his marriage to Mary. On November 25, 1695, she married a distant cousin, Lord George Hamilton (1666–1737), fifth son of William, Duke of Hamilton; on January 3, 1696, Lord George was created Earl of Orkney.

4. *Katherine* was a Maid of Honor to Queen Catherine. On May 20, 1680, a gossip reported that "Fine Mrs. Frazier, one of the Maids of Honor, is lately withdrawn from Court & Coll. Villiers daughter sworn in her place" (Newdigate Newsletter). The best dancers at a Court ball in November, 1684, were said to be "the Duchesses of Norfolk and Grafton, Lady Mary Tudor, Mrs. Fox, and Villers, the maid of honor" (*Portland MS*, III, 383). On July 20, 1685, Katherine married James Lewis du Puissar, second son of a French refugee, the Marquis de Thouars. After Puissar's death in 1701, Katherine married a cousin, William Villiers. She died in 1709.

5. *Barbara* (1657–1708) married in 1677 John Berkeley (1650–1712), an officer in the Guards. Barbara became governess to Princess Anne's children. On June 13, 1690, Berkeley succeeded as fourth Viscount Fitzharding.

6. *Anne*, a Maid of Honor to Princess Mary of Orange, married on February 1, 1678, at The Hague, Hans Willem Bentinck (1649–1709), who was created Earl of Portland on April 9, 1689. Anne died in Holland, November 20, 1680.

7. *Henrietta* married, as his second wife, on May 23, 1695, John Campbell, Earl of Breadalbane (1662–1752). She died on February 1, 1720.

8. *Mary*, a Maid of Honor to Queen Mary, married, as his second wife, William O'Brien (1666–1719), known as Lord O'Brien until 1692 when he inherited as third Earl of Inchiquin. On April 12, 1691, Luttrell reported, "The lord Obryan has married Mrs. Villiers, one of the maids of honor to the queen; her majesty gave them their wedding supper at Kensington, where many of the nobility were present at a great ball. Her portion is £4,000 given by their majesties, and £1,000 in clothes and jewels" (II, 208). Mary died April 17, 1753.

Complete Peerage; *Westminster Abbey Registers*; *The Diary of Dr. Edward Lake*; *Rutland MS*, II, 37); *London Marriage Licenses*; Collins, *Peerage*.

WHARTON

Philip Wharton, fourth Baron Wharton (1613–96), was a Puritan and in the reign of Charles II an ardent Whig. By his first wife, Elizabeth Wandesford, he had a daughter, Elizabeth, who married Lord Willoughby of Eresby. By his second wife, Jane Goodwin, Wharton had four daughters and three sons who survived the perils of infancy: Thomas, Goodwin, and Henry. By his third wife, Anne Carr, Wharton had one son, William.

1. *Thomas* (1646–1715), "Honest Tom," was also a Whig. In spite of his Puritan background he became one of the greatest rakes in England. A modern historian described him as "Bluff, blasphemous and randy, possessing the social confidence engendered by great wealth, high social position, a commanding charm for women, and the reputation of the first swordsman of his age—and yet with it all an organizer of genius, an effective speaker, and a powerful electioneer" (J. F. Kenyon, *Robert Spencer, Earl of Sunderland,* 1958, p. 270).

Thomas held a number of political posts under King William and Queen Anne. He succeeded as fifth Baron Wharton in February, 1696; on December 23, 1706, he became Earl of Wharton, and on February 5, 1715, Marquess of Wharton. He married (1) on September 16, 1673, Anne, daughter of Sir Henry Lee of Ditchley, a gentle poetess with £10,000 dowry and £2,500 a year, who died in 1685; and (2), in July, 1692, Lucy, daughter of Adam Loftus, Viscount Lisburne—"her estate," wrote Luttrell, "said to be 3 or 4,000 £ per annum" (II, 313). Lucy died February 5, 1716, leaving an eighteen-year-old son, Philip, who became notorious as the "infamous" Duke of Wharton. Perhaps Thomas should be better remembered as the author of a famous political song, *Lilliburlero,* 1688.

Macky commented on Thomas, "He is certainly the completest Gentleman in England, hath a very clear understanding and manly expressions, with abundance of wit. He is brave in his person, much of a libertine, of a middle stature, fair complexion" (*Memoirs,* p. 92).

2. *Goodwin Wharton,* a flighty, addle-brained man, was once arrested and sent to the Tower (October, 1688), "for viewing the fortifications at Portsmouth" (Luttrell, I, 468). He said he "went to Portsmouth only out of curiosity to see the new fortifications" (*Le Fleming*

292

MS, p. 214). Goodwin was something of a projector, a Member of Parliament for Grinstead, Sussex, and in 1697 one of the Lords of the Admiralty. He died in 1704.

3. *Henry Wharton*, first commissioned in the army in 1674, became a colonel and died at Dundalk, Ireland, October 28, 1689. He was a notorious duelist and wencher.

4. In December, 1687, *William Wharton* was killed by Robert Wolseley in a duel, the result of a poetomachia between the two whiffling poets. In Dryden's *Miscellany*, II, 19, "A New Song of the Times, 1683" is attributed to William.

Thomas and *Henry* were notable bullies and fighters. The following items record some of their exploits.

November 24, 1679, "On Saturday night young Porter, Wharton [Henry?], and Jack Howe came and broke down Mrs. Willis's balls [on her gate posts] and called her all to naught, upon which she sent for the constable, but he was so civil as not to secure them" (*Seventh Report*, p. 477B).

February 28, 1680, "In a duel between Sir William Poultney's son and young Warcup, the first disarmed the second." Poultney's second, "a son of My Lord Wharton's, was hurt in the side by one Oglethorpe, not Theophilus" (*Hatton Correspondence*, I, 223). The Wharton was Henry, who was "so dangerously wounded that he is more like to die than to live" (*Ormonde MS*, N.S., V, 281).

January 24, 1682, "Mr. Henry Wharton is forbid ye Cot for running one of Madm Guin's coach horses thro wch drove too near him" (Newdigate Newsletter).

1682, "Our country talk is that my Lord Scarsdale, Ld. Spencer, Mr. Thos: Wharton and his brother Henry went to Ethrop & whipped the Earle of Carnarvan in his own house & didd some other Peccadillos in his Castle besides. . . . Capt. Bertie was sent for to reliefe the Castle & I hear he did come accordingly, but the bravos were all gone first" (*Verney Memoirs*, II, 402).

July 8, 1682, "I hear two of Lord Wharton's sons played a grievous prank in Burford Church, how true I know not" (*Seventh Report*, p. 497B). This episode was remembered by Swift (*Examiner*, no. 23). Thomas Wharton, he wrote, "felt a pious impulse to be a benefactor to the Cathedral of Gloucester [error for Burford Church, corrected in *Examiner*, no. 25] . . . one morning or night he stole into the church, mounted upon the altar, and then did that which in cleanly phrase is called disburdening of nature." According to Swift, Wharton was prosecuted and fined £1,000. Truly "one of the completest gentlemen in England!"

August 16, 1685, "Yesterday morning Capt. Henry Wharton comeing to [Tunbridge] Wells, bade a coachman drive out of the way for the D. of Norfolk was comeing, but the coachman having broke some harness said the D. of Norfolk must waite if he came, or words to that effect, on which Harry W. knockt him down." Dr. Jeffreys, brother to Lord Chief Justice Jeffreys, looked out of the coach and protested; "the captain bade him come out of the coach, & he would serve him soe too" (*Verney Memoirs*, II, 401).

February 4, 1686, "On Tuesday night one Moxon, a lieutenant in the Duke of Norfolk's regiment, was killed at the Blue Posts in the Haymarket by Harry Wharton upon some words aris[ing] between them after having been at play" (*Downshire MS*, I, Part 1, 116).

Complete Peerage; *Memoirs of the Life of the Most Noble Thomas, Late Marquess of Wharton*, 1715; E. B. Chancellor, *Colonel Charteris and the Duke of Wharton*, 1926; Harris, *Dorset*, pp. 110–12.

WILLIS, SUE

The origins of Sue Willis, a famous prostitute and bawd, are unknown. The first recorded attack on her appears in "Lampoons," c. 1673 (Harvard MS. English 636F),

> Willis the expensive is now grown old;
> In her youth she was ugly as I have been told.
> For herself by-the-by some pricks to engage
> Turns governess bawd to the young whores of the stage;
> Near Whetstone keeps school to teach jilting tricks,
> To give running diseases to purses and pricks.

In "Satire on Bentinck," 1689 (see above), we have a brief account of her career. She is now said to be the mistress of William Bentinck, Groom of the Stole to King William.

> This whore at first her life with Moseley led,
> The bawd's least profit, not her bully's bread;

Thence in a playhouse, where a goatish peer
Feeling her c--t liked it, but never her.

There is no evidence that Mrs. Willis was ever on the stage, but she may have been a "playhouse punk" in the audience. The "goatish peer" is identifiable as Thomas, Lord Colepeper of Thoresby (1633–89).

On June 24, 1677, Henry Savile wrote, "My Ld Culpepper is also returned from Paris with Mrs. Willis, whom he carried thither to buy whatsoever pleased her there and this nation could not afford" (*Savile Correspondence*, p. 62). The affair must have begun some years earlier, because by Mrs. Willis Colepeper had a daughter, Susan, who by February, 1686, was old enough to marry Sir Charles Englefield, Bart., of Englefield, Berks.

From 1675 to 1683 "Maddam Willis" kept a bawdyhouse in Lincolns Inn Fields, with two white balls on the gateposts. In November, 1679, young Porter, Wharton, and Howe, according to the custom which permitted them to beat up the quarters of bawds and whores, "came and broke down Mrs. Willis's balls and called her all to naught" (*Seventh Report*, p. 477B). In 1686 she had moved to Park Place, where her house narrowly escaped a fire which consumed fourteen houses. She was still in business in 1687; on May 22, Sir George Etherege wrote from Ratisbon, asking his correspondent to "make the kindest compliment you can for me to Mrs. Willis, and let me know how she and her little family does" (*Letters*, p. 118).

Among Mrs. Willis's putative lovers were Captain Edward Lee, Sir Scroope Howe, Sir George Hewitt, and perhaps John, Earl of Rochester. D. M. Vieth (*Rochester*, p. 137) printed as possibly by Rochester an obscene libel titled "On Mrs. Willis."

Complete Baronetage; *Herbert Correspondence*, p. 326; *Ellis Correspondence*, I, 132; London County Council, *Survey of London*, 1912, III, 32.

INDEX

297